CHA

HOUSE OF FALLEN WOMEN

CHARLES DICKENS

and the

HOUSE OF
FALLEN WOMEN

Jenny Hartley

Methuen

Published by Methuen 2009

3 5 7 9 10 8 6 4 2

Copyright © Jenny Hartley 2008

First published in Great Britain in 2008 by
Methuen
35 Hospital Fields Road
York
YO10 4DZ

www.methuen.co.uk

A CIP catalogue record for this book is available from the British Library

ISBN 978-0-413-77644-0

Printed and bound CPI Group (UK) Ltd, Croydon, CR0 4YY

For Nick

CONTENTS

LIST OF ILLUSTRATIONS

ACKNOWLEDGEMENTS

ALL THE HELP I have received has made this book a great pleasure to write. I am glad to be able to express my thanks to the many individuals and institutions who have been such a support.

Funding from Roehampton University Internationalisation Fund, headed by Dr Heather Forland, and a period of study leave awarded by the School of Arts Research Committee gave me the opportunity to visit Australia. I would also like to thank Professor Neil Taylor in the University Research Office.

Invitations to speak about Dickens and Urania Cottage at Leicester University, Leeds Metropolitan University, San Francisco State University and Flinders University Adelaide have helped to develop my thinking and provided valuable feedback. Thanks are due to Mary Eagleton, Joanne Shattock and Eric Richards. The 'Dickens and Sex' Conference at the University of London's Institute of English Studies in 2004 was the ideal forum to give a paper, exchange ideas and learn from Dickens scholars. I am also grateful for invitations to speak at the Dickens Fellowship, the Dickens Society Symposium, and to the Friends of the Charles Dickens Museum.

Archivists and librarians have been generous with their support and expertise. I would like to thank Gilly King at Whitelands College, Anne Wheeldon at Hammersmith and Fulham Archives and Local History Centre, Robert Walker at the Highgate Literary and Scientific Institution, Andrew Russell at the Victoria and Albert Museum, Isobel Long and Tracey Earl at Messrs Coutts & Co, and the late Earl of Harrowby and Michael Bosson, the archivist at Sandon Hall. The staff and librarians at Lambeth Palace Library, the City of Westminster Archives Centre, London Metropolitan Archives, the Hertford County Archive, the West Sussex Record Office, the Guildhall Library, the Public Records

Office at Kew, the London Library and the British Library have all been unfailingly helpful and efficient. Christine Nelson at the Pierpont Morgan Library in New York generously provided information and sent photocopied material. Florian Schweizer and Andrew Xavier made visits to the Charles Dickens Museum in Doughty Street a pleasure. In Cambridge Margaret Brown gave me access to the archives of the Pilgrim Edition of Dickens's *Letters* – and much else besides by way of guidance, expert knowledge, kindness and hospitality. In Australia Kathi Spinks at the State Library of New South Wales, Irene Turpie at the National Library of Australia, and librarians at the State Library of South Australia all located and provided information, as did archivists at the South Australia Genealogy and Heraldry Society in Adelaide, and the Public Record Office Victoria in Melbourne.

I am indebted to the late Robin Fenner and to Sheila Fenner in Tavistock for information about the Morson family, to Lady Healey for details about Angela Burdett Coutts, and to Rebecca Langton, Judy Jeffery, Anthony McNicholas, Jan Gothard and Jenny Elson for data and advice on Australian emigrants and emigration.

In Adelaide Robin Haines stands out as an inspirational scholar; Judy Georgiou and Dr Brian Dickey could not have been more generous in sharing their research findings, and Paddy Burrowes extended liberal hospitality. In Melbourne the Ivanhoe Reading Circle kindly entertained me with tea and insights into the lives of early settler women; Gwenyth Cadwallader's unhesitating welcome and continuing interest have blessed my research as its presiding spirit. In Canada and North America Jim Larsen, Kat Rytych, Dave Lee and the Cole family have kindly passed on invaluable information. I have been especially fortunate in finding my way to June Gillies: she has shared her family history and helped me understand rural Canadian life.

I have benefited from the many friends, colleagues and Dickensians who have talked to me, and offered advice, help and encouragement: Malcolm Andrews, Meg Arnot, Nicola Beauman, Norma Clarke, Peter Conradi, Joan Dicks, Holly Furneaux, Juliet Gardiner, Thelma Grove, Pamela Janes, Julia Jones, Jane Jordan, Pippa Lewis, Elizabeth Maslen, David Parker, George Rigal, Jane Rogers, Clive and Kathleen Saville, Anne Schwan, Elaine Showalter, Michael Slater and Tony Williams.

Gabriel Pearson at the University of Essex gave me an exhilarating introduction to studying Dickens.

Reading and teaching Dickens with students and colleagues at Roehampton University over many years has been a joy. I am privileged to acknowledge the huge debt I owe to countless students, and to my colleagues from whom I learn so much: Steve Bamlett, Simon Edwards, Ian Haywood, Nicola Humble, Tim Jordan, Mark Knight, Zachary Leader, Susan Matthews, Laura Peters, Kate Teltscher and Mark Turner. Sarah Turvey and Cathy Wells-Cole have, as ever, sustained me by engaging so wholeheartedly with this project and contributing so many insights.

For all the work on my behalf by my agent Laura Morris, who saw the story in Urania Cottage and has been a mainstay throughout, I am most grateful. Jean Seaton has been a rock of encouragement, wisdom and interest. To my husband Nick, who has kept me and the book going at every stage, I owe more than I can say.

Permission to quote from manuscripts in their collections has been kindly granted by: the editors of the Pilgrim Edition of *The Letters of Charles Dickens*; the Trustees of Lambeth Palace Library; the Pierpont Morgan Library, New York; the Director of The House of St Barnabas-in-Soho; and Mark Dickens for access to Dickens's account-book at Messrs Coutts and Co.

Jenny Hartley, London 2008

It is most encouraging and delightful! Imagining backward to what these women were and might have been, and forward to what their children may be.

Charles Dickens to Angela Burdett Coutts, 21 March 1851

PROLOGUE

A Rainy Day on the Calcutta

LONDON, JANUARY 1849. A drenchingly wet day. Henry Morley starts his report by writing himself into the scene as 'a motionless damp substance'. He has already tried his hand at medicine and teaching; now he wants to make his name as a journalist. He is waiting at Blackwall pier for the train bringing three young women. His assignment is to follow them as they say goodbye to England and take ship for Australia and the rest of their lives.

A whistle shrieks and the train pulls in. The three young women get out: Julia Mosley, Martha Goldsmith and Jane Westaway. With them is Mrs Holdsworth, the matron of the Home they have come from. Cloaked and hooded against the rain, the young women huddle together fidgeting. They touch each other's clothes and fiddle with their bonnets.

'High water in the puddles, low water on the Thames,' observes Morley. He watches as the nervy little group negotiates the slippery step-ladder to the floating barge and climbs the swaying plank on to the steam-boat for Gravesend. There they will embark on the *Calcutta*, a three-masted sailing barque bound for Adelaide, a new colony on the south coast of Australia. A voyage of three to four months – and then what? No wonder the girls cling closely to each other, and to Mrs Holdsworth who has been mother to them for the last year. They have been inmates at Urania Cottage, a Home for Fallen Women in Shepherd's Bush, and guinea pigs in a small-scale experiment in reinvention. Julia, Martha and Jane are the forerunners. They are the first to get this far: sturdy emigrants, frontierswomen heading off over the empty seas into the completely unknown.

Now the girls and Mrs Holdsworth are all in tears. Getting their emigration kits and outfits organised has been a heroic effort. Mrs Holdsworth only managed two hours sleep last night and, what with all the excitement, the young women not much more. This morning there were more tearful and elaborate farewells, extending to every tree and shrub in the garden.

The rain drives down in stair-rods. 'Them gals', the stubby, weather-beaten captain tells Morley, 'would be much better down out of the rain, but they *will* be after looking at the ship that is to carry 'em'. Then the *Calcutta* looms suddenly huge above them. Within moments they are hoisting themselves precariously up to the paddle-box of the steamer and wobbling across another plank on to the ship.

Chaos everywhere, all bustle and boxes, 'wild work with the packages' notes Morley. Mrs Holdsworth goes below with Julia, Martha and Jane. Her last responsibility is to settle them into their new quarters. Her steadying practical presence is a boon, as she helps to unpack what they need for the voyage, stowing away the outfits they have lavished so much care over. She busies herself putting up hooks everywhere and getting to grips with the 'miraculous cupboard system'. Thanks to her the lost soup bowls are located in time for lunch, their first meal on board ship. Not that they can eat much, but the novelty entrances – 'Look, look; *do* look at the little pepper-boxes!'

When the steamer comes alongside to escort those not sailing, the girls will not let Mrs Holdsworth go. 'A prisoner of love' scribbles Morley sentimentally as he watches the crying and the kissing. Before she finally leaves, Mrs Holdsworth makes them promise to write to her; they have all learnt to read and write during their year at Urania Cottage. Attempts at parting cheers choke in their throats. A mutual waving of handkerchiefs and hats, and the *Calcutta* creaks slowly away on her long voyage.

Who were Julia, Martha and Jane, and all the other young women at Urania Cottage? Where did they come from, and what sort of place was it? Readers familiar with the life of Charles Dickens will know the name. Urania Cottage was the Home in Shepherd's Bush he was involved with for more than ten years, the 'Home for Homeless Women' as he called it in his magazine *Household Words*. Fallen women and emigration to Australia were to be two of the magazine's headline issues.

Details of Urania Cottage – its personalities and its dramas – survive in the treasure-trove of letters which Dickens wrote to the woman who put up the money for it, Angela Burdett Coutts. We have not, until now, known much about the girls themselves, their lives before and after their time there. What impact did Dickens have on them, was it for good? Does his attempt to turn a small group of young people's lives around have anything to tell us now?

Although biographers have paid attention to Urania Cottage, it features mainly in the story of the extra-curricular Dickens, the side of him which is not writing fiction. Dickens the social reformer, Dickens the hyperactive and relentlessly busy, Dickens the champion of the urban underclass, and also of course Dickens the obsessed with prisons and criminals. Urania does connect with all these aspects of Dickens, and to no other social project would he commit himself with equal intensity. So yes, Urania is important for all these reasons.

What about its consequences for his fiction? Dickens made it his business to get to know these young women closely. In return they win starring roles in his novels. Little Em'ly in *David Copperfield* is one of literature's most famous fallen women. They also infiltrate themselves less directly, more insidiously and to stunning effect, as they work their way into his imagination. The Urania years were the years of *Dombey and Son*, *David Copperfield*, *Bleak House*, *Hard Times* and *Little Dorrit*, some of the greatest novels Dickens (or indeed anyone) ever wrote. Finding out more about Urania and its inmates threads us back through his creative landscape in new and exciting ways.

I also wanted to know what happened to the real young women once they arrived in Australia. Life in the colonies could be tough during those early years, especially for single women. Did they survive, did they thrive, did they leave any traces? I wanted to follow the women who had been at Urania Cottage down through their daughters and granddaughters. This is the story of what I found.

PART ONE

THE EXPERIMENT

CHAPTER ONE

Where to Go?

The means of return to Happiness are now about to be
put into her own hands.
  Charles Dickens to Angela Burdett Coutts, 26 May 1846

JULIA MOSLEY SPENT the summer of 1847 in Tothill Fields,
Westminster – a central address but not a fashionable one. She was
doing six months in the Westminster House of Correction for stealing
a handkerchief and thirty shillings from 'the person' of Henry Meyers;
Julia was a pickpocket, though obviously not successful that time. She
was twenty-one and originally from Stroud in Gloucestershire, where
her father was a tailor. While she was in prison Julia would be set
to picking oakum, which meant unraveling lengths of old rope and
separating the threads for recycling. Or she would be given uniforms
to repair. As she worked in the rigorously enforced silence she would be
wondering what lay ahead once her six months were up. Realistically,
she knew she had little alternative to going back on the streets again.

The governor of Tothill Fields, Augustus Tracey, was an enlightened
man, but he could offer little in the way of support to his ex-prisoners,
especially the women. All he could suggest were a few temporary refuges. No hostels or half-way houses, no job centres or training, and no
employment. The one thing a young woman needed to get a job – a
good reference – was exactly what Julia had lost by being in prison.
While a man with no reference could hope to pick up manual unskilled
labour, practically the only work for a woman was domestic, for which
she needed a 'character'. This Julia had forfeited. She had left home

before she was fifteen. Although her younger brother followed their father into the tailor's shop on Stroud High Street, there was no room for Julia. Or maybe she chose not to; perhaps she wanted to spread her wings, see more of life. She could read and write a bit, but that, she well knew, would not get her far now. She was not, a visitor to the prison noticed, in good spirits.

A few miles away in Clerkenwell another 21-year-old, Rosina Gale, was also spending summer in prison. Rosina was a Londoner and an orphan; her father had been a seaman. She did have a skill, but not one you could make a living by: she was a needlewoman. Rosina's prison was Coldbath Fields, the Middlesex House of Correction. She had probably been convicted of a minor theft, since these cases outnumbered all the others put together. Probably theft, but we will have to guess at Rosina's crime because the records are now lost.

For all the Victorian obsession with cataloguing, ticketing, filing and form-filling (for which all historians must be eternally grateful), together with the efficiency of twenty-first-century retrieval systems, it is still much easier to trace the bishop than the prostitute, the politician than the petty thief. So this attempt to track the homeless, the penniless and the feckless will run into blank spots, silences, gaps. Rosina's crime is one such blank, but we can assume that it was quite minor as we know she was only serving a short sentence. She was looking forward to a release date in November, though with little cause for celebration.

Julia and Rosina: two of the thousands of young women on the streets of London at mid-century. This was where a third 21-year-old, Martha Goldsmith, found herself six months later in the freezing January of 1848. She was one of three sisters who had come up to London from Berkshire in search of work after their mother died. Country girls made steady, reliable servants, it was thought, and Martha went into service. But by the time she was twenty she had been a prostitute long enough to know that she wanted to change her life for the better, so she asked to be admitted to what was unpromisingly called a Penitentiary.

Martha knocked at the door of the London Magdalen Hospital in Blackfriars Road, established nearly a century earlier 'for the reception of penitent prostitutes'. In those days a 'Hospital' could mean any charitable institution and not just somewhere for the sick. Application was by personal petition only, and on specified days; you truly had to want to 'repent' your previous life. There were usually well over a hundred women inmates, and here Martha flourished. 'A civil and amiable manner, tidy in her person', ran the testimony for her written by Ann Bourchill, Matron of the Magdalen.

Martha worked hard in the laundry and proved 'a very industrious needlewoman'. But after twelve months there her time was up, and she must make way for the next batch of prostitutes hoping to reshape their lives. Her younger sister was in domestic service, her older sister was poor; neither had room to take her in. Martha was out on the streets with a change of clothes, three shillings, and Ann Bourchill's encouraging reference. With no job and nowhere to go, her principal emotion was one of dread that she would meet up with old companions and lapse into her old way of life. A quiet, ordinary-looking sort of girl, Martha seemed to possess little of the resilience needed to make it on her own. Never a good month for the homeless, that particular January saw constant rain and black skies, with temperatures often well below freezing. 'An unusually fatal season', commented *The Times*. No wonder Martha was observed to be 'terribly depressed' and in tears.

She knew she would be one of many. At any one time, according to the estimate of that acute and sympathetic eye-witness of London life Henry Mayhew, there would be ten thousand homeless young female servants out on the streets on the move between jobs. Some of them had been dismissed, some were moving voluntarily, and not always for the best of motives. Mary Anne Church, for example, had only worked for Eliza and George Banks for two days, at the end of August 1850, before absconding with twelve towels, some clothes and a gown belonging to Mrs Banks. As a thief, eighteen-year-old Mary Anne was hopeless. She was caught almost immediately, parading the streets in Mrs Banks's nice dress. She willingly led the policeman to where she had hidden the rest of the stuff in a neat bundle. This sort of offence was all too common, and her name fitted the crime – the courts of London overflowed with Mary Annes. When this one came up at the Old Bailey she got six months. It would not be her last brush with the law.

You had to be tough to survive on the streets. The wildest girls went round in marauding gangs; they were usually from the workhouses, those prison-like barracks disgracing the face of England. Workhouses combined the functions of orphanage, school, shelter for the homeless, hospital and old people's home, but unpleasantly enough to deter all but the desperate. They could be huge: the workhouse at Marylebone held well over two thousand.

Regimes were harsh. Inmates were rigidly segregated, men from women, old from young, children from their mothers. In some work-houses unmarried mothers would be constantly reminded of their pariah status by their distinctive yellow uniforms. More than a third of the inmates were under sixteen, and more than 60 percent of these had been orphaned or deserted. Horror stories abounded about the work-house where children were killed to put into pies, or where the corpses of the aged poor were used to manure the guardian's fields. There was no training on offer, little education, and no toys for the children. In the words of those exhaustive historians of English Poor Law policy, Sidney and Beatrice Webb, the workhouse 'starved both the will and the intel-ligence, and forced the pauper into a condition of blank-mindedness'.

Girls who had been there since birth or infancy would grow up together and know no other environment. When they were sent out to domestic service they would be returned as unemployable. Bursting with energy and physical aggression, they enjoyed rioting and whip-ping up reigns of terror. So much so that 'Misbehaviour in Workhouse' was now a separate indictable offence. The girls got their moment in court and made the most of it, a brief hour of glory much appreciated by *The Times* reporters.

In the early weeks of 1848 the press gave star billing to the Chelsea Five, 'stout hearty-looking young women from Chelsea workhouse', repeatedly committed for disorderly conduct. Their 'outrageous behav-iour' included singing, hooting, assaulting the staff, and 'rendering themselves the objects of general terror'. Armed with iron weights from the laundry, they set fire to the detested oakum and hurled it round the room. They broke all the windows. Their language was 'disgusting and abominable', and their trial frequently disrupted by their 'hearty fits of laughter'. After the magistrate committed them for six weeks' hard labour 'they shouted with laughter and exclaimed, What of that? We don't care about six months.'

Two weeks later it was the turn of the Bermondsey Seven, charged with creating a riot and threatening to murder the workhouse master. 'When remonstrated with, three of them took from under their garments open knives, and flourishing them over their heads, threatened to rip up the master's belly or murder any person who dared to attack them.' In court they repeated their threats, 'even if we get hung for it; he is a tyrant and ought to be murdered.' This time the magistrate threw up his hands in despair and sent them on to a higher court.

This was the beginning of 1848, the year of revolutions throughout continental Europe and of potential Chartist rebellion at home. *The Times* was clearly casting the workhouse girls as another incendiary mob. Throughout the early months of the year, battles and run-ins between young women and the institutions of the state continued to fill the column inches.

Defiance became a point of honour, and the attention flattering. For her fifteen seconds of fame Mary Anne Smith tried to smuggle two stale loaves into court under her clothes. She planned to 'throw them at the head of the — judge, for he had given her six months last time, and she owed him a score'. Even the apparently lady-like could succumb to this sort of temptation. Felicia Skene, one of the very few professional prison visitors at this time (she distanced herself firmly from the casual and curious), met an elegant ex-governess who had concealed her shoe under her shawl so she could throw it at the chief magistrate, which she managed with great accuracy.

> Of course the result of such an outrage on the judicial dignity was the immediate doubling of her sentence under severe conditions. But that was simply nothing to her, in comparison with the exquisite enjoyment of the moment, when she saw her muddy old shoe flying through the air to lodge on the magisterial cranium. Even when she spoke of it afterwards in the presence of the visitor, to whom she wished to be abnormally respectful, she had difficulty in repressing her shrieks of delight at the recollection of that ineffable moment.

Violence in the courtroom, rowdiness on the streets. These were rough times. Middle-class women could not go out without some sort of escort, even when they went out in pairs. Christina and Maria Rossetti regretfully declined an invitation to visit their good friend Amelia Heimann because they needed a reliable brotherly escort, and 'Willie has an appointment for Monday; and Gabriel is always of difficult attainment'. This was in the mid 1850s. At the end of that decade the young Sophia Jex-Blake, later pioneer physician and feminist, was studying at the newly opened Queen's College in Harley Street. She astounded her country cousins with her independent ways. 'You seem to be spending rather a jolly time of it,' Ellie wrote to her from Norfolk, 'but still it seems to me rather queer that a lot of girls should walk about London when and where they please.' Sophia's mother put her foot down. 'Good-looking girls do not needlessly go about London without chaperones.' The streets were still a liability for the respectable woman. From his window at Coldbath Fields Prison in Clerkenwell, governor George Chesterton watched the noisy crowd waiting outside to reclaim their friends released back on to the killing streets of London. In November 1847 they were waiting for Rosina Gale.

For once Chesterton had something positive to offer, some hope. He had a letter, intended he told Rosina, specially for her. First he read it out to her, then he left it in her cell for her to work her way through for herself. It was printed, which made it easier to read. And what a letter! Never before had she been appealed to with such force of feeling, such insight into her own mind and heart. The writer began by speaking directly to her: 'You will see, on beginning to read this letter, that it is not addressed to you by name. But I address it to a woman – a very young woman still – who was born to be happy and has lived miserably; who has no prospect before her but sorrow, or behind her but a wasted youth; who, if she has ever been a mother, has felt shame instead of pride in her own unhappy child.' Four pages later he signed himself off, 'Believe me that I am, indeed, YOUR FRIEND.'

As Rosina listened to George Chesterton reading to her, she heard her own thoughts played back to her with uncanny accuracy.

> Think for a moment what your present situation is. Think how impossible it is that it can ever be better if you continue to live as you have lived, and how certain it is that it must be worse. You know what the streets are; you know how cruel the companions you find there are; you know the vices practised there, and to what wretched consequences they bring you, even while you are young.

So what was this friend offering her instead? Chesterton paused when he reached the main feature: 'a HOME'. The word was written in capital letters for maximum effect. Here Rosina would be treated 'with the greatest kindness', she would learn 'many things' that would be useful once she got a home of her own. She could even have her own little flower garden – all the details seemed to be in place, Rosina could almost see it for herself. But that was not all. The next part of the letter went on to talk about the next stage of her life. She would, the writer foretold, be 'restored to society': not here but in a vague 'distant country' where she could marry an honest man and 'die in peace'.

What an extraordinary invitation. Chesterton read the letter slowly to Rosina in her cell, and to a few other carefully selected girls. He patiently answered their questions, as the letter-writer promised he would. Across town at the Westminster House of Correction in Tothill Fields, Augustus Tracey read the same letter out to Julia Mosley. He and Chesterton had both been roped in to support this radical new project. An ambitious scheme, and probably a hare-brained one, but how could they say no? Designed as it was, and dragooned as they were, by the most famous man in England, and the most irresistible, the 'Inimitable' as he liked to call himself: Charles Dickens. It was his words Chesterton and Tracey were reading out, to girls who could barely understand them.

The two prison governors were both friends of Dickens, mobilised by him as recruiting agents for his new scheme. He was planning to open a small-scale refuge, a home for fallen women which would take girls from the prisons, workhouses and streets of London. Here they would be educated and given a second chance. Then they would be dispatched abroad to start new lives. They would go to England's colonies, where good servants were always in demand. This is what the home would train the girls to be. It was a unique opportunity for reinvention.

Further, the place itself would be unlike anywhere else at the time. It would be a real home, not an institution or a penitentiary; a family, not a temporary dormitory or crowded rough-house. The money came from Angela Burdett Coutts, the millionaire philanthropist. The ideas all came from Dickens.

Dickens had known both prison governors for some time. He and George Laval Chesterton (his mother was 'a Frenchwoman and sister of the French General Laval', he was proud of saying) went back to 1835. Chesterton could tell a good story, and when his sensational *Revelations of Prison Life* came out in 1856 it was an instant bestseller. He and Dickens shared a fascination with what Chesterton called the 'flash language' of the criminal community. Disgusting, said Chesterton, 'but still, so wickedly ingenious as to constitute a startling science'. Curious about its 'endless variety', he asked a well-educated prisoner to compile a glossary for him, so that he could savour the subtle differences between '*cadgers*', '*high-flyers*' and '*showful-pitchers*' (all types of vagrant), and appreciate the jokes about 'how neatly the *skins* (purses) were drawn from the *kicks* (trowsers pockets), the *thimbles* (watches) from the *gurrells* (fobs) or *wedge* (silver) *sneezers* (snuff-boxes) from the *fans* (waistcoat-pockets)'.

When Chesterton arrived at Coldbath Fields in 1829 he found a 'hot bed of vice' with male and female prisoners mixing freely. But he soon got the measure of the 'loquaciously self-laudatory' matron and the chief warder who moved 'at minimum speed'; also of the dodges and hiding places in which prisoners secreted everything from weapons to fish-sauce.

The watchwords of Chesterton's new regime were 'discipline, industry, and progressive morality'. He had little time for 'mawkish theory', adopted the silent system because he believed that prisoners talking among themselves would corrupt each other, and favoured the tread-mill, at least to start with. Prisoners could then earn the right to learn a more interesting occupation. Chesterton arranged training in tailoring, shoe-making, and rug-making.

He missed his women prisoners once they were removed in 1850. He was amused by their audacity and spirit, and liked to tell racy anecdotes about them. He warmed to the 'old beggar-woman committed under the vagrant act' whom he ticked off for disobedience. This 'nettled' her so much that she

> shouted in a shrill voice – 'I'm a gentlewoman! My father wasn't governor of a gaol, he was governor of the West Indies!' The scene was so comical, that I, the female warders, and the prisoners burst into a fit of irrepressible laughter; and the old woman, on seeing the mirth she had occasioned, recovered her temper, and laughed too. From that time forth, she could not forbear to smile whenever she saw me.

Both Chesterton and Tracey were the real thing: tough men of action who had fought for their country during the Napoleonic wars, Chesterton in the army and Tracey in the navy. Chesterton's taste for battle and 'hopes for honourable advancement' subsequently impelled him to enlist in Simon Bolivar's liberation movement. '"South America!" I ejaculated, and strange imaginations seemed instantly to invade my senses.' Guerrilla warfare, hurricanes, tigers, naked tribesmen, toxic fevers and even worse jails: Chesterton wrote them all up for his rip-roaring autobiography entitled *Peace, War and Adventure* – on none of which fronts is the reader left short-changed. Tracey stuck it out in the navy for over twenty years, before taking up his post at Tothill Fields in Westminster. Dickens was fond of him and their families enjoyed each other's company. For this new scheme both Chesterton and Tracey could be relied on to help pick both staff and inmates. Just as importantly, they would underwrite some of Dickens's wilder notions.

But while Dickens was fizzing with missionary fervour, the young women were slow to see the light. Although Chesterton did his best, he had a gloomy report to make. 'Objections would be raised, conditions critically sifted, and disdainful rejections of the offer would ensue.' Or what started as a yes would melt away. 'Some would appear gratefully to assent, but as their enlargement approached, a change of mind would arise, and some plausible pretext be advanced to give colour to the ultimate refusal.' What did they not like about Dickens's great idea? According to Chesterton there were two obstacles: 'the irksomeness of quiet domesticity, and the prospect of expatriation'. These, unfortunately, were what Dickens considered his two trump cards.

This was not the first place to offer shelter to women from the streets. But when Dickens writes to Angela Burdett Coutts about their project as 'your "Home" (that is the name I propose to give it)', we can see from his turn of phrase that calling it a Home was something new. The other words Dickens used before were 'Asylum' and 'Institution'. A Home, however, is definitely and explicitly what he wants it to be, with its invocation of the healing powers of domesticity. To create for these young women 'an innocently cheerful Family' was the point of the thing, to be at once both cosy and daring. The small scale was crucial: no more than a dozen or so.

How would this new place differ from what was already on offer? There was in fact quite a batch of penitentiaries and refuges opening their doors at this time. Many were run by Anglican nuns and were big institutions, employing their inmates in industrial work such as large-scale laundry. 'Penitents' slept in dormitories, attended Chapel three times a day, and observed long periods of silence. It was a philosophy of abjection. In order to turn her life round the prostitute must take responsibility for her actions. Her fall was her fault, she must take blame and shame as her deserved lot. 'Pernicious and unnatural' was Dickens's swift verdict on the proposal for a House of Mercy which a canvassing vicar had sent Miss Coutts. 'The suggested place is but a kind of Nunnery.' Miss Coutts herself objected to the amateurism, the use of untrained volunteer ladies as teachers and supervisors.

Christina Rossetti was one such volunteer at the St Mary Magdalene Penitentiary in Highgate. Stirred by its high religious tone, she enrolled as an Associate Sister, and dressed in the black nun's habit and veil. 'Very simple, elegant even', wrote an admiring family friend. 'Self-devoted and unpaid ladies' like Rossetti, as the Highgate Penitentiary's annual report flatteringly described them, were needed to enforce its strict rules. No inmate was ever to be left on her own without a 'sister', even when asleep. The surveillance was constant and intrusive. Rossetti visited Highgate regularly and spent several weeks there a year, reading and praying with the inmates.

Very admirable no doubt, if not very attractive, at least to young women like Julia and Rosina. But nor was domestic much of a draw either. To them it mainly meant dull. They were used to the adrenalin rush of life on the streets, and the buzz of workhouse and prison – even the silent system had its moments of hysteria and excitement, as Chesterton himself recognised and enjoyed. The picture of a quiet home 'in a pleasant country lane' near London sounded like monotony itself.

We no longer maintain our prisons on the silent system. The women's prison where I help run a reading group can be a place of volatile mood swings. It is always full of energy, partly because most of the inmates are young. Moments of high drama are relished: the times when the place becomes most alive, when inmates feel briefly that they are getting their lives back. A century and a half ago Chesterton watched as a shrieking band of 'young furies divested themselves of their upper garments'. A month ago I was told about the woman who had been refused a visit; she removed all her clothes in the prison dining room. 'Pussy and all': the women who told me appreciated the drama of the action, its pace and timing. For them it was an event rather than a protest, something to spice the tedium, life by proxy. The woman was statuesque and stripped in style. 'Last thing to come off was her wig, she saved that till the end.'

So Julia and Rosina would have to be coaxed, and the home itself would have to be lively. And if that was not enough, the young women also had to buy into the grand finale of emigration. To do that, they first of all had to understand what it meant.

This was the mid 1840s. Emigration was *the* idea in the minds of the British public, the best remedy for all the economic and social ills of the time, and the only escape from the Irish famine. A million and a half people left Ireland between 1845 and 1855. The stampede brought problems of its own: pressure on shipping and atrocious conditions on board, which were at best chaotic and at worst fatal. In 1847 nearly a fifth of those bound for North America died before they arrived. So while emigration was a solution – almost the only one according to Dickens's mentor Thomas Carlyle – its image was tarnished and compromised.

If you asked the young women Chesterton and Tracey were valiantly reading out Dickens's letter to, most of them would associate going abroad either with the destitute and ragged Irish, or with transportation. They could see the hulks, the huge prison ships moored on the Thames, with convicted criminals waiting to be sent to the colonies. By then, transportation was coming under heavy criticism. It would be cut back hard during the 1840s, but it did not stop completely until 1868.

The new emigration projects had to distance themselves from the older, compulsory and punitive system. Above all, critics must not be given grounds for painting the new projects as cynical attempts to solve the country's troubles by dumping them abroad, transportation under another name. Any emigration venture could all too easily be labelled as an excuse for 'shovelling out paupers'. Women were particularly in demand in Australia, to redress the balance between the sexes. But could it really benefit the emigrant herself? That was one of the questions I wanted to answer about Dickens's meddling in the lives of these now almost invisible young women.

The scheme he was hatching aimed to work with carrots not sticks. The juiciest carrot on offer was the new start: all that fall could be wiped out. But this was 1847, and the most hardened female criminals, as Rosina and Julia well knew, were still being sent abroad as the severest punishment. Mary Anne Smith, who had hidden the stale loaves under her clothes to throw at the judge, was sentenced to be transported for ten years. She had already been convicted more than twenty times for pick-pocketing, Julia's own offence.

It was even longer – fourteen years' transportation – for celebrity thief Anne Simons. Titled and fashionable folk flocked to her trial and blocked the traffic in Marylebone High Street; *The Times* reporter spotted the Swedish Ambassador 'and other nobility' in the throng. Anne Simons had worked as a shop assistant in Marshalls' store in Oxford Street (on the corner of Vere Street, it later became Marshall and Snelgrove's). While serving the smart set she also managed to filch vast quantities of goods. A staggering two thousand pounds worth of stock deftly packed in boxes and trunks made its way to her father's house in Leicestershire.

Tracey and Chesterton had an uphill job. Could emigration be made attractive? Would the cutting-edge concept of a half-way house/training centre/family find its target group? This was an attempt at rehab in an age which did not believe in rehab. Could it work? What hope could it offer Julia and Rosina and Martha?

CHAPTER TWO

Leap of Faith

We have now eight, and I have as much confidence
in five of them, as one *can* have in the beginning of
anything so new. As we go on, I sincerely trust and
believe you will do more good than your most sanguine
expectations picture now.

Dickens to Angela Burdett Coutts, 28 October 1847

A SLOW START. The girls (Dickens called them girls, and so shall I)
whom Tracey and Chesterton had originally targeted were not
keen. So they made a second selection, this time with more success.
Julia Mosley and Rosina Gale both said yes: really, to the unknown.
They were not the only ones taking a risk. It would be new territory for
everyone involved: a new way of life for Julia and Rosina, new working
patterns for those who were going to care for them, and an attempt
on the part of the organisers to put into practice a set of radical and
bold ideas.

Julia was the first one in, even before the official opening in mid-
November 1847. She had finished her prison sentence, and been allowed
to stay on an extra three weeks. This was a long time for Julia to choose to
stay inside; she must have believed that the new project could work.
Admittedly, there was little else on offer for her, but her commitment
made a welcome contrast to the setbacks and false starts.

Chesterton felt badly let down by Julia's best friend. She was, said
Dickens, 'the matron's model, and the head female turnkey's model,
and the peculiar pet and protégée of Mr Rotch the magistrate.' She was

better educated and better spoken than most, 'but she impressed me as being something too grateful, and too voluble in her earnestness, and she seemed, in a vague, indescribable, uneasy way, to be doubtful of me, which I suppose made me doubtful of her.' Dickens describes the scene in great detail for Miss Coutts, partly because of their common interest in these crucial first steps, and because it casts his judgement of character in a good light:

> I observed her as closely as I could, and when they had all gone, told Chesterton that he would be amazed at what I was going to say, but that I doubted the model more than any of them, and believed that if we failed with anybody, we should fail with her. This made such a rebellion among the matrons and turnkeys that I was almost ashamed of myself, and heartily wished I had kept my opinion quiet. But we have always talked about her since, naturally; and when she stayed in prison on her own accord, I gave way altogether, and became quite abject. Last Saturday, Chesterton and I were at the Home together, and the model was still in great force. Last Sunday, I went to him by appointment on this same theme, and the model was gone!

She would reappear three years later, at the end of *David Copperfield*, as Number Twenty-Seven the Favourite Model Prisoner, the overly grateful 'umble Uriah Heep.

Meanwhile, back at Tothill Fields prison, tender-hearted Julia 'cried all day' and was still crying when Dickens saw her three days later. She had hoped that she and the model would stick together and 'become like sisters'. Impatient to reinforce Julia's good intentions to 'reform', Dickens sent a new dress over to the prison for her. If only she would stay on the few extra days until the Home was ready, 'I have no doubt of her, and hope we may count upon her reclamation as almost certain.' But prison was still prison; its 'heavy discipline' and gloom were oppressing her spirits, and Dickens worried lest she might defect too. So he jumped the gun on opening day, and arranged for her to be taken by coach to Shepherd's Bush. Here was the house he had chosen, in what was then a rural area of fields and market gardens. It was big enough for about a dozen inmates and called Urania Cottage. You could get there by omnibus from Oxford Street, or from Piccadilly to Hammersmith and then a walk of half a mile. Both these bus routes are still running.

Julia was set to work making more new clothes for herself, and in helping to get the place ready. Head of ops and obsessively involved with every single decision was Dickens himself. At last his vision was starting to take shape: it had to be exactly as he had conceived it.

For Dickens it had all begun with a bang eighteen months before, in May 1846. He was in mid-career, at the height of his success. That very month reviews of his new book, *Pictures from Italy*, were proclaiming him 'the great master of the age'. He was certainly one of the most famous men of his time, and at thirty-four still young, cutting the figure of a dandy with his flashy waistcoats. He was also the head of a rapidly expanding family with six children under the age of ten. His latest spur-of-the-moment decision had them all packing up for a long trip to Switzerland; he planned to be away for a year.

Before he left for the peaceful shores of Lake Geneva, he wanted the super-wealthy Angela Burdett Coutts to come with him to Limehouse, down in the east London docks. They would visit a ragged school, a charitable school providing free education to the poorest children. The Ragged School movement dated back to the Sunday schools of the eighteenth century, and to the early nineteenth century, when the disabled cobbler John Pounds taught up to forty children while he worked in his shop. In 1844 nineteen schools in London joined to form the Ragged School Union with Lord Shaftesbury as their president. Reaching out to children referred to in one government report as 'the sweepings of the street', these schools improvised premises for themselves in disused coach factories and granaries, in old distilleries and warehouses.

Dickens and Angela Burdett Coutts had been friends for many years; he often acted on her behalf in a host of good causes. Her 'unofficial almoner', he was sometimes called. Now she was planning to endow a school for poor children alongside her new church in Rochester Row, Westminster, and Dickens wanted her to see for herself 'a lively and most encouraging picture of the Good you will do'. During that visit the idea of a home for fallen women came up for the first time.

In the hectic few days before his departure for Switzerland, Dickens found the time to sit down amid the bustle, and write Miss Coutts, as he addressed her, a truly mammoth letter. One of the longest he ever wrote, it spelled out his vision for such a home in minute detail. Why? What was it about this idea which grabbed him, and was to engage so much of his time, his practical talents and his emotional involvement for the next twelve years?

The answer lies in this extraordinary letter. In it Urania Cottage springs to life fully fledged, the creature of Dickens's imagination and energy. Like the *Daily News* which he had been planning to edit (an ill-conceived notion, and the main reason for the flight to Switzerland), like the amateur dramatics he put on and persuaded his friends to act in with him – and even more, like his novels and stories, this home for fallen women would be another total world for him to control. Here he could create and run everything according to his rules. The more he thinks about the idea, the more he loves it: the systematic invention of a little universe of his own. And not only that. He is hooked by the idea of changing people.

On the day he picked up his pen to put this vision into words, his breakfast copy of *The Times* would have informed him at obsequious length about the 'great and important news, the Accouchement of Her Majesty'. This was Queen Victoria's fifth child, Princess Helena (she turned out fat and lachrymose, dutiful and unremarkable, although capable of surprisingly advanced epistolary flirtation with her father's librarian – he lost his job as a consequence). Column after column of the newspaper bulged with the names of all the Princes and Princesses, Dukes and Duchesses, Bishops, Right Honourables and 'very numerous inquirers' who had called upon Buckingham Palace to pay their respects. But the paper also told of little girls born into altogether less fortunate circumstances. A classified advertisement placed on the front page by the Infant Orphan Asylum in Wanstead appealed on behalf of two-year-old Mary Anne Grave, one of eight children whose father, a butcher, had just been killed in an accident.

On its other pages his newspaper documented the famine in Ireland and threats of unrest at home. On the rare occasion when a woman does make an appearance in the columns of *The Times* (unless she is a Queen or newborn Princess), she is either in the crime reports, where the workhouse girls were excelling themselves, or in a scene of acute distress. Earlier in May, for instance, 24-year-old Eliza Clark had thrown two of her children over Battersea Bridge and was about to jump herself. Her drunken husband had hit her so hard that her head 'went through the door panel'. 'I have done all I could,' she told the court incoherently; she talked of her children as if they were still alive. 'It's a hard struggle now to get them a bit of bread.' Then there was 26-year-old Elizabeth Pulling, who lived with a brickmaker in Westminster. He was accused of attempted murder after he had beaten her and thrown her out of the window with such force that 'not a feature of her face could be distinguished from the violence she had received'. Or again in the same month and still in London, Ann Desmond, a suicide off Blackfriars Bridge: the verdict on her was 'Temporary Insanity'.

Over the years Dickens supported many charities and benevolent funds. While he never had much faith in governments, he did have faith in the power of the individual to change for good. In his books and stories, his characters can convert suddenly, turn their lives round for the better. But it was easier for men than women. One sexual mistake was enough to condemn a woman as fallen: this was the conventional Victorian line. It was a line Dickens was never happy with.

Strangely enough though, it is not the fallen women themselves who furnish the fuel for Dickens's first bright vision. He starts, not with the woman herself, nor even with what the home will be like, but with the end-point of emigration, and the 'distant parts of the World [where] women could be sent for marriage'. For him emigration is what sets the whole thing going. Emigration plus marriage, with the young women featuring to begin with as parcels, mail-order brides. Dickens himself looks like a one-man transportation scheme.

His creation of a home for fallen women in his letter to Miss Coutts ran to fourteen pages. It is a short story, manifesto and sales brochure all rolled into one. And when he had finished stacking the stall, Dickens ended by pitching for himself as the man to run it. 'I need not say that I should enter on such a task with my whole heart and soul.'

Miss Coutts evidently agreed, and throughout the next months they argued their different views of it. She had two main objections.

One was the incentive of marriage which Dickens rated so highly. Nor did she warm to his plan that exposure to temptation would be part of the training (unless they can learn to resist they will not do well on the outside, was Dickens's line). He only made matters worse by drawing parallels with the young men who worked at Coutts Bank and were exposed to temptation daily. This annoyed Miss Coutts. She took it as a personal slur on her clerks. But she fell in with his plans to meet Tracey and Chesterton, and obediently worked her way through the reading list Dickens set her. By now he was taking a more liberal stand than his mentors. He wants to argue the toss about drink. Of course these women will have drink problems; given their lives how could it be otherwise? Over the next months the plans would mature, partly waiting for Dickens's return to London the following February. For now, both he and Miss Coutts had other things on their minds.

Angela Burdett Coutts was two years younger than Dickens, and in her early thirties at this time. The two had met during the late 1830s. 'It must have been on a Friday', Dickens wrote later – he believed that 'anything of importance' to him always happened on a Friday. She was the youngest daughter of Francis Burdett, MP for Westminster and in former times a political firebrand who had caused riots and been imprisoned in the Tower of London. He and his daughter were early admirers of the young novelist. She read *The Pickwick Papers* to him as it came out in parts, and Sir Francis quoted *Oliver Twist* in his speeches. Angela invited the rising star to smart parties at her grand house which glowed with masterpieces by Raphael, Tintoretto and Rembrandt, prompting some social twitchiness on his part. He wrote to a mutual friend, 'Miss Coutts's card for the fifteenth has solemn mention of a Royal Duke and Duchess – *are* gentlemen expected to wear Court dresses in consequence? . . . I have no confidence in my legs, and should be glad to hear that the etiquette went in favour of Trowsers.'

In 1837 Angela had, to everyone's surprise, inherited her step-grandmother's half share in Coutts Bank along with the extra surname, making her what the press liked to call 'The Richest Heiress of All

England'. Naturally all England, including Queen Victoria, liked to gossip about whom she would marry; the Queen was also glad to borrow money from her. For suitors about to boil up to a proposal Angela and her companion, Hannah Meredith, went into a well-established routine. Hannah would leave the room but keep the door open; when she heard the discreet cough she knew it was time to come back in.

The beginning of 1847 was particularly eventful for Angela. Wary and weary of the young suitors, and prone to hero-worshipping strong older men, she had been devoting her attentions to the Duke of Wellington. The Iron Duke had retained his air of 'an eagle of the Gods' well into his seventies, in the estimation of the portrait painter Benjamin Haydon. And he had a softer side too. He and Angela exchanged tender letters complete with pressed flowers. They spent much time in each other's large houses. In February she proposed to him. His refusal is a model of tact and kindness, entreating 'My dearest Angela . . . not to throw yourself away upon a man old enough to be your grandfather'. Rejection notwithstanding, they continued to enjoy each other's company. A private winding staircase was built to connect their rooms in the Duke's house at Stratfield Saye, and by the autumn rumours of their impending marriage were speeding round Europe. Dickens found it hard to fix meetings with her; she would forget arrangements they had made.

There was another preoccupation too, in the shape of Richard Dunn. He was an Irish barrister who had stalked Angela for years, his persistence sometimes landing him up in jail. Now he was turning his hand to blackmail. He presented himself at Coutts Bank with a draft for £100,000 plus some lame doggerel which he claimed to have been written by Angela. This time her customary tactic of ignoring him would not do, and things came to a head in February 1847 with Dunn standing trial for wilful and corrupt perjury. 'Laughter in court' as the poem Dunn said Angela had composed for him while he was in prison was read out. The verses which were printed in *The Times* next morning gave Angela the tones of a bouncing music-hall comedienne:

Send to Coutt's your bill –
There are lots in the till –
I'll give the clerks orders to do it.
Then get your discharge,

27

Your dear body enlarge,
And in Stratton-street do let me view it.

Dunn was permitted to cross-question Angela, an unnerving experience for a woman who detested publicity. He lost, of course, and found himself in and out of prison for the next decade. He was banged up for good – in a lunatic asylum – only after he had transferred his attentions from Angela to her friend Princess Mary Adelaide of Cambridge, first cousin to the Queen. Dickens got the point: 'It is remarkable how brisk people are to perceive his madness, the moment he begins to trouble the blood royal.'

Dickens sympathised and fulminated, but in Lausanne he had other projects. No sooner arrived and unpacked than he was at his desk and announcing to his friend John Forster, 'BEGAN DOMBEY!' This is the end of June 1846. He was beginning his novel within the month of his inspired invention of a home for fallen women. Monthly publication of the new novel started at the end of September 1846 and went on until the end of March 1848, exactly those months during which Urania Cottage moved from Dickens's mind's eye to living reality. The shelter for the homeless girl kept pace with the progress of his novel.

It is clear from *Dombey and Son* that girls are much on Dickens's mind. 'Girls are thrown away in this house', we are told in the first monthly episode. At the heart of the novel is the unloved and neglected Florence Dombey. Before the end of the second episode the little girl is alone on the streets, separated from her nurse (the wonderful Susan Nipper – not her fault).

> With a wild confusion before her, of people running up and down, and shouting, and wheels running over them, and boys fighting, and mad bulls coming up, and the nurse in the midst of all these dangers being torn to pieces, Florence screamed and ran.

Worse is to come. Florence is kidnapped by a horrible old woman who strips off her pretty clothes and threatens her with a large pair of scissors, 'ruffling her curls with a furious pleasure'.

If these streets were a liability for well-born little Florence, they were just as dangerous in their way for Julia, Martha and Rosina. Old companions they would fall back in with, rowdy gangs of workhouse girls, brothel-keepers and pimps on the lookout, pockets to pick and men to accost: all made their threats and demands. Miss Coutts suggested that being allowed out alone might be a privilege for good conduct, as one of those small exposures to temptation which Dickens favoured. But he vigorously opposed the idea. 'If a girl goes out by herself, where is she to go? Every one she knows now is, to a greater or lesser extent, an infamous associate; and suffering her to go out by herself would be to expose her to the arts and temptations and recognitions of fifty such.' Privileges indoors, with keys perhaps, yes, 'But the streets of London, I confess I view with very great apprehension.' These are the streets which Dickens himself walked incessantly as he wrote his novels in his head. He knew what he was talking about.

Back in London in the early months of 1847, it was time to get down to practicalities. Where should the Home be? Dickens gave the thumbs down to Miss Coutts's initial choice of somewhere central. What would the girls do for exercise? He had another reason: 'The cultivation of little gardens, if they be no bigger than graves, is a great resource and a great reward.' After investigating various possibilities he finally plumped for a house called Urania Cottage in Shepherd's Bush. It would comfortably accommodate the thirteen inmates he judged the ideal number (he originally suggested thirty but smaller was better). The house was surrounded by fields, which later came up for rent. Dickens advised taking them, and let one of them to the milkman. They would create a sort of buffer zone between the house and the outside world.

During the summer he itched to launch his new ship. 'May I impress upon you', he wrote to Miss Coutts at the end of June, 'that it would be an immense thing for the Institution to begin before it is Winter weather, and while the garden is green and sunny.' In the event they did not open until mid-November.

Urania Cottage was nearly new, built in the early 1820s for a widow called Elizabeth Scott who lived nearby in Orville Cottage. Despite being called cottages, these were substantial well-proportioned houses in spacious gardens. A stable, coach-house and 'offices' had been added on to Urania Cottage in 1830. Dickens thought the stable would convert easily to a wash-house.

Once the solicitors had agreed a lease at sixty guineas a year and completed the paperwork Dickens threw himself into the preparations. He spent Miss Coutts's money – she put a thousand pounds into his bank account – but insisted 'you must not see the house until it is quite ready'. It was his dolls' house, and he revelled in manoeuvring all the pieces, both animate and inanimate, into place.

Dickens always loved domestic. 'No man', wrote his eldest daughter Mamie, 'was so inclined naturally to derive his happiness from home affairs. He was full of the kind of interest in a house which is commonly confined to women.' It is often said that Dickens did not do women well, either in books or life. There is no denying his indefensible treatment of his wife in the all too public breakdown of their marriage, behaving 'like a madman', said his younger daughter Katey. 'This affair brought out all that was worst – all that was weakest in him. He did not care a damn what happened to any of us. Nothing could surpass the misery and unhappiness of our home.' But that was all to come, more than ten years in the future. The story of Dickens and women which Urania Cottage tells us is about him working well with Angela Burdett Coutts, with the staff at the Home and with the inmates, to make the venture a success.

Everything for the new Home went through Dickens's hands: builders' alterations, furniture, bedsteads, bookcases and the books to go in them, and all 'from the most respectable wholesale warehouses'. He went on shopping expeditions for the material to make the girls' clothes. 'I have laid in all the dresses and linen of every sort for the whole house', he told Miss Coutts. He was pleased as Punch at negotiating wholesale prices at Shoolbred's in Tottenham Court Road.

As Julia Mosley sat sewing the fabrics Dickens had picked out for her, she was giving shape to the threshold ritual he put so much store by. The dress she was making marked her initiation. Dickens's first idea had been for a house divided into two halves, with probationers earning the right to cross the inner threshold. This had to be abandoned because it was not physically possible. Instead, he devised an elaborate ritual of reclothing: a cross between layette and trousseau. As they entered the Home the girls would be clad from the inside out in totally new clothes, even down to that 'linen of every sort' which presumably means underwear.

These clothes would be both uniform and not uniform. Dickens chose surprisingly bright fabrics. 'I have made them as cheerful in appearance as they reasonably could be – at the same time very neat and modest. Three of them will be dressed alike, so that there are four colours of dresses in the Home at once; and those who go out together, with Mrs Holdsworth, will not attract attention, or feel themselves marked out, by being dressed alike.'

The clothes mark the step change in philosophy. For the previous six months Julia had been wearing stiff drab prison uniform. Workhouse girls and Magdalenes (penitentiary women) were also clad in coarse uniforms whose message was clear. They spoke the language of society's disapproval: punishment, abasement, atonement. The laundry work which the penitentiaries favoured reinforced this message. The Magdalenes would, it was thought, be washing their souls clean along with the dirty clothes.

Urania was new thinking, and new spending too. From the first it was high-end philanthropy. With the cushion of Miss Coutts's money, though Dickens was always a careful bursar, the inmates would not have to bring in earnings as the Magdalenes did with their laundry work. Just as importantly, the small band of organisers had the freedom to try out their progressive notions untrammelled by the opinions of other sponsors or subscribers. They were heading away from the rest of the pack with their first assumption that anything which smacked of either religion or prison would be anathema.

The Urania risk meant taking a punt on optimism. It opposed current thinking on 'fallenness'; it championed Chesterton's belief that 'by far the majority exhibit many redeeming virtues', and it put its faith in the possibility of reform. But this was a time when the 'downward path' of the fallen woman was assumed to be inevitable and irreversible. '*The tendency is all downwards*,' Ralph Wardlaw emphasised in italics, in his often-quoted *Lectures on Female Prostitution*, published in 1842. 'Even in thievery, there may be an advance. . . But in the present case, *rising is a thing unknown*. It cannot be. It is all descent.'

Further, women prisoners, who were to form the Home's first constituency, were currently featuring in press and parliamentary reports as peculiarly unpredictable, prone to violent outbursts known as 'breaking out'. The other refuges which were starting up, such as the House of Mercy at Clewer two years after Urania, coped by attempting to break the spirits of their inmates. Susan Mumm, historian of these religious penitentiaries, describes their atmosphere as 'prison-like'. The inmates' heads were shaved, and their unruliness punished by solitary confinement. When Marianne George refused to eat the bullocks-head soup at Clewer she was fed nothing else: she gave in after a few days. The socially-minded novelists who dramatised fallen-women issues could see what was going wrong. Books with titles like *Hidden Depths* and *Out of the Depths* denounced the 'grim old matrons' and agreed that 'the good people who have established Refuges and Homes for those who repent have succeeded in making them repellent and intolerable'.

Dickens and Miss Coutts's new Home would have nothing to do with depths or debts to society. Shepherd's Bush was to be a one-way street to the future, with no looking back. Dickens insisted that neither the owner of the house nor its neighbours should know what kind of an institution it was to be. The neat servants' dresses which the inmates stepped out in would deflect any taunts about 'reformatory girls'. They would also begin to create the characters the young women would grow into under Dickens's vigilant eye. They were dressed to progress.

Urania would focus not on the wreck of the soul, but much more pragmatically on possibility and potential. And, it should be said, on pleasure. Dickens nudged Miss Coutts when he thought she was overdoing the spiritual salvation angle. 'The design is simply, as you and I agreed, to appeal to them by means of affectionate kindness and trustfulness.' 'Dealing gently' should be the guide. 'These unfortunate creatures are to be *tempted* to virtue.'

If Julia was walking on to Dickens's stage set, she was also walking into a marvellous new world. She was given a bedroom to share with two other girls: just the three of them and no supervision. The arrangements were much the same as for a large middle-class family at that time. When she saw her smart little bed Julia was understandably overwhelmed and 'cried very much'. She seems to have been quite a weeper. 'Happy and grateful' was how Dickens found her in these early days.

Of the first intake of five, so carefully interviewed and selected by him – 'All these girls I have seen repeatedly, and know very well, and I believe they have the strongest disposition to be confiding and faithful' – three would stay the course. Two, Frances Bewley and Mary Anne Stonnell, would not. Julia Mosley, Rosina Gale and Rubina Waller are some of the girls we know most about because Dickens took most interest in them. So did Miss Coutts, as she carefully annotated the letter Dickens wrote to tell her all about them. Miss Coutts made a point of noting their family backgrounds: 'Julia Mosley, Not bad parents, Mary Anne Stonnell Bad Parents, Rosina Gale Parents dead, Frances Bewley Mother living, Rubina Waller Father in law bad.'

She and Dickens and the prison governors had talked through these cases long and hard, although Dickens had to lean on her to get her inside prison. 'I still remain in the hope that you will come with me to Mr Chesterton's, where there is nothing to shock you but the sight of women in captivity – and where there is very much to gratify you in the humanity with which they are treated – for unless you see them now, you never can sufficiently feel what you have done for those who turn out well.'

With these transformation stories in mind, Dickens wanted Miss Coutts as sponsor to be the first reader of them. His letters, during Urania's birth and infancy, overflow with ideas and plans. How would these play out with the flesh and blood young women? He knew well that they would not be meek and passive receptacles for middle-class benevolence. But meek and passive he did not want. That was the stuff of horrors to him. It would mean defeat, as he recognised in the image of the young woman whom he was to describe nine years later in an article for his magazine *Household Words*. No more than a heap of rags, she collapsed outside the workhouse where she had been refused lodging.

> I put the money into her hand, and she feebly rose up and went away. She never thanked me, never looked at me – melted away into the miserable night, in the strangest manner I ever saw. I have seen many strange things, but not one that has left a deeper impression on my memory than the dull impassive way in which that worn-out heap of misery took that piece of money, and was lost.

As he interviewed prisoners at Coldbath Fields and Tothill Fields in the autumn of 1847 and made his choice of Julia Mosley and Rosina Gale, he knew he was not looking for passive – but nor was he looking for stroppy. After all, these girls had to be controllable. They also had to buy into his vision actively, be imaginative enough to see what was in it for them. He overrode Miss Coutts's doubts about the wisdom of luring the girls with promises of marriage in the far-off colonies, and crowed with delight when a matron at one of the feeder prisons agreed with him. 'Nothing would touch them so much, she said.'

The staff whom Dickens and his team of prison governors were also interviewing were as much an unknown quantity as the girls, and could be even more difficult to get right. Women who worked in hospitals and prisons relied on heavy discipline. They tended to be rough and uneducated: this was well before the time when such work was seen as suitable for a lady. Two women were needed, a matron and a second-in-command. Mrs Holdsworth did not immediately impress Dickens as the answer – 'I had no leaning towards her, at first' – but eighteen months later he admitted that he had 'really come to like her without the least inclination to do so'.

Once Mrs Holdsworth had been appointed Dickens instigated all sorts of elaborate preparations, including 'some Rehearsals of the routine of each day's life'. She must have tolerated his busy-bodying with good grace, as he marked which prayers in the prayer book she should use, but at the same time absolutely prohibited her, on pain of losing her job, from talking to the girls about their past lives. She learned to fall in with his demands, and would write to update him with the latest developments if he was out of town. She could make difficulties. Washday was one of her bugbears; she objected to the getting up early. 'She informed me, with a face of most portentous woe and intensity, that "she couldn't do it".' Dickens would grumble about 'such mincing nonsense', but then it all became yet one more aspect of the theatre of Urania Cottage. 'I wish I could draw Mrs Holdsworth's face for you, as she appeared when she opened her objection to me.'

It is because of Dickens himself that we know anything about this singular little world at all. His involvement mounted to obsession, certainly in its early days. He was 'in a state of great anxiety', 'unspeakably interested', and always 'very busy' with it. If he was making inroads into the lives of these young women, they in their turn were making an impact on him. At the beginning he was out there 'on alternate evenings'. He made it his business to get to know especially these first girls intimately. Indeed it *was* his business. 'I have taken some pains', he told Miss Coutts, 'to find out the dispositions and natures of every individual we take; and I think I know them pretty well, and may be able to give the matron some useful foreknowledge of them, and to exercise some personal influence with them in case of need.' Rather irritating for matron one might think, but Dickens had other priorities. What an entrée these girls gave him into the street life and underclass of London.

Further, he knew he had to get Miss Coutts on board; her money was what kept the ship afloat. To do this he had to keep her close and personally involved. A shy woman, Miss Coutts did not relish the face-to-face aspect of philanthropy. She did visit Urania Cottage with her companion Hannah (Saturday was their day), though much less often than Dickens did. So his letters had to do the job of bringing the place to life for her, personalising the characters in the drama – people she obviously knew a bit, enough to be interested, but not as well as Dickens did. Practically all of the eighty-seven names we have of Urania inmates come from this correspondence. The hundreds of letters he wrote to her over the decade from 1847 brim with details designed to engage her, and presumably keep the funds flowing. Charities these days appeal to our feelings by showing us the few rather than the many – one face rather than the starving millions – and no one knew better than Dickens how to write a character. And he adored being part of the drama himself.

CHAPTER THREE

Guinea Pigs

'I'm glad you like it,' said Mr Jarndyce . . . 'It makes
no pretensions; but it is a comfortable little place,
I hope, and will be more so with such bright young
looks in it.'
Bleak House, Chapter Six

THE END OF November 1847: Urania had been open less than a
week and already there was a huge difference to be seen in Julia
Mosley and Rubina Waller. Dickens claimed that they were 'altered
in appearance in a most extraordinary manner', but then he had a lot
invested in this 'experiment' as he called it. This was to be his most
sustained work with real people rather than fictional characters, his
one attempt to do a novel in three dimensions. Two decades later, Dr
Barnado would have his orphan charges photographed; we have no
such pictures of the Urania girls. But we do have the unique legacy of
their voices in what Dickens wrote about them.

Three years before Urania Cottage started he had made the world
weep copiously over the melodramatic what-if scenario of his Christmas
story 'The Chimes'. His friends had wept over it too, at one of the first
readings Dickens ever gave, a private affair to a group of male friends.
One of them, the artist Daniel Maclise, sketched the scene with two of
the men crying openly. 'If you had seen Macready,' wrote Dickens to

his wife Catherine, 'undisguisedly sobbing, and crying on the sofa, as I read – you would felt (as I did) what a thing it is to have Power.'

The Christmas hit of 1844, 'The Chimes' features two starving young needlewomen. Lilian becomes a prostitute: the chinking purse of money signals what is going on but keeps it suitable for family reading by the fireside. Poverty-stricken Meg is on the verge of drowning herself and her baby. The point of the misery, which is luckily reversible – after all, it's Christmas – is to teach a lesson. We must learn mercy towards such women and 'mothers rendered desperate'. They are not bad but wretched, to be pitied and helped.

So much for fiction, what about life? Could the misery of real women's lives be put into reverse? Could Dickens bring his 'Power' to bear on the down-and-outs, the petty thieves, prostitutes and attempted suicides whom he read about in his newspaper every day, whom he recognised from his habitual prison visiting and nightly walks? There is more than a whiff of the lab-rat about the Urania women for Dickens. They will be the case-studies for his philosophy of practical benevolence. They were to be his own controlled experiment, set to live under the conditions he dictated, a world run according to his rules and under his observation.

Out at Shepherd's Bush the first specimen was proving far from straightforward. Julia Mosley was a mercurial and emotional young woman, subject to extreme mood swings. She had been depressed in prison, even when reaching the end of her sentence; the move to Urania made her, Dickens said, 'wonderfully happy'. But it was all too much for her. She could not eat, and threw herself into the work of the new household with a manic energy which prompted Dickens to tell Mrs Holdsworth that Julia's industry, while beyond praise, should not 'be carried too far'.

She could not settle easily, and wrote a letter to an old friend or lover, which Dickens 'immediately forwarded to its destination'. He thought it unlikely that her correspondent would want to 'renew the broken intercourse', and odd that Julia did not realise this. The next day – and this was all within two months of her arrival at Urania Cottage – Julia was in big trouble, causing the first major incident at the Home. Dickens recreated it, or created it, at great length for William Brown. Brown was the doctor on the Home's management committee, he was married to Angela Burdett Coutts's former governess and now companion, Hannah Meredith. They lived next door to Miss Coutts in Piccadilly.

Julia, Dickens told William Brown, had roused Mrs Holdsworth's suspicions through her recent habit of leaving the long room after tea for twenty minutes or so each evening, sometimes alone, sometimes with one other girl. Mrs Holdsworth thought she might be meeting someone in secret and set the gardener to watch. Sure enough, a young man was spotted 'going along the fence' by the wash-house. The gardener coughed and the man ran away, though not before the gardener had grabbed his coat and ripped it badly. He recognised him as a brick-maker from up the road, a youngster of about seventeen currently out of work. The kilns were only fired during the summer months and this was mid-January. He later gave the gardener a reasonable explanation as to why he had been there, so he may have had nothing to do with Julia, and they were never seen together. But it was at this time she suffered one of her mood changes. 'She has been low-spirited, silent, and churlish ever since.'

Dickens sped out to Shepherd's Bush to interrogate Julia, who denied everything: no meetings, no communication, no young man. Dickens's close attention to her brings her voice momentarily back from oblivion. 'On my saying "you seem changed in your manner. Is there anything the matter with you?" she replied "Not as I knows on."' A tiny sound bite of the moody Julia, and a reminder that Uranians were girls with attitude.

Dickens's protracted account of the little fracas marshalled its points legalistically. '1stly', '2ndly', 'there seems no doubt'. He stressed the lack of direct evidence against Julia, but could not let the matter go. He paid the gardener lavishly for extra surveillance work and ordered Mrs Holdsworth to tell him of any change in Julia. A complicated scenario was invented to account for her behaviour. 'My own impression is, that she is in the restless state which precedes the determination to go away. I think it possible that she may have got this man to go to some other man with whom she was formerly acquainted, and that this other man has returned some message importing that he has no desire to renew the acquaintance. Which would depress and irritate her.'

Why such involvement on Dickens's part? Was it sentimental, a warm-hearted attachment to the first inmate, his first pet as it were?

The motive he suggests is altogether cooler. 'My reason for desiring to know accurately what she is about, is, that we may be beforehand with her, and, if we have any new reason to believe that she is going, that we may – for the general example – discharge her. I will go out on Thursday night, and see her again.' While he was acutely interested, it was in her as a case as much as an individual. Julia the experimental specimen. He did indeed make that trip to Shepherd's Bush on Thursday, just to see her, but although he 'spoke very kindly' to her, 'her manner of replying, in the presence of the rest, was so very sullen and insolent that I fear some strong notice of it must be taken' – though not yet.

Part of Julia's problem seems to have been her poor health. We get another of those rare sound traces when she asks Dickens to arrange a private appointment for her with Dr Brown. The medicine he has prescribed is making her sick, and she needs to be frank about her condition. 'She has not told you that she believed her illness to be "along of her past misconduct".' This sounds like some kind of sexually transmitted disease, and brings us to the tricky issue of prostitution and the idea of the sexual fall, which is so central to the Urania experiment. Prostitution was a big public issue of the time, social evil number one. Estimates about numbers of prostitutes in London veered wildly from eight thousand up to more than eighty thousand. No one really knew and there was panic talk about 'the multitudinous Amazonian army the devil keeps in constant field service'.

Two major assumptions dominated thinking: once you've fallen, as the word suggests, you can never be the same again, there is no going back. 'The career of these women is a brief one,' wrote the social commentator William Greg in his essay on 'Prostitution' for the *Westminster Review* in 1850, 'their downward path a marked and inevitable one; and they know this well. They are almost never rescued, escape themselves they cannot.' Thinking had not changed much since William Hogarth's graphic series 'The Harlot's Progress' in the eighteenth century, with its inevitable descent via prison and disease to early death – in the same prison, Tothill Fields, where Julia Mosley found herself a hundred years later. In the mid 1830s a massively documented study of prostitution in Paris had demonstrated that it was in fact a transient occupation for many women. The majority of prostitutes moved on after a few years, and many of them married. But this trajectory of transience did not cross the Channel well. The British clung to the idea of irreversibility, and to profiles of prostitutes as contaminating threats. In the 1860s, the decade after Urania Cottage, the Contagious Diseases Acts would be passed – and fiercely contested – in attempts to regulate their behaviour.

The second assumption is to do with choice: women choose this life and are therefore to be held responsible for it. Over the next few years, from 1849 onwards, attitudes would begin to shift, especially among the liberal-minded. Henry Mayhew's interviews with working women made a big impression. Many of them were seamstresses, forced on to the streets simply to stay alive. Poverty rather than vice came to be recognised by many commentators as the prime cause. Until 1875 the age of consent was twelve. No one knew how many child prostitutes there were, but the young girls migrating from the protection of their families as they flocked into domestic service were an obviously vulnerable group.

Urania was in the vanguard in treating fallenness as a reversible process. The greatest gift Dickens brought to the experiment was his ability to see the world through the eyes of the young woman herself. Right from the beginning he thinks himself into her outsider stance, indeed this is where the whole thing starts for him, as he writes to Miss Coutts about the kind of young woman they should try to reach. 'Society has used her ill and turned away from her, and she cannot be expected to take much heed of its rights or wrongs.' 'Never mind society' – that is what Dickens thinks she thinks. His aim is to make her care, to make her part of that world. He will do this by giving her agency. 'The means of return to Happiness are now about to be put into her own hands, and trusted to her own keeping.' Self-respect will give her the key, and although Dickens's first ideas look heavy-handed (a lot about 'habits of firmness and self-restraint') the core idea is radical.

Dickens knew from Chesterton and Tracey that resettlement was the big problem for prostitutes. Later he referred to the Urania Cottage women as 'homeless', but in his first letter to Miss Coutts he was explicit about the fallen nature of his target-group. Their only crime is 'their original one of having fallen from virtue'. Caught in a set of vicious revolving doors, these women are in and out of prison because they have nowhere else to go but the streets. While prostitution itself was not a crime, the fine for loitering and importuning for the purposes of prostitution was two pounds. Sometimes, Dickens told Miss Coutts, they bribe policemen to turn a blind eye, and sometimes the money is not enough or they drink it away.

Other rescue societies and institutions, such as the Lock Hospitals which treated patients with venereal disease, had taken in prostitutes since the mid-eighteenth century. But there was, in the words of historian Frank Prochaska, 'a phenomenal upsurge in interest in the mid- and late Victorian years'. Urania Cottage came at the beginning of this wave, more than ten years before the Female Mission to the Fallen. Rescue work in the streets then became the fashionable thing, with midnight meetings (tea and buns for the prostitutes), brothel visiting, 'cruising' in Regent Street, slumming in the East End, and other exhilarating tactics. But this would be all towards the end of the nineteenth century. Urania Cottage was to be quite different from any existing refuges and religious institutions. It was to be a family, and it was to produce emigrants.

Dickens also wanted to keep a healthy distance from the religiosity which he felt infected rescue work. The choice of chaplain was a ticklish one. Dickens was reluctant to offend Miss Coutts, but he did not want the girls harangued by a tub-thumping Old Testament moralist. Nor did he want a chaplain addressing each girl individually before she got to the Home. This, he thought, 'would decidedly involve the risk of their refusing to come to us'. The absence of sermonising was to be Urania's strong suit. Young Mrs Fisher, the first appointment as second-in-command, was exactly right. A widow of twenty-six and looking even younger, she was an intelligent woman, energetic and responsive, and with experience of this age group. She saw what Dickens wanted straight away, and as her pet canary hopped about the table in the long room the first night she was there, she helped the girls to feel at home. A great start for the experiment in atmosphere.

A few years ago fourteen letters from Dickens to Georgiana Morson, one of the matrons at the Home, came on to the market. The auction-eer was quoted as saying 'Some passages suggest that his interest in the girls was less than healthy'. Well, yes and no. If Dickens had wanted to have sex with prostitutes and working-class girls, I do not think he would have set up a bordello to do it under the nose and sponsorship of Angela Burdett Coutts. After all, he had other ways of finding such women, as he told his friend, the artist Daniel Maclise, about the pros-titutes at Margate: 'I know where they live'. On the other hand, there had to be something in it for him. Of course he genuinely wanted to help the young women, but he was undeniably much more involved with them than he ever was with the Ragged School boys, another of the charitable causes he worked on with Miss Coutts.

Dickens had always preferred girls, as he told his friend Clarkson Stanfield on the birth of yet another son. The novel of the early Ura-nia months shows this preference, as *Dombey and Son* turns out to be 'a Daughter after all!' Saving his fictional Florence from the infernal streets of London, Dickens will be saviour for real in Shepherd's Bush. He will also be stage manager of the make-over show. In fact the whole thing has a modern flavour. No one better suited than Dickens to be Big Brother; nor would he be the last celebrity to use his charisma in order to lead a small do-good project from the front.

Getting to know the young women intimately was always part of his enterprise. Can he be accused of trading in their woes, of being a voyeur? This has been a criticism put to me while I have been com-mending his good works; and I suppose that, yes, he was a voyeur in the sense that for a novelist, everything must be grist to the mill. The Urania women certainly came to have many uses for Dickens, they were a positive goldmine. He would give his fictional women edited versions of the lives of the real young women, and send them where they went. But more than that, his very way of writing would change in ways he could not have foreseen, as the stories the young women told him helped him find his way back to his own past.

The house in Shepherd's Bush was already called Urania Cottage in fire insurance documents dating back to the 1820s; Dickens and Miss Coutts decided to stick with the name. Classicist Dickensians liked to think it referred to Aphrodite Urania, the pure goddess of love, as against Aphrodite Pandemos, the goddess of the streets. This would chime in with Dickens's fear of the streets for the young woman. Urania is also one of the nine muses, the muse of Astronomy. Her name means 'Heavenly' in Greek; in Renaissance times she was associated with exalted inspiration. Milton invokes her as his muse in a beautiful passage in *Paradise Lost*, which Dickens would have read. Milton praises her 'voice divine' and prays to her:

> Still govern thou my song,
> Urania, and fit audience find, though few.

Dickens's audience was, as he well knew, considerably larger than Milton's; but I think the idea of the Urania inmates as his muses is not so far-fetched.

Muses or not, history has left us little to go on about these young women. But there is a bit. The census returns for 1851 record most of the Urania inmates as coming from London, although in a distressing number of cases they did not seem to know where they had been born. In 1861 some of the ten inmates came from as far afield as Cornwall and France. While practically all of them were in their late teens, some were as young as fourteen and Charlotte Glyn claimed that she was thirteen. Dickens did not believe her: 'its ridiculous impossibility is self-evident'.

Not all these women were ex-convicts. From the first Dickens spread his net widely, always in the interests of Urania as research project. In 1850 he was trying to see if the 'class' of girls to be found in Ragged Schools 'are worth the experiment'. For fifteen-year-old Emma Spencer, Urania Cottage would be her third institution; she came via Clerkenwell Workhouse and the Field Lane Ragged School. Dickens looked over four girls from the school, all 'pretty strong and healthy'. He picked Ellen Glyn, sister of the fibbing Charlotte, along with Emma Spencer. Both looked 'terribly destitute and wretched'. Neither had been in prison, and 'each assured me, separately, that she in no sense belonged to the class from whom the greater part of our inmates have been taken', which sounds as though they were insisting that they were not prostitutes. Dickens commented: 'I cannot say that I quite believe this, but I have no other reason to doubt it, than the suspicion which their faces awaken within me.' Their fake assurances did not deter him. 'I don't know, from their stories, how they very well could have been less wretched than they are.' They must have enthused about emigration, at least for his sake. So he took them in.

Institutional overload would wash many candidates up on the Urania doorstep. Martha Goldsmith from the Magdalen Hospital was getting on well, which suggested a new plan to Dickens: hiring a room 'near the Magdalen on their receiving-days, and seeing the girls whom they cannot take in'. He was no stranger to the world of ragged schools, foundling hospitals and orphanages. He knew that you had to look past what you saw: girls such as the 'desolate creature without father or mother', nineteen-year-old Mary Anne Wilson, who 'answered me plainly, and said she had been about the streets for a year'. Dickens guessed that once out of the workhouse and into Urania, 'she would be a robust strong girl, after a little regular food and shelter'.

A visit to the workhouse could kill two birds with one stone. While on the lookout for likely girls, he would also be collecting material for a crackling piece of journalism. 'The dragon, pauperism' was the villain, but it was the size of the place and its institutionalising effect which struck him so profoundly:

> Groves of babies in arms; groves of mothers and other sick women in bed; groves of lunatics; jungles of men in stone-paved down-stairs day-rooms, waiting for their dinners; longer and longer groves of old people, in up-stairs Infirmary wards, wearing out life, God knows how – this was the scenery through which the walk lay, for two hours.

He was dismayed by the 'lethargic indifference' all this induced. Small was better, homely was best. That was the lesson he took back with him along with the workhouse girls.

At least one Urania girl started life in the infamous orphanage run by Benjamin Drouet, 'that amiable victim of popular prejudice'. Dickens led attacks on 'The Paradise at Tooting', as he savagely called Mr Drouet's Pauper Asylum for Children, in a series of front-page articles for the *Examiner* in 1849. When cholera broke out at the end of 1848 Drouet had over thirteen hundred children in his care, or rather neglect, sent by workhouse authorities across London. At that time Tooting was a quiet little village. A violent man, Drouet kept the children in squalour and was known to beat them. He repeatedly ignored detailed guidelines specified by the Board of Health, whose general secretary was Dickens's brother-in-law Henry Austin.

While the starved, abused and over-crowded children died in their hundreds, the authorities looked the other way or shrugged the responsibility on to someone else. After eighty infant burials in Tooting churchyard, the Surrey coroner had still not ordered any inquests. Eventually, some infected children were moved out of Tooting and died in the neighbouring area of West Middlesex, and here the coroner did take action. He was Thomas Wakley, surgeon, radical politician and founder of the *Lancet* medical journal. Dickens admired him, and with good cause, having served on one of his juries nine years earlier. 'Nobly patient and humane' was Dickens's verdict on him.

Over a hundred and fifty of the Tooting children died in January 1849. Drouet landed up in the dock of the Old Bailey, but got off on a technicality. His barrister insisted that the children might have died anyway, and the judge directed the jury to acquit the defendant. All this made a big impression on Dickens, who later described it as 'an enormity which, a hundred years hence, will still be vividly remembered in the bye-ways of English life'. He did not forget or forgive Drouet, and frequently returned to the attack. Servants like Guster in *Bleak House* have never recovered from their ordeal at Tooting. The dummy book-backs which Dickens designed for his study include *Drouet's Farming. Vols. I-V.*

The girl from Tooting at Urania bore its unmistakable stamp. She had no idea of her age or her birthday. 'Not naturally stupid, but her intellect had been so dulled by neglect that she was in the Home many months before she could be imbued with a thorough understanding that Christmas Day was so called as the birthday of Jesus Christ. But when she acquired this piece of learning, she was amazingly proud of it.' Rosina Gale, who was among the first intake at Urania, was one of the thousands of young women who failed to make their living by needlework. Here Urania was again in the vanguard. Over the next few years the distressed needlewoman was to become a famous icon, an image of suffering and exploitation. Pictures of her filled exhibitions and galleries; campaigns were waged on her behalf.

The needlewoman was in some ways the opposite of the prostitute. She was virtuous suffering, she could be openly discussed as a problem, she could be pitied and helped. She was the working woman you would all come into contact with, sometimes literally, as she fitted and made your clothes. You wore the work of her fingers next to your skin, displayed her skills for the admiration of others. You also knew that you did not pay her enough. Thomas Hood's 'Song of the Shirt' started to put her on the map of good causes at the end of 1843, and Henry Mayhew's journalism of 1849-50 gave the campaign a big boost. His interviews showed that these women could not earn enough to live on by their needlework, and that some had to supplement their income by petty theft or sex-work. Needlewoman and prostitute were not, then, so far apart; but one you could campaign on behalf of, the other you could not, at least not until Josephine Butler's work later in the century.

Girls would also come via Dickens's diverse connections and contacts. Sometimes he canvassed actively. In 1850 he invited a couple of magistrates from the London courts, whom he knew. 'It has occurred to me that you might, at some time or other, have some miserable girl before you, for whom you would be happy to make such good provision.' He spelt out the Home's conditions clearly: fallen or not. 'We don't consider a Magdalen qualification indispensable, but we don't object to it, and we are glad (when we are not full) to receive any reasonably hopeful case of distress or offence.'

William Broderip, who presided over Westminster Police Court, responded fulsomely in the manner of the day about trusting 'that we may have the gratification of helping to heal the broken-hearted and gently leading back those who have erred in the right way.' Gilbert A' Beckett, who was a comic writer as well as a magistrate (as 'Poz' he had done rip-off imitations of Dickens back in the 1830s) replied more concisely. He was glad to have the Urania card up his sleeve for the 'girl who had been brought before him for trying to get admission into the workhouse at an unseasonable hour.' This was in 1851. Dickens told Miss Coutts how he went to A' Beckett's court 'immediately, and found her to be a little country girl of 17 – rather pretty – who had been deserted by her father, and had been tramping and hop-picking and vagabondizing generally, all her life.' He accepted her for the Home on the spot.

Sometimes people approached Dickens. Elizabeth Mackin from Clerkenwell Green was the daughter of a warder at Coldbath Fields prison who appealed to Dickens while he was visiting. He was happy to take her in. As the word spread about the new Home, magistrates from as far away as Birmingham and Leeds contacted him with deserving cases. Clergymen would write to him. Even the Home Secretary, Sir George Grey, was part of the network. Were they soft touches, swayed by a pretty face? Perhaps, but wouldn't you rather a soft touch than a heart of flint?

Only occasionally did Dickens suspect the men who wrote in on a girl's behalf. 'I am not at all clear of the innocent nature of her knowledge of the Mr Vernon whose letter you gave me,' he told Miss Coutts in 1852. He guessed that the letter purportedly by the girl herself was also a Vernon composition. 'I doubted one expression in her letter to you as not being what the girl herself would be likely to use; and, on pressing her, I found that the letter had been written for her by someone else.' He hoped these subterfuges would not scupper the girl's chances. 'She seems quite earnest in her application,' and was keen to emigrate to Port Phillip (in what is now Victoria) 'because she has been told she has an uncle there, who is rich'.

In Bristol Mary Carpenter was organising Ragged Schools and trying to improve the lives of poor children. The influential book she wrote on *Reformatory Schools for the Children of the Perishing and Dangerous Classes* avowed her admiration for Dickens. He returned the compliment and would have liked to show her round Urania Cottage himself, but 'I fear it would hardly worth your while to visit it, unless it were in my power to go with you and tell you the private history of the different cases.' Alas, he was behindhand with *Bleak House* and could not spare the time.

Mary Carpenter was a pioneer too. In 1854 she founded and superintended Red Lodge in Bristol, the first girls' reformatory school in England. Her philosophy matched Dickens's. 'Love must be the ruling sentiment and guide of all those who attempt to influence and guide these children' – love and a legion of rules. Outwardly, noted her biographer, Mary was 'sharp of tongue and sharper of pen', but she softened towards the girls she liked best. She confessed that she 'had a hand in spoiling' ten-year-old Kitty, who came from a family of tramps and looked like the pony she was supposed to have stolen. Although Mary bent the rules to keep Kitty on beyond the usual leaving age, she had to let her go when her mother called for her. Kitty left loaded with presents and kisses, but was dead within a few months, killed by the life on the road. When Mary heard the news she put her head down on her desk and cried.

A few years later she intervened more drastically, this time with five-year-old Rosanna, who had been sent to the reformatory for the 'crime' of possibly being illegitimate, which closed the doors of the local orphanage to her. 'God put it into my mind that I ought to be a mother to the little thing,' wrote Mary, who was unmarried and fifty-one, and proceeded to lavish maternal blessings on the 'darling little thing'. 'I feel already a *mère de famille*, happy in buying little hats and socks and a little bed to stand in my own room, out of *my own* money. It is a wonderful feeling!' When Rosanna's real mother pressed charges of child-stealing, she was no match for the seasoned philanthropist, who accused the mother of abandoning her child. 'My own dear R' lived with Mary until her death, and was well provided for in her will.

From Manchester Elizabeth Gaskell was an early enquirer for a prospectus – she got back a letter from Dickens riding his hobby horse of emigration. Remembering this a few years later in 1850, she wrote to ask his help for sixteen-year-old Pasley. We do not know her first name but it might as well have been Ruth. She provided the model for Gaskell's fallen woman novel of 1853, the book which provoked so much scandal and controversy that it gave its author 'Ruth fever'.

Pasley's story was, inevitably, more interesting than the white-washed Ruth's, and Gaskell enjoyed sharing its details with her fellow novelist. She told Dickens that Pasley had been seduced by a local doctor. Her progress takes the predictable turns: drinking, pawning her clothes, stealing, prison. Now 'pining to redeem herself', abroad was the only hope, but only in 'a *good* ship', so this is where Dickens comes in. 'You see the message you sent about emigration some years ago has been the mother of all this mischief.' Pasley duly got safe passage under the protection of a couple going to the Cape, and Dickens got the post-script Gaskell knew he would appreciate. When in prison Pasley needs a doctor and guess who is summoned – none other than her seducer. 'The girl just fainted dead away, and he was so affected he had to sit down, – he said "Good God how did you come here." He has been dismissed from his post in consequence.'

Dickens's own novel of 1853, *Bleak House*, comes from the heart of the Urania years. Homes, homeliness and houselessness run through the warp of the book. As the critic Rosemarie Bodenheimer points out, 'Just about every character in the novel's enormous cast is judged through his or her style of household management.' Dickens celebrates John Jarndyce's honourable attempt to create a family home for Ada Clare, Richard Carstone and Esther Summerson, three young victims of legal and social blight. An enterprise not so different from that of his creator.

PART TWO

ALTERNATIVE DOMESTICITY
AT SHEPHERD'S BUSH

CHAPTER FOUR

Charles in Charge

I was obliged to run away to Shepherd's Bush and my
virgin charges there.
Dickens to Frank Stone, 5 September 1851

IT WAS RISE and shine at six o'clock sharp for everyone at Urania
Cottage. From then on every moment of the day was timetabled by
Dickens, until bedtime at ten o'clock. About which he had strong views
of course, as he did about all the arrangements. Ten o'clock was right,
he thought, because of the dangers of shutting up 'unoccupied minds
at preposterously early hours.' So how did his experiment play out in
reality? What was life like behind those doors which were locked to
keep people in as well as out?

The close fit of the road-map in the monster letter Dickens wrote
back in 1846 to the regime he enforced for the next eleven years does, it
has to be said, look like inflexibility on his part. But for him the whole
point of the place was to work through his seminal vision. The intensity of its hold on him had something to do with his fascination with
institutions, and with prisons in particular. No one knew more than
Dickens about the different forms a prison could take. The fenced-in
family was a version he knew at first hand.

Dickens's childhood experience is well known. When his father was
imprisoned in the Marshalsea debtors' prison in 1824, the rest of the
family moved in too. Twelve-year-old Charles was alone on the outside.

He kept that small epoch of desolation and his work in the blacking warehouse a profound secret, but he began his writing career with a visit to the notoriously shameful Newgate. For the rest of his life he would be making capital out of prisons. Once he was even accused, much to his amusement, of being an ex-convict himself.

He was walking along the Edgware Road with his friend Mark Lemon (the editor of *Punch* magazine), when nineteen-year-old Cornelius Hearne tried to steal Lemon's watch from his pocket. 'We pursued him,' Dickens told the court the next day, and 'when he was taken he was most violent; he is a very desperate fellow, and he kicked about in all directions.' Dickens thought he recognised Hearne, he said, from seeing him at the House of Correction. This gave Hearne his moment. 'Now, your worship,' he confided to the judge, 'he must have been in quod himself, or he couldn't have seen me. I know these two gentlemen well; they're no better than swell mobsmen, and get their living by buying stolen goods. That one [he pointed to Mr Dickens] keeps a "fence", and I recollect him at the prison, where he was put in for six months, while I was only there for two.' *The Times* reporter was in court to see both 'literary gentlemen' roaring with laughter at the 'honour which the prisoner had with such unblushing effrontery conferred upon them'. Hearne got three months' hard labour.

Urania, though, was not to be a prison, and its regime was entirely different. No, this was to be 'an innocently Cheerful family'. But the first thing Dickens did was to order the garden to be fenced all round. Security was tight. 'What do you think of a very big dog in a barrel?' he suggested to Miss Coutts. The house should be under special police watch, with the gardener as back-up. He himself stood firm at the door, guarding all entrances and exits. Adamant that the girls should not be allowed out on their own, he recognised the importance of keys, and what they would mean to the inmates. They were never to be left lying about. Girls would take it in turn to act as 'porteress' on the gate but always under supervision.

'Active management' was how Dickens described his role at Urania Cottage to Harriet Martineau. Accurate on both counts. Active certainly: in the early years he was there at least once a week, for the Monday afternoon committee meetings which he chaired. Later the committee meetings shifted to once a month, but Dickens was always ready to make the trip from his home in north London if something came up which he wanted to be involved in. He took what he called 'the showman's pride' in taking round friends or interested social workers. When he was outside London he would come up to town specially if he thought it was necessary.

As for managing: quite simply, all the decisions and all the money went through him. How closely he worked with the staff is clear from the letters he wrote to Georgiana Morson, who was matron at Urania for five years. One of them just says 'Yes, to both your enquiries.' Every girl applying to the Home would be interviewed by him at least twice: once before she was admitted, and then again when she had settled in. It was up to him to decide which girls they should accept and when they were ready to emigrate, usually after about a year. He also insisted that the committee should see each girl separately every time they met, to check on her progress. So he must have got to know the inmates well. And because of his management of their routine, when he was not there he could look at his watch and know what they were doing every half-hour of the day.

Dickens's own children testified to his mania for tidiness. 'He made a point of visiting every room in the house once each morning,' remembered his eldest daughter Mamie, 'and if a chair was out of its place, or a blind not quite straight, or a crumb left on the floor, woe betide the offender!' Thus would it be at Urania too. Everyone and everything must be clean, fresh and bright. The house was equipped with all mod cons. As soon as gas was laid to the road in 1857 Dickens wanted it brought inside. 'I would recommend a jet in the fanlight, kitchen, wash-house, bathroom, over the chimney piece in each bedroom. Then no light would Ever be carried about the house. Just as we do here.' His anxiety makes sense after an accident in 1850 which seems to have singed off Mrs Morson's eyebrows.

Saturday night was bath-night for everyone at Urania. Dickens himself took a shower every day. On one holiday he even employed a local carpenter to shut a 'noble waterfall' with a drop of a hundred and fifty feet into 'an immense wooden caravan' for the purpose. Before they arrived at the Home girls might have to be given money to buy themselves a bath. Very unusually a girl might have to have her head shaved, such as Campbell (we do not know her first name), whose hair was falling out. Dickens noticed she was 'low spirited in consequence. As well she may be, looking something between the knob on the top of a pair of tongs – a Chinese – and a scraped dutch cheese.'

In his letters drains are a constant refrain. But what might appear to be fussing over 'the Great Drainage Question' is understandable in the light of the cholera epidemics sweeping London during these years. His exertions paid off. Only once is there any mention of an infectious disease at Urania. 'This disaster of Itch [scabies] at the Home is a little unfortunate,' he tells Miss Coutts in 1856; 'but I have a strong hope that it will not spread in the least. The place being so extremely clean and well kept, there is every ground for feeling confident that it will not occasion much inconvenience.' It does not seem to have done. The only recorded death is Harriet Tanner's in June 1856; from what, we do not know.

Dickens would move swiftly if necessary. 'No time must be lost,' he told William Brown, 'in getting the unfortunate Brighton girl into some Hospital. Her condition is so horrible, that she is obliged to be kept apart; the very odor from her sores, being unendurable as they say.' Most importantly, the dreaded cholera was kept well at bay. Dickens sent round a prescription for the pills which his own family were taking as a preventative during the epidemic of 1849.

Under his regime the girls were healthier than at other institutions. Miss Coutts could afford to subsidise a good diet to feed them up properly. And while the inmates at Clewer were allowed outside only once a week for a walk in Windsor Great Park, Urania girls were often out and about – always with a matron of course – running errands, going to Church and shopping locally. In the summer they cultivated their gardens: healthy exercise for the young women, a supply of fresh flowers and produce for the house, and excellent preparation for the colonial housewife.

Just how much did Urania Cottage cost to run? Although the bill book in which Dickens itemised the accounts so sedulously is lost, we can make some educated guesses from references in his correspondence and his own bank book at Coutts Bank. The start-up was expensive because all the furniture and clothes had to be bought. Dickens mentions bills of nearly twenty pounds each on books and blinds alone. Six months or so after Urania opened he devoted a whole letter to reassuring Miss Coutts about his careful husbandry. He admitted he had been startled by 'the increasing row of items' which 'rather took my breath away, when I was writing it out', and was relieved 'to find that you had formed so liberal an idea of the expences' (sic).

As for the running costs: in April 1850 Dickens tells Miss Coutts that 'the Monthly book (including fire insurance, gardener's salary &c) was £44.1.11 ½, in addition to which I have given Mrs Morson, she having no money, £5 for petty cash.' This did not include the salary for the two matrons, which cannot have come to less than sixty pounds a year. In December 1852 he 'paid the bills for last month, which (with £5 petty cash to Mrs Morson) amounted to £43.16.0'. October 1852 was an unusually heavy month, 'some Seventy Pounds' because it included three months' worth of drapers' and carpenters' bills. Dickens's account book at Coutts and Co suggests an erratic pattern of payments, due partly to all the improvements he was forever urging: 'my infirmity in the arrangement way' as he acknowledged to Miss Coutts.

The evidence of Miss Coutts's payments gives a clearer picture. She transferred two and a half thousand pounds to his account between January 1848 and January 1853, which works out at five hundred pounds a year – forty-two pounds per girl. This does not include the rent of sixty-three pounds a year. And that was not all. On Miss Coutts would fall the full costs of emigration, which she paid through her own secretary. Fares would be about twelve pounds each; then add at least another four pounds for the outfit for each emigrant, plus the 'reward' money she had earned while at Urania. If, say, ten girls emigrated each year, that would be at least a hundred and sixty pounds. The grand total could not come in at under seven hundred and twenty pounds a year.

Was this lavish by the standards of the time? The most a work-house girl would have had spent on her was twenty pounds a year, less than half the Uranian forty-two pounds running costs. By Victorian standards of social welfare, Urania was top of the range. The sums might not have been much to Miss Coutts, given her annual income of more than £50,000 a year. During these years Dickens too, though on a more modest level, could at last feel financially secure. In 1847, his friend John Forster reports, 'all embarrassments connected with money were brought to a close'; over the next decade his profits soared spectacularly.

To see what these figures look like in today's money we need to multiply by a hundred. Thus, Miss Coutts could be seen as spending £72,000 a year on Urania, out of an income of five million. In the twenty-first century, to provide an equivalent service for twelve young women you could put together a package of foyer accommodation (foyers provide housing and skills training for young people), plus Jobseekers' allowances and fares to Australia. Twelve of these over a year would cost not far short of £250,000. Such enterprises are never cheap. Some of the Urania success was due to the time and devotion of the best-selling novelist of the time, as he sorted, scrutinised and entered every bill and expense. 'I went over the accounts and paid them all', Dickens tells Miss Coutts in the autumn of 1852: as he habitually did, down to the last halfpenny.

Over the years Dickens recognised that he could be difficult to work with. 'I am always for the promptest measures,' he admitted to Miss Coutts, 'and I suppose made you laugh by my ferocity.' She agreed that she did indeed sometimes find him 'rather overpoweringly energetic'; they were in many ways such opposites. Shy and retiring herself, she preferred giving her charitable donations under the name of 'Lady Unknown'. But to join forces with Dickens on Urania Cottage was to share a pleasure. While they both took it seriously, there were jokes to be had too. Dickens gave the girls nicknames, as he did his own children. He entertained Miss Coutts with tales of the volatile little Fairy, or Stallion, or the 'brownish-yellow' girl. Only once was he provoked into a head-on collision with the Home's benefactor.

Miss Coutts believed in sensible clothes for the girls. She herself might have a weakness for expensive frocks and jewellery (her outfit for the royal ball last night was worth 'about a hundred thousand pounds', she once told a suitably impressed visitor), but to her bright colours on working women could mean only one thing. Dickens disagreed strenuously. Loving bold colours himself (those flashy waistcoats), he wanted his girls to enjoy them too. When it came to the clothes in which they should start their new lives, the brighter the better. 'I return Derry' he wrote to Miss Coutts in 1856, nine years into the life of Urania and as passionate as ever for his cause. According to Dickens's biographer Edgar Johnson, Derry was 'a cotton material from which Miss Coutts proposed that overalls and other articles of clothing be made for inhabitants of the Home.' Swatches of the material are still attached to the letter, 'in different dull colours . . . and very drab they all are', in Johnson's opinion. Colour, Dickens claims in a wonderful passage, 'these people always want, and colour (as allied to fancy), I would always give them. In these cast-iron and mechanical days, I think even such a garnish to the dish of their monotonous and hard lives, of unspeakable importance. One colour, and that of the earth earthy, is too much with them early and late. Derry might just as well break out into a stripe, or put forth a bud, or even burst into a full blown flower. Who is Derry that he is to make quakers of us all, whether we will or no!'

One might, in the nature of things, expect that a young woman applying to Urania would sometimes have a child in tow. Dickens acknowledges this openly at the beginning of his 'Appeal to Fallen Women', which he directs explicitly to the kind of woman 'who, if she has ever been a mother, has felt shame instead of pride in her own unhappy child'. What about the fate of an 'unhappy child' at Urania?

It was a proposition Miss Coutts categorically opposed. 'We have not, and never had, any such instance,' Dickens told a magistrate enquiring on behalf of a mother and baby. The Urania family could not stretch to another generation. Since Dickens hated turning likely candidates away, he would try to make other arrangements.

In 1852 he sent Miss Coutts an account of his interview with 'Almina (!) Holgate'. While her name amused him, his interest was engaged by her 'exceedingly respectable appearance' and expertise as 'a good Milliner and Dress Maker. You would have no suspicion of her history from seeing her.' The sticking point was that Almina had a nine-month-old baby whom 'she has no idea of abandoning'. She planned to make a new start abroad and send for the child later. Dickens wanted to help but did not see her as Urania material. Both the child and her age told against her: although she looked much younger, she was twenty-seven. His solution was to propose a system of out-door relief, whereby the matron at Urania would come to his own house and work with Almina there on the necessary preparations for emigration.

No Urania babies: that was policy. But what if a new inmate turned out to be pregnant? The preliminary enquiries and interviews were designed to screen for this, and when there was a slip-up Dickens took immediate action. Susan Mayne did not make much of an impression on him in the first place: 'I was not so propitiated by her manner as Mr Hardwick was.' John Hardwick, the magistrate at Great Marlborough Street, had given Susan seven days for disorderly conduct in January 1855, but after doubt was cast on the 'hasty and mistaken' police evidence he put pressure on Dickens to get her into Urania. Dickens gave in, on his usual condition 'that the account she gave of herself should be closely enquired into'.

Susan managed to pass this test, only to falter a couple of weeks later, as Dickens reported back to Hardwick. 'Our ladies have great apprehensions that Susan Mayne is in the family way. On the other hand, our usual medical attendant is rather of the contrary opinion. A fortnight or so will probably decide the question; but if she *should* be in this state, it will be necessary for her to be taken away as soon as the fact is ascertained.' Dickens's instinct was to shield Miss Coutts, to whom 'the matter would necessarily be painful'. If need be he would hastily bundle Susan back to Hardwick – a victim of Miss Coutts's sensibilities.

If Dickens's control was tight, his regime was liberal when compared with other institutions. His most important insight was that coercion was not the way. Not for Urania the shaven heads in vogue at the Houses of Mercy, or the silence of the nation's prisons. He put his faith in kindness and the warm supportive atmosphere, in rewards and incentives rather than penitence or punishment. Staff were chosen and directed expressly to this end.

On the other hand, this was not Liberty Hall. Although girls could earn increasing independence during their time there, Dickens saw them as people to be protected and guarded. Most of all, he thought, they needed to be guarded from themselves. This had to be done subtly. Inmates should always be 'overlooked', usually by each other. You would have your own space – 'each inmate has a separate bed', and this would be a first for many of them – but no privacy. The girls slept three or four to a room, with no supervision from anyone else, but enough from each other. 'As no girl makes her own bed, no girl has the opportunity of safely hiding any secret correspondence, or anything else, in it.' An intrusive trick this: Dickens enlists the women to spy on each other. 'Any inmate missing from her usual place for ten minutes would be looked after. Any suspicious circumstance would be quickly and quietly investigated.'

No privacy, decreed the rules of the house, and no private property. Girls made and mended their own clothes but they did not keep them, and their outdoor clothes were kept locked up too. 'When temper is awakened, the possession of a shawl and bonnet would often lead to an abrupt departure.' All visits from outsiders were strictly controlled and monitored. Parents could come once a month, other friends and relatives once in three months. Any letters going in and out were to be read by the matron. Dickens seems to have covered every base.

Urania would be run on kindness, informal surveillance, and a third element: a reward scheme cribbed from the most avant-garde penal philosophy of the time. Dickens's latest prison fad was for the writings of Captain Alexander Maconochie, the 'Philanthropic Ruler' as one of his admirers called him. Dickens acquired an advance copy of his latest work, *Crime and Punishment*, and had him round to dinner.

Like Dickens, Maconochie had tasted prison life at first hand, in his case as a prisoner of war during the Napoleonic wars. He was a naval man, and served as private secretary to John Franklin, Arctic explorer and one of Dickens's heroes. Dickens and Maconochie met shortly after Maconochie's stint as Governor of Norfolk Island, which must then have been one of the remotest inhabited places on the globe, a tiny island a thousand miles off the coast of New South Wales. In the 1840s it was reserved for double offenders, the men who had committed crimes within the penal colonies of Australia. Even now Maconochie's radicalism takes your breath away. Since he and his island were so cut off he could try out schemes which would have been vetoed by sedate civil servants in London. As it was he only lasted four years: not because his precepts failed in practice, but because London finally got wind of them.

Maconochie's reforms were highly experimental (a word he liked as much as Dickens did) and progressive. His innovative proposal that men should earn the right to early release was blocked by his powerful critics. But his core idea, that even hardened criminals can improve if you work on their self-respect, was a beacon they could not put out. For years after, when the island had long since returned to the brutalised regime of violence and fear, there was talk of the extraordinary days of Captain Maconochie.

'A more demoniacal looking assemblage could not be imagined,' said Maconochie on first calling together the old hands on the island. He persisted in treating them as civilised human beings, set up programmes for work and training, and turned the place round. He succeeded so well that some convicts asked to stay after they had been released. Dickens enthused to Miss Coutts at length about 'Captain Maconochie's Mark System' with its daily tally of good and bad behaviour. She was less than keen, and in the frenetic month before Urania Cottage opened, Dickens had to agree that the scheme was 'perhaps unsuited to so small an establishment'.

But he did not give up, and once the Home was up and running, he managed to foist the full Maconochie on Miss Coutts and the two women in charge – for whom it meant a daunting amount of paperwork. Inmates would be marked out of four under nine separate headings each day: Truthfulness, Industry, Temper, Propriety of Conduct and Conversation, Temperance, Order, Punctuality, Economy, and Cleanliness. That is a lot of behaviour to assess every day and a lot of sums for the girls to do. Good for their arithmetic, thought Dickens. 'Personal interest' is a powerful motive.

His laboured exposition of the system to Miss Coutts makes it sound both heavy-going and rather punitive. In his example Emma Lea loses marks under four different headings for calling another girl 'by opprobrious names'. He had thousands of forms specially printed. They were in duplicate, with one for matron and one for the girl herself. Every Saturday evening the matron conducted a 'kind of Savings Bank' session to tot up and record each girl's points. She entered all the points into her large house book, and each girl entered her own score into her own little book, which must have been about her only possession. Points meant prizes: marks for good behaviour were pegged to the wages of a basic domestic servant. The money was banked for the inmate to draw when she emigrated.

Did Dickens trawl the streets himself for likely Urania candidates? In April 1850 he wrote to Miss Coutts about his 'nightly wanderings into strange places', where he has spoken to women and girls. He has been pitching for the Home, with emigration as the selling point. The women are, he tells Miss Coutts, 'very thankful, but make a fatal and decisive confusion between emigration and transportation'. His irritation at their 'astonishing and horrible' ignorance suggests that some of these encounters might have been quite abrasive. And maybe the women did not find emigration the attractive prospect which Dickens thought it was.

Encounters of a rather different kind are suggested by a letter written within a fortnight of this one, this time to his old friend Daniel Maclise. The two men had been out together the night before, and Dickens had been waylaid. But 'the young lady was *not* interesting, and I was after you in three or four minutes.' What kept him the three or four minutes, and what did he mean by 'interesting'? On the face of it, the answer is obvious. 'Mac' was an artist, one of the raffish set of actors and painters whose company Dickens enjoyed. It was to Mac he had given the tourist tips about the prostitutes of Margate.

This 'lady', though, was not 'interesting'. Perhaps he lost interest in her – whatever his interest had been – or perhaps she was not interested in his offer, whatever that had been. 'Interesting' is, well, an interesting word. In descriptions of women it can mean 'pregnant'; Dickens himself used the word this way. But that is not, I think, the meaning here. More to the point might be its popular usage by the newspaper-men of the time. Police reports in *The Times* describe Jane Elliott, a dressmaker charged with stealing a roll of calico from the doorway of a draper's shop in the Edgware Road, as 'an interesting-looking young woman'. Sixteen-year-old Emma Payne, a servant who had been indecently assaulted by her employer, is 'an interesting looking girl'. Attractive? Intelligent? *The Times* thought that boys could be interesting too: the son of a bankrupt woman is characterised as 'an interesting boy of thirteen'. It seems to mean 'worthy of having an interest taken in them'.

Dickens was not the only eminent gent prowling the London streets in the spring nights of 1850. William Gladstone, later to be Prime Minister no fewer than four times, and whose career spanned sixty-three years in the House of Commons, was out there too. 'Conv. at night with an unhappy woman', he noted in his diary in early May 1850. Two days later he tracked 'the same poor creature' down again and heard her story. 'She has a son to support: and working *very* hard with her needle *may* reach 6/- per week as a maximum . . . Lives no 6 Duke's Court.'

Gladstone was another pioneer in the field. His rescue work and regular meetings with prostitutes are well known: he made no attempt to hide them. He and Dickens could have met during their night walks, but neither mentions it. They seem to have met only once, much later, at a breakfast event to which Gladstone invited Dickens with about a dozen others. This would not have been the moment to compare their various efforts at rescue work, although Gladstone was the first to acknowledge his own lack of success. By 1854 he reckoned he had spoken, 'indoors or out', to nearly ninety prostitutes, and so far as he knew, only one had changed her way of life through his influence. Perhaps he should have heeded the words of Jane Bywater, who wrote to thank him for his efforts in getting her into the House of Mercy which he had helped found. She knew he meant well, but would rather kill herself than be 'shut up in such a place as that'. Dickens would have sympathised. Where Gladstone was preaching salvation, he was more practically pushing emigration – if only they had understood what he meant.

And what are we to make of these two men on their nocturnal patrols? Both of them were always open about them. Mrs Gladstone and Miss Coutts knew all about it; Gladstone used to invite the prostitutes home. These days the encounters which Dickens and Gladstone engineered with women on the streets would cause a few raised eyebrows, and there is no doubt that they both found it exciting. But attitudes change and boundaries shift. What looks like a good idea at one time doesn't at another. With no social services or welfare state to step in, the two men were doing the work which middle-class women would take up later in the century.

'He told me much', wrote Susan Norton, an American visitor to Dickens's country house, Gad's Hill, in 1868, 'of Miss Coutts's "refuge", or whatever it was called, for the unhappy prostitutes of London', and of much else besides, showing his extensive knowledge of the relief schemes operating for such women; 'of the Parish Refuges where by night they might expect a shelter, but which being small provided one might almost say for *none*. How he had often been of a winter's night to one or other of these wretched places, and had seen the crowds of these poor starving creatures so great that there was no possibility of sheltering them.' Benevolent stalkers: this might be an accurate description of Dickens and Gladstone. They could stand in for the picture of Arthur Clennam following Little Dorrit which graces the cover of a child's version of the novel from the 1940s.

As to what else they might have done: at the end of his life Gladstone denied very precisely that he had been 'guilty of the act which is known as that of infidelity to the marriage bed'. Although Dickens's biographer Peter Ackroyd considers it 'a very remote possibility' that Dickens ever consorted with prostitutes, he does quote a conversation with Emerson in 1848 during which Dickens said that 'if his own son were particularly chaste, he should be alarmed on his account, as if he could not be in good health'. But his eldest son Charley was only eleven at the time, so perhaps Dickens was talking tongue-in-cheek.

Dickens had in fact been the prostitutes' champion since his earliest writings. Nancy bounces into Dickens's second novel, *Oliver Twist*, and has been more or less stealing the show in all its guises ever since. We are inclined to remember her as a figure of pathos, at the mercy of her ambitious young author as much as of her pimp, Bill Sikes. But before her shockingly bloody murder she is a woman with vitality and appetite. She dishes up porter and sheep's heads, and tucks into plates of boiled beef at the bar.

Nancy also has a powerful imagination. On what will be her last night alive she is overcome by 'fear and dread'. To distract herself she tries to read but 'I'll swear I saw "coffin" written in every page of the book in large black letters.' 'Imagination', Mr Brownlow tries to reassure her soothingly. He is missing the point. Imagination is exactly the force inspiring Nancy's author, thrilling his readers and selling *Oliver Twist* like hot-cakes. It is also the quality which Dickens recognised and identified with in the Urania Cottage women. This is how he characterises them to Miss Coutts: 'All people who have led hazardous and forbidden lives are, in a certain sense, imaginative'. These women were kindred spirits.

The pale, well-spoken Oliver is one of literature's most famous victims and Fagin one of its most famous villains. But the true victim of *Oliver Twist* is Nancy, and the villain is the street-life of London. Dickens spells it out for us. 'The girl's life had been squandered in the streets.' His own identification with these lost girls taps into the sources of his most intense creativity. And if he traded in the death of Nancy, she could also be said to be the death of him. He prepared a reading of the 'Oliver murder' as he called it, but put off performing it for several years, aware of the hysteria it might provoke. It was spectacular, horrific stuff, and he saved it for his farewell tour. Performing it sent his pulse racing to three times its normal rate and hastened his death. 'I shall tear myself to pieces', Dickens famously muttered to his friend Charles Kent before the final reading of 'Sikes and Nancy'.

The rough urban life which Dickens suffered as a boy energised him and became one of the sources of his creative genius. But no such good fortune can be found in the streets for his fictional young women forced to work there. Bet has to identify the corpse of her friend Nancy 'and went off mad, screaming and raving, and beating her head against the boards; so they put a strait-weskut on her and took her to the hospital – and there she is'. The good characters in the book talk to Nancy of emigration and 'a home in some foreign country where I could end my days in solitude and peace'. Eleven years later Dickens would give a real girl of the streets the chance that Nancy was denied.

To begin with Dickens had not wanted to take Martha Goldsmith, the 21-year-old ex-prostitute from the Magdalen Hospital. His reason seems to have been some early policy, maybe about women from the Magdalen. 'I explained the general objection to her, which she very reasonably received.' But he was swayed by her tears and by her persistent sister, who 'implored me so earnestly to make another appeal to Miss Coutts'. Once Martha settled in and he got to know her, he liked her better than he expected. 'Her manner pleased me greatly', he reported back to Miss Coutts. The Magdalen had not done much for her health, and she took some time to recover from her 'ricketty' state.

Over the months Martha proved her worth. She was such a steady and conscientious worker that an offer of employment outside came her way. As Dickens refused on her behalf, she probably knew nothing about it. He assured Miss Coutts that he was acting in Martha's best interests. The offer was from someone in London, and 'I cannot forget the strong emphatic exception that was made by the Matron of the Magdalen as to the hopefulness of any disposal of Martha Goldsmith, *at home.*' Not only did Ann Bourchill's warning about the temptations of Martha's 'old companions' on the streets strike a chord; he had other plans for Martha. She had made friends with Jane Westaway and Julia Mosley – they may have shared a bedroom – and Dickens was slating all three for his first boat to Australia.

CHAPTER FIVE

Isabella's Gang

It would be a beautiful thing, and would give us a
wonderful power over them, if they would form strong
attachments among themselves.
  Dickens to Angela Burdett Coutts, 3 November 1847

URANIA PUT A high premium on friendship. From the beginning
Dickens decreed that 'no one should Ever be sent abroad alone'. In
his mind's eye the plucky emigrants sallied forth to meet the challenges
of an alien world in brave little clusters of two or three. Urania graduates should stick together; the friendships they forged at Shepherd's
Bush would stand them in good stead in the future. Accordingly, he
encouraged what he called 'affectionate feelings' among the inmates. 'I
. . . told them to be friends' was his recipe for harmony. The girls liked
to gossip about who was going to emigrate with whom, and Dickens
liked listening. But there was always the danger that a friendship group
would mutate into a gang. Then Dickens and his team would have to
move swiftly.

By the time Isabella Gordon arrived at Urania Cottage in February 1849, the place had been running for over a year. It was now on
a reasonably even keel, though staff troubles often threatened to erupt.
The first intake of young women was leaving for the colonies in their
twos and threes, to be replaced by a new set of girls; one of them
was Isabella.

She started off sly. During her initial interview with Dickens she told him that the assistant matron Miss Cunliffe had been plying her with questions. Isabella knew as well as everyone else that silence about the past was the cardinal rule. She also knew that Miss Cunliffe was out of favour, and currently refusing to leave her room. Pretty and plausible enough to get Dickens on her side, Isabella 'incidentally' let slip about Miss Cunliffe's prying. She must have thought it was fun to land someone else in yet more trouble.

Over the next few months Isabella turned out to be a mixer. She squabbled with the other girls, and made life difficult for the newly arrived Georgiana Morson in her first weeks as head matron. Indeed, trouble with Isabella got a whole Dickens letter to itself. He was impressed by the way Mrs Morson had patched up a feud between Isabella and Rachael Bradley by writing a letter to Isabella, not an obvious thing to do as they were all living under the same roof. But it worked. Isabella simmered down, and Dickens praised Mrs Morson's tactics. 'I am truly glad to hear that your letter to Isabella Gordon has produced so good an effect. I hope it will be a lasting one, and that an attachment to you may get the better of a restlessness which I have no doubt will sometimes come upon her.' 'Restlessness' is the word Dickens tends to choose when he sympathises with a problem girl.

High-spirited Isabella was always the one who caught his eye. She was sparky and not at all intimidated by him. Augustus Tracey remembered her fondly from her prison days so Dickens made a point of passing on Isabella news. She was 'looking very well again', he had 'heard a good account of her'. He enjoyed her chat. 'She was a little envious of the people going by to Hampton Races, and said "how she would like to be going with em"!'

Isabella comes across as a girl who liked to enjoy herself; she added to the gaiety of the house. This endeared her all the more to Dickens, keen as he was to foster an agreeable atmosphere. He loved the buzz of the place, and fretted when it felt 'too grim and gloomy'. He was sometimes surprised how much the girls bickered, particularly in bad weather when they could not go out. But on the whole he reckoned 'they perhaps quarrel less than the average of passengers in the state cabin on a voyage out to India.'

Alexander Maconochie had pushed, unsuccessfully, for the inclusion of wives and children on his island, arguing that the family unit was the only way forward. Dickens agreed. Shepherd's Bush should be a family, with all the warmth which his novels celebrated, but which seemed to be draining from his own home. While his wife was still 'my dearest Kate', the children were arriving with alarming rapidity. In 1846 he declared himself 'past all congratulations on that score'. By 1852 he was confessing that he could not 'afford to receive' his seventh son (his tenth and last child) 'with perfect cordiality, as on the whole I could have dispensed with him.' He often referred to his charges at Urania as his family, and who is to say he did not sometimes prefer this one to his own?

If Urania Cottage was Dickens's alternative family – and it was about the same size as his real one – it was also a beguiling spectacle, a cross between soap opera and reality show. Over the years he enjoyed dramatising its scenes of everyday life, in some of the liveliest letters he ever wrote. 'Little Willis', for instance, who misbehaved with the 'Key and Bible business': you put a key in your Bible at the Book of Ruth to find out your future husband's name by reciting the alphabet and waiting for the Bible to move. Willis had been trying her hand at it 'in bed and in the dark, knowing it to be wrong'. To punish her Dickens said he would dock all her marks for a month, 'unless she behaved very well'. Willis pondered the matter, and when he was next at Urania she tried to strike a deal with him. 'I wish you could have seen her', Dickens wrote to Miss Coutts, 'come in diplomatically to make terms with the establishment.' His fascination with these girls' voices, and his generosity in sharing them with their benefactor, gives little Willis her place in posterity.

> O! Without her marks, she found she couldn't do her work agreeable to herself – 'If you do it agreeable to us,' said I, 'that'll do.' – 'O! But' she said 'I could wish not to have my marks took away.' –'Exactly so,' said I. 'That's quite right; and the only way to get them back again, is to do as well as you can.' – 'Ho! But if she didn't have 'em giv' up at once, she could wish fur to go.' –'Very well,' said I. 'You shall go tomorrow morning.'

Isabella Gordon was just the girl to fill Urania with the spirit Dickens wanted. She brought colour and vivacity; she had a sense of humour and a sense of style. But she was pushing it, as Dickens eventually spotted. Not only had she been 'in the habit of talking in a disorderly manner', she had also 'certainly said (and believed) she could do what she liked with us.' So, no more chat. Dickens deliberately changed his manner. He adopted 'a severity towards her which should have an effect upon her, and through her upon the rest of them.' Isabella is not to be allowed to rock his little boat, even if he can foresee the consequences. 'I am not sanguine of her remaining with us.'

He went on noticing her though, and soon reneged on severe. Less than two weeks later 'I spoke to my poor friend Isabella Gordon, who was very white when she saw me come in; but whether with vengeance or contrition, I don't know.' This was at the beginning of July 1849. When the next news of her came in August he was on holiday on the Isle of Wight and deep in *David Copperfield*. He was sorry, though not surprised, to hear that she had crossed the line and was facing expulsion. He would have come to the committee meeting set to deal with her on Tuesday 'but for my friend David, who has a tight hold upon me'. Still intensely interested in David's rival, 'my poor friend Isabella', Dickens had an urgent favour to ask of Miss Coutts. 'Will you ask Mrs. Morson, if she be expelled, to write and tell me exactly *how she goes away*. I have a particular reason, as a point of experience, for asking this, and for hoping that she will observe her behaviour particularly.'

The reason was Martha Endell, the prostitute Dickens was writing into *David Copperfield* at this very moment, with Isabella as template. Part of him hoped she would weather the committee's castigation. Could they be absolutely sure it was all her fault? Dickens is still batting on her side. 'The only point I should be particularly careful about, if I were at the Committee on Tuesday', he tells Miss Coutts, 'would be to ascertain beyond all question that the charge against Isabella Gordon is an undoubted matter of fact, and does not originate in any league against her.'

She was on his radar all that summer. He was 'all in suspense' to know if she had been allowed to stay; then he was full of hopes that she was justifying the 'clemency' which the committee decided to extend to her. Finally she got just too cheeky to keep. Whenever there was trouble, there was Isabella, 'disturbing the general peace again'. Attractive and outspoken, she had to be Queen Bee. Her speciality was getting the new girls on her side – how like boarding school Urania sounds at times – and ganging up against the staff.

Things came to a head in the autumn, when Dickens was back in London. Champion of Isabella though he had been, and charmed by her though he still was, he could not allow her to destabilise the family. So he set up a show trial to denounce her. There is a blow-by-blow account of it in a letter Dickens wrote to William Brown, the Home's medical attendant, who had missed the committee meeting because he was on holiday in Paris with Miss Coutts. Isabella, 'we found', was fomenting rebellion against Mrs Morson and Mrs Macartney, and organising a complaints posse in readiness for the committee meeting. It was a gang of three: Isabella and her sidekicks Hannah and Sesina, the latter only just arrived from Tothill Fields prison. Dickens convened a kangaroo court to deal with them. He and his committee investigated all the complaints 'with the utmost care, confronted Isabella with Mrs Morson, and were convinced that her whole story was utterly false and malicious'.

He and Isabella both basked in the limelight. 'We ordered her to her room while we considered the subject, and she danced upstairs before Mrs Morson, holding her skirts like a lady at a ball.' Much as Dickens was amused by her drama queen antics, Isabella had picked her moment badly. News of the first girls to emigrate to Australia had just come back, and, as we will see, it was not good. The committee were moved to sternness. 'We were all of opinion that the authority of the place *must* be upheld.' There was now only 'one way' forward, the court decided, however much Dickens squirmed about it being 'repugnant to our own feelings'. Isabella would have to go. 'We therefore had her down again some time afterwards, and, to her utter bewilderment and amazement and that of the whole house, dismissed her.'

Next in the dock was Hannah Myers. Once again the committee confronted the culprit, whereupon Hannah convicted herself with a series of obvious lies. Dickens knew she was headstrong; even so he was startled by the rage she vented on the matrons, 'her malignity against them (for the time) very intense and passionate'. But one expulsion was enough for the time being. The committee let her stay with the punishment of losing a week's points and the dire warning that 'on the first repetition of such behaviour' she would be 'inexorably dismissed'. This seemed to come out of the blue to Hannah, who was as 'amazed' as Isabella had been. Their little plot to drive a wedge between the matrons and the committee had misfired badly.

The third member of Isabella's gang and catalyst for the catastrophe was the show-stopper Anna Maria Sisini, or Sesina as she preferred to call herself. A pint-sized prima donna, she was twenty years old; she could read a bit but not write. Like Hannah and Isabella, she came from Tothill Fields, where she had just served six months for stealing a bed. That sounds like a crime which took a bit of nerve, something Sesina had in abundance. To begin with of course, Dickens lapped it up. His initial interview to take down her history proved highly entertaining. 'P.P.S.' he ended a letter to Tracey, the governor of the prison Sesina had just come from, 'I have a good (and very short) story about Miss Sesini. Whom I consider a rum 'un.'

He was right. Within hours of her arrival at the beginning of November, Sesina was in cahoots with Isabella. Urania was not the haven it was supposed to be, Isabella told the new girl, plying her with petty tales of staff cruelties. Sesina did not take much convincing. She loved the idea of taking centre stage with Isabella as noble crusaders for justice. They launched themselves into a frenzy of gratifying self-righteousness. Within two days Sesina found herself in Dickens's court, alongside Isabella and Hannah and cast as 'the third party'. Because she was so new, the committee gave her the benefit of the doubt. Maybe she had not found her feet yet, and did not understand how Urania worked. It was, after all, like nowhere else she could ever have been.

At this point Dickens's attitude still inclines towards amused tolerance. He is 'persuaded', he tells William Brown, that Sesina 'is the pertest, vainest, (preposterous as the word seems in such a connexion) and most deceitful little Minx in this town.' Morally speaking, his judgement is caustic: 'I never saw such a draggled piece of fringe upon the skirts of all that is bad.' But he felt he could afford to exercise a lighter touch than he could with Isabella. He does not know her as well, he hasn't invested so much in her, and there is a chance that the Minx will reform. He decided to subject her to a headmasterly pep-talk.

> I gave this young lady to understand, in the plainest and most emphatic words, that she appeared to us to misunderstand the place – and its object. That she must thoroughly change her whole feelings and demeanour, and put on a very different character, and conduct herself towards both the superintendents as a new creature altogether, if she had the least hope of remaining.

He was offering Sesina a second chance, though he thought she would not take it. Three days earlier he had interviewed her at length, as he did every new entrant to the Home. In his opinion she would most probably '*not* remain; and I have no doubt, after taking her history and observing her closely while she tried to gloze it [explain it away], that it will be much better for us if she goes away.'

The trial of Isabella and her minions took up the whole afternoon. Dickens's letter paints a vivid picture of the four committee members – himself, prison governor George Chesterton and the two clergymen, Edward Illingworth and William Tennant, both co-opted via the prison governors – together with the two matrons, Mrs Morson and Mrs Macartney, all of them trying to do their best by these strong-willed young women, in the fading light of the November day.

When Dickens returned to Shepherd's Bush the day after the trial he found Hannah 'very much subdued'. It did not last. Four months later she crashed out of Urania by way of the fence, breaking down the palings as she went. She could easily have left by the front door, but preferred the more extravagant exit. This time Dickens could feel only relief. 'I really think it an extraordinary good thing to be rid of Myers,' he told Miss Coutts. 'I don't know where she could have been sent, or what could have been hoped of her.'

Sure enough, within a month Hannah was back in court for real, at the Middlesex Sessions. Here she was tried for theft and found guilty.

The emigration talk at Urania seems to have percolated into her consciousness because 'she begged very hard to be transported, and probably would have been gratified, but that Mr Chesterton, not thinking her gratification advisable under the circumstances, exerted himself against it with the Judge.' So it was back to Tothill Fields for another twelve months. When she had finished that, more of the same. Dickens saw her four years later in Tothill Fields yet again, 'sitting next to the last girl who robbed the Home'.

As for Sesina: after Dickens's departure that afternoon Urania remained in uproar. The girl could not contain herself; she boiled over with outrage and insults. Finally even the easy-going Mrs Morson had had enough. She ordered Sesina to her bedroom, and was so rattled by the girl's wildness that she kept the gardener in the house all night. The precaution made Dickens laugh, 'when I thought of its object being a little dumpy atom of a girl whose head may be somewhere on a level with Mrs Macartney's waist.'

On rare emergencies Mrs Morson would cross town in a hired coach, known as a fly, to get instructions from Dickens on how he wanted things handled. This time she appeared at half past eight in the morning: what should they do with Sesina? Dickens told her to 'go back, give her her own clothes, and tell her she was to dress herself, and leave the place directly.' He himself would be at Shepherd's Bush half an hour after Mrs Morson. If he found Sesina still in bed, or in the house at all, he would 'send for a policeman and give her in custody for being there without our consent and making a disturbance.'

Back went Mrs Morson, closely followed by Dickens. By now Sesina was a lost cause, but she would not surrender without a few fireworks. Dickens looked forward to watching them. In his letter her exit is transfigured into a comic turn; you can hear how Urania must have featured in his conversation. This time, because William Brown and Miss Coutts were out of town and because Dickens enjoys it all so much, we can join in as privileged eavesdroppers.

Sesina was determined to make the most of her last moments. She would keep the staff on their toes right up to the final curtain. Dickens obviously relished the interlude in her bedroom, which Mrs Morson relayed to him. Sesina was giving the scene her best. 'On receipt of this message [to leave immediately] she parleyed a little, and, after making a slight pretence of being ill, threw her nightcap to one end of the room and her nightgown to the other, and proceeded, very leisurely, to dress herself.' Eventually she appeared downstairs, with yet more delaying tactics. 'She objected that she couldn't go away in the rain on which she was told that she had better sit in the long room then, "till I came".' That did it. 'Declining this offer, she walked off', though not without a parting shot. 'Before she went, she told Mrs Morson "that she know'd Miss Coutts's address, and would write her a good long letter, telling her what treatment was had there."'

So far as we know the letter never arrived, and anyway Sesina could not write. Always prone to predicting the next steps of his Urania women, Dickens now foresaw her joining up with Isabella 'somewhere, today'. He bumped into her in the lane as he was arriving to deal with her. Shortly afterwards he passed her again on his way back home. She was ostentatiously enjoying her liberty, 'walking in a jaunty way up Notting Hill, and refreshing herself with an occasional contemplation of the shop windows'. What a performance. 'I think', concluded Dickens, 'she would corrupt a Nunnery in a fortnight.'

How would Isabella ride the storm? By the time they passed sentence on her it was five o'clock on a dark afternoon. She begged to stay until tomorrow. Dickens was intransigent: she must leave now. Sensing what a charismatic figure she cut, he would not trust her alone with the other girls to say her goodbyes. He insisted on staying until she left, and he made Chesterton wait too. She did manage to keep the good Urania dress she was wearing, because she claimed it was the only one she had. Dickens would allow her only the roughest of shawls to go over it. He and Chesterton gave her half a crown (12 ½ pence) for a night's lodging 'and directed her to a certain charity where she is *sure* to be taken in if she chooses, and if she means to work'. And that was it.

During her nine months at Urania, Isabella's larger-than-life character had put her at the heart of the place. Now the whole household dissolved in tears. 'They all cried bitterly (Mrs Morson and Mrs Macartney included).' Rachael Bradley, the girl she had squabbled with, 'held to her skirts as she went out at the door, and implored us to let her stay and to give her one more trial – sobbing and weeping terribly'. It was, as Dickens said, 'a most pitiable sight'. This was the crisis he had had in mind since August, so he watched intently.

> The girl herself, now that it had really come to this, cried, and hung down her head, and when she got out at the door, stopped and leaned against the house for a minute or two before she went to the gate – in a most miserable and wretched state. As it was impossible to relent, with any hope of doing good, we could not do so. We passed her in the lane, afterwards, going slowly away, and wiping her face with her shawl. A more forlorn and hopeless thing altogether, I never saw.

'It has', commented Dickens, 'made a great impression on the rest, unquestionably.' That was of course just what he wanted. Isabella and her gang had to be dealt with summarily, and publicly. In her final moments at Urania the girl whose company he had enjoyed so much becomes nothing more than an object lesson to the other inmates. 'How long it may last, Heaven knows.' Dickens himself returned home exhausted. He went to bed 'in a dull state . . . with the whole of the sad picture in my mind'. Soon it would be transmuted into fiction.

Is that why Dickens turned against Isabella so abruptly? Could he be accused of cannibalism, of hastening her departure to get the drama he wanted for his next number? Admittedly, she was hanging on by a thread. At any rate, she left in the first week of November, and within days Dickens was rewriting her expulsion for Part Eight of *David Copperfield*, which appeared at the end of that month. Here we have the scene of Martha, the girl gone wrong, leaving Yarmouth for London, 'gathering her shawl about her, covering her face with it, and weeping aloud'. Even failure could have its upside for the novelist.

And what of the real young woman? The census for 1851, eighteen months after her expulsion from Urania, lists two Isabella Gordons who might be her. They are both London servants of about the right age. One was working for a schoolmaster: a respectable result if that is our Isabella. But women like her are hard to trace for sure.

1 **Dickens in 1855 by Ary Scheffer.**
The 'nightmare portrait', as Dickens called it, demanded 'interminable sittings' and 'does not look to me at all like'. The studio in Paris where Dickens sat for Ary Scheffer and his brother Henri is now part of the Musée de la Vie Romantique.

2 **Angela Burdett Coutts in about 1840, artist unknown** (detail). Angela enjoyed fine clothes and parties, but suffered badly from eczema. Her mother advised: 'You take a good deal of coffee you know but you should take NONE!'

3 **The women's work-room at Tothill Fields Prison in the 1850s.** The women were strictly supervised and worked in total silence. Other institutions for homeless or fallen women tended to be large, temporary and prison-like.

4 **The only known photograph of Urania Cottage**, which was in Shepherd's Bush, dates from 1915, long after it had ceased to be a home for homeless and fallen women. It is the middle house.

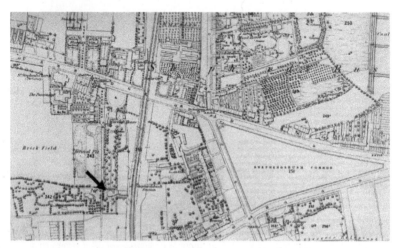

5 As the **Ordnance Survey map** (of 1871) shows, Urania Cottage sat in its own ample garden surrounded by fields. In Dickens's day the railway to the east had not yet been built.

CHAPTER SIX

School for Servants

> She never went out, or came into the office, or had a
> clean face, or took off the coarse apron, or looked out
> of any one of the windows, or stood at the street-door
> for a breath of air, or had any rest or enjoyment what-
> ever. Nobody ever came to see her, nobody spoke of
> her, nobody cared about her.
>
> *The Old Curiosity Shop, Chapter 36*

O N THE ONLY occasion that the most famous man and woman of
their day ever met, their talk turned, inevitably, to the servant
question. In March 1870 Queen Victoria invited Dickens to Buckingham Palace. He told George Dolby, the man who managed his
public readings, all about it over dinner that evening at the Blue Posts
in Cork Street. 'Her Majesty . . . graciously asked his opinion: could
he account for the fact that we have no good servants in England as in
the olden times?' Dickens just as graciously hedged his reply. He had
more views on the servant question than Her Majesty would care to
hear. Urania girls were destined to be servants in the colonies; Dickens's ideas for training them were, as you might guess, idiosyncratic.

His paternal grandparents had been in service, but he never mentioned that. He himself had been an inventor of servants before he was
an employer. The eccentric love-match of Sam Weller and Mr Pickwick
made Dickens a bestselling author with his first novel. Is Sam friend
or servant? '"Not exactly a friend," replied Mr Pickwick in a low tone.
"The fact is, he is my servant, but I allow him to take a good many

liberties; for, between ourselves, I flatter myself he is an original, and I am rather proud of him.'" The closing image of the book celebrates their perfect partnership: the 'somewhat infirm' Mr Pickwick 'invariably attended by the faithful Sam, between whom and his master there exists a steady and reciprocal attachment which nothing but death will terminate.'

Thereafter, servants will be one of Dickens's hallmarks, his stock-in-trade. Whether singly – as heroes or villains – or collectively as the Greek chorus in the servants' hall of *Dombey and Son*, this is Dickens's fictional fourth estate. They can come into our line of vision unexpectedly, 'a little voice very low down in the doorway' of Sampson Brass's office in another early novel, *The Old Curiosity Shop*. 'A small slipshod girl in a dirty coarse apron and bib, which left nothing of her visible but her face and feet. She might as well have been dressed in a violin-case.' She has no name, she does not know how old she is; the sublime Dick Swiveller calls her the Marchioness. While Little Nell dwindles and dies, the Marchioness finds the key to unlock herself from her dungeon of a cellar, and escapes to nurse Dick back to health. Hers will be reward on earth rather than Nell's heaven. Named by Dick ('Sophronia Sphynx' is his happy choice) and educated by Dick, she finally marries him.

Servant girls such as the Marchioness are Dickens's bleakest little characters, but they also bear the sparks of their creator inside them. During the months he was gestating Urania Cottage, he came up with one his boldest servant girls, fourteen-year-old Susan Nipper in *Dombey and Son*, with her 'little snub nose, and black eyes like jet beads . . . so desperately sharp and biting that she seemed to make one's eyes water'. Whatever Susan does, she does redoubled. When she sews, it is 'with the concentrated zeal of fifty sempstresses'. Energy explodes out of her. 'Bursting' is the word Dickens uses most often about her – bursts of laughter, tears (loud sobbing where her mistress Florence quietly weeps), a 'busting' heart as she says. Her very breathing speaks volumes. She chokes, sneezes, and 'drew in her breath with an amount of expression not easily described, further relieving her feelings with a smart cough'. What we get with Susan is a young woman with a vigorous body. She struggles with the urchins in the streets, pokes Rob in the ribs, gets kissed by Toots, grabbed and hugged by the rough sea captains.

Sending Forster the manuscript of the first four chapters, Dickens commented, 'I rely very much on Susan Nipper . . . for a strong character throughout the book'. And strong she certainly is: she is the only one to stand up to Mr Dombey. In a bravura performance she berates him for the 'sinful shame' of his treatment of his daughter Florence, and loses her job as a result. Loyalty is Susan's big thing and Dickens pulls out the grand words for her. She is gallant, valiant and undaunted in the service of her slighted mistress. She makes a wonderful knight militant.

> Miss Nipper threw away the scabbard the first morning she arose in Mrs Pipchin's house. She asked and gave no quarter. She said it must be war, and war it was; and Mrs Pipchin lived from that time in the midst of surprises, harassings, and defiances; and skirmishing attacks that came bouncing in upon her from the passage, even in unguarded moments of chops, and carried desolation to her very toast.

Would that the Urania girls might make such competent servants as the Nipper. A trustworthy, capable domestic servant could expect a comfortable standard of living. Both Dickens and his wife Catherine were good at keeping servants, though she had better luck. Anne Brown, Catherine's maid, accompanied them on all their trips abroad to America, Switzerland and Italy. Dickens called her 'invaluable' and had the utmost faith in her. He offered her as a nurse for Macready's dying daughter; when Catherine was ill she escorted her to Malvern for the water cure.

'A servant who is our friend also' is how Dickens described her to Hans Christian Andersen. Anne embodied his notion of the perfect servant. She was one of the family who would enjoy a bit of joshing – 'I shall require Anne to fall into fits of admiration' at a natty new portmanteau – but also someone who could be completely reliable and discreet. 'Bad news', grumbled Dickens to a friend when Anne announced her marriage to Edward Cornelius. He was a French polisher, and one can imagine Tavistock House requiring extended attention on that front. Dickens's letter of congratulation assures her of the 'affectionate remembrance I shall preserve of your friendship and fidelity during sixteen years together'.

Anne left the family in 1855 but lived nearby in Regent's Park. She kept in touch and waited at table on Dickens's birthday in 1856. He was pleased that she looked 'brighter' than she had recently. That summer she gave birth to a daughter. By the turbulent autumn of 1857 she was back at Tavistock House, the Dickens family home. It was to her Dickens entrusted the infamous directions to board up the matrimonial bedroom. He had bought a small iron bedstead and bedding: Anne was to convert his dressing room into his bedroom and supervise the blocking up of the door between this room and 'Mrs Dickens's room'. Sensitive to possible scandal, he relied on Anne's discretion. 'As I would rather not have [these arrangements] talked about by comparative strangers, I shall be much obliged to you, my old friend, if you will see them completed before you leave Tavistock House.' Dickens seems to be leaning on her. Wouldn't her first allegiance be to Catherine?

Seven months later in May 1858 he leant even more heavily and this time openly, enlisting Anne's support for one of the nastiest episodes in his life. Dickens claimed that the 'violated letter' as he called it, was made public against his wishes. In fact he gave this statement about the end of his marriage to Arthur Smith, the manager of his public readings, with instructions to show it to anyone interested. Thackeray was one of those who saw it. In the letter Catherine is accused of 'mental disorder', of 'peculiarity' of character, and of being the one who wants a separation. Anne is summoned as witness to the protracted misery of the Dickens marriage. The first paragraph puts her centre stage as 'an attached woman servant (more friend to both of us than a servant)' who 'will bear testimony' to 'this unhappiness . . . wherever we have been, year after year, month after month, week after week, day after day.'

On the other hand, a letter which Dickens wrote to Miss Coutts at the beginning of that May casts Anne as the 'only hope' he could envisage for Catherine after the separation. 'She took care of her, like a poor child, for sixteen years', and could solve all their problems now. Which way would Anne jump? Would she stick by the excommunicated wife, evicted almost like a Urania delinquent and bereft of all her children except for grown-up Charley (the youngest, Plorn, was only six years old)? Or would Dickens succeed in poaching her?

It seems that he did. By August she was again employed at Tavistock House, keeping house for Dickens and preparing mustard poultices for his 'exceedingly bad cold'. She would work there until the house was sold in 1860. Two years later she was at Gad's Hill, but this time for a holiday with her small daughter Kate. Dickens nicknamed the child The Demon and enjoyed casting her as one of Wilkie Collins's sensational heroines. He wrote to Collins:

> She grows exactly like a Pre-Raphaelite she-saint, or Virgin. With her beastly little head on one side as she twines at the table, and a pickled eel disporting itself in her bowels, she looks as religious as the National Gallery. . . . Worms of various species are her meat, and Vinegar her drink; and after whopping Tizzy, the Groom's child, yesterday behind a door, she emerged to say that she had not done it, 'because it were her dooty to dough unto others as she would have them dough unto her'. – I am lying by for an opportunity of tripping her backwards down the Tunnel steps.

Anne and The Demon were invited back to Gad's Hill more than once over the next few years. Anne must have felt then that her allegiance was to Dickens rather than Catherine. Later she fell on hard times. Her husband was sick, and Dickens showed tact in alleviating her troubles. Don't think about how much money to give her, he told his daughter Mamie as he uncharacteristically granted her '*carte blanche*', but rather 'how *most efficiently* to ease her mind and help *her*. To do this at once kindly and sensibly is the only consideration.' Dickens continued to support her from beyond the grave. In his will she is the second legatee and her daughter the third; she comes second only to Nelly Ternan. No other servant is named.

Dickens's long-serving man-servant, John Thompson, would have deserved a mention, had he not blotted his copybook irrevocably three years before Dickens's death. He had come to work for Dickens way back in the early 1840s, and could be a bit feeble at times. When he was driving Catherine in the little phaeton and the pony bolted down a steep hill, 'what does John do but jump out!' He pretended he had been thrown out, but no one in the Dickens household believed him. They all thought the worse of him for abandoning Catherine, luckily unhurt though 'rending the Isle of Thanet with her screams'. But Dickens was used to him and trusted him implicitly.

In 1850 John asked to move to the newly opened *Household Words* office. Dickens was sorry to lose him as his valet – 'An excellent servant and a most ingenious fellow'. He consented because John was about to marry and wanted to live in the quarters above the office. We get glimpses of him at work over the ensuing years, 'waiting for the Post, with his mouth open, like a Post office in itself'. He could be a useful pair of hands at the office for Dickens: seeing the boys off to school, buying furniture for Gad's Hill, and always to be trusted with money. He helped out on the tours too, and had his part in the adventures on the road which Dickens threw himself into with such energy. He particularly liked John's hopeless imitations of Irishmen, ending in 'the absurdest little gingerbeery giggle'. And he was genuinely impressed by John's open-mindedness. From Paris he sent the 'astounding intelligence' that 'John has *no* British prejudices – a very remarkable phenomenon in a man of his station in life, unacquainted with the language, and left here for a week to subsist wholly on Pantomime!'

In 1864 John fell desperately ill. 'His life still hangs on a hair' Dickens wrote to Harry Wills, his sub-editor at *Household Words*, horrified by the behaviour of John's 'diabolical' wife and her sister. 'Being left last night to watch him' they 'got themselves blind drunk together on Gin – omitted everything they had undertaken to do – dropped Gin and God knows what over his poor dying figure.' Dickens intervened with his customary briskness. He 'tumbled' John's wife out of the sick-chamber and barred the 'abominable bitch' permanently from the house. John recovered, to be entrusted with sensitive errands such as creating tempting baskets of delicacies for Nelly Ternan after the Staplehurst railway accident: 'a little fresh fruit, a jar of clotted cream from Tuckers, and a chicken, a pair of pigeons, or some nice little bird. Also on Wednesday morning and on Friday morning, take her some other things of the same sort – making a little variety each day.'

By now John had been with Dickens for more than twenty years. Dickens was contributing to the school fees for John's children; it looked like a perfect master-servant relationship, and Dickens believed it was. 'I have been so fortunate in servants,' he told his friend Edward Bulwer Lytton. He liked to think that good employers made good servants.

But then came the 'horrible business'. Writing to his sister-in-law Georgina in the autumn of 1866, Dickens started with a melodramatic warning not to 'be betrayed into any expression of surprise' in front of her guests at Gad's Hill. The horrible business was theft and betrayal. Eight sovereigns had gone missing from the cash box in the office. 'Yesterday morning (there having been a great disturbance in the meantime) they were replaced. It was the clumsy manner of the restoration, that most helped the discovery of the culprit.' Having no clue who it could be, Dickens sent Harry Wills to Scotland Yard, 'for Walker, the head Inspector of the Detective Police'. He rather enjoyed the commotion until the police investigation led to 'the irresistible conclusion that the thief was – John!'

So much for loyalty. More than twenty years of jokes, affection and trust. Mortified though he was, Dickens took it upon himself to deal with the consequences himself. 'What I am to do with, or for, the miserable man, God knows. But we must make our gloomy way through it alone together, and it would be inexpressibly painful to me to have any third person present who knew him through his old long service.' Keeping it hushed up was also the only way John might be able to get another job, but John did not seem to see things the same way, as Dickens reported to Georgina three days later. 'I am afraid John very little feels the enormity of his offence, except as it inconveniences himself. Wills telling him today that he might be able to get him made a Waiter at the Reform Club, he replied "Oh I couldn't do that, Sir."'

The material which the team at Urania was working with could look rather unemployable. Though many of the young women might have been in domestic service, it was at the slovenly slipshod end of the market. They must learn to be good servants, and Dickens customised their curriculum with this in mind. Urania Cottage was to be its own best teaching aid. In learning how to run it, the girls would master the essentials of housework and housekeeping. The house kept no servants but them. They did all the cleaning, cooking, washing and ironing. They carried the coals and emptied the chamber pots. They baked their own bread, and made and mended their own clothes. All this had to be done to Dickens's obsessive and meticulous standards. He even had rules about 'arrangements for washing and dressing, and putting away of clothes'.

As she crossed the threshold of Urania Cottage in her fresh clothes, each girl would be handed her timetable. It was rather like the first day at school. Dickens had the timetables specially printed – although most of the girls could barely read them – with each domestic task neatly allocated its slot. There had not, he considered, been enough shape to their lives, so the rigidity of the syllabus was itself formative. Running Urania along his guidelines put Victorian philosophy into practice. The 'order, punctuality, cleanliness, the whole routine of household duties' which Dickens prescribed would fetch his bedraggled flock back into the fold.

The day began with prayers and breakfast at quarter to eight. Then the thirteen inmates divided into twos and threes to do their work in the bedrooms, kitchen, scullery and laundry. But also squeezed into the timetable was a generous amount of free time. They had half an hour before dinner at one o'clock and an hour afterwards. If possible they would go outside for some exercise or to tend their gardens. Then they had another half hour to themselves before tea at six, and an hour after that, when they sat together at their needlework, listening to someone reading aloud. Evening prayers were at half past eight.

In order to learn everything properly, each girl was allocated a different set of tasks each week. The rota itself had a role. 'In every room, every Monday morning, there is hung up, framed and glazed, the names of the girls who are in charge there for the week and who are, consequently, responsible for its neat condition and the proper execution of the work belonging to it. This is found to inspire them with a great pride in good housewifery.' Efficiency and economy were the watchwords of the house. 'Nothing is wasted or thrown away.' This was not just for the sake of frugality; there was a moral in it for the inmates. 'From the bones, and remnants of food, the girls are taught to make soup for the poor and sick. This at once extends their domestic knowledge, and preserves their sympathy for the distressed.' What a clear signal this would give that, with others below them, they now had their feet firmly on the ladder of recovery.

In drawing up his opinionated agenda, Dickens did have one model which both he and Miss Coutts knew at first hand. This was White-lands College in Chelsea, founded in 1841 and the first teacher training institution for women in the country. Its students were the daughters of butlers, bakers and drapers, and here they were trained to teach little girls how to become responsible servants. Miss Coutts supported the college by awarding annual 'Prizes for Common Things'. While Dickens disparaged her praise for the students (hypocrites in his opinion) who piously rejected 'gay colours for gowns or ribbons', he was happy to borrow from their books of instruction. Miss Coutts liked observing the students on teaching practice, and voiced her approval for a lesson she watched on the weekly expenditure of a working man. The children were told to imagine they were shopping with the labourer's wife; how would they test the quality of the butter and cheese? ('Taste them' was the practical advice.) 'The children were much interested and their attention never flagged,' commented Miss Coutts. The students' diligent work survives in the Whitelands Archive: perfect miniature nightshirts and samplers of different stitches.

Dickens always aspired for the best for his girls. There was even talk of cookery lessons from the celebrity chef of the day, Alexis Soyer. Naturally the servant classes would attend at different hours and on different terms from either the young ladies or the working men's wives and daughters. Every so often new skills such as straw-plaiting might be added. Sometimes a vicar among Miss Coutts's extensive acquaintance made helpful suggestions. 'A Mrs Bangham in King Street Hammersmith near Flintoff's Library would be a very fit person to teach the inmates of your Home the art of staymaking,' offered the Reverend Atwood from his vicarage in Lincolnshire. 'She can instruct them to make a good stout Article.'

Apart from the straws and stays, there would without fail – and this was an amazing innovation – be 'school' every morning for two hours. Appalled by their illiteracy, Dickens took the progressive step of decreeing that part of the Urania project was to give the young women a basic education.

The connection between ignorance and crime had always struck him forcibly. For his journalism he scoured government reports to extract the statistics he needed. Seventeen thousand of the twenty thousand women taken into custody by the Metropolitan Police in 1847, he thundered at readers of the *Examiner* in 1848, had no trade or occupation; and of this seventeen thousand 'only *fourteen* can read and write well!' At Urania the matrons taught from his lesson plans, mainly the three Rs plus spelling. He scanned catalogues for teaching aids and chose realistically: the elementary rules of arithmetic set out on stiffened sheets, and large pictures of birds and animals with short descriptions underneath. The series Dickens picked started with a gothic-looking long-eared bat and introduced the prospective emigrants to their first kangaroo. Its caption informed them that it was an 'interesting and good-tempered animal'.

He was surprised at what slow learners some of the inmates were. When a better educated candidate did present herself he was prepared to be flexible, but he knew he would have to talk it past Miss Coutts. She did not like making exceptions. So he took some pains with Eliza Clayton, a young widow just out of Coldbath Fields prison. 'Whose curtsey is certainly low, but is meant to be very respectful, and who is exceedingly humble and grateful.' Banishing Heepisms from his mind, Dickens decided to offer Eliza a special deal.

> Finding her very different from the rest of our people – able to work and embroider, and a much better 'Scholar' than we are ever able to make – I thought it right to give her some encouragement. I told her that as she already knew what we usually taught, I had no doubt you would be disposed to send her abroad much sooner than usual, *if* you were satisfied with her general conduct and behaviour.

But she would have to buckle down, do what she was told, and go 'cheerfully to work'. Eliza said she would, although 'she had been in much distress of mind'. On Miss Coutts, however, the widow's accomplishments made less of an impression. Her rigorous standards condemned

Eliza Clayton as 'sloppy'. Dickens responded with a nice balance of tact and practical suggestion:

> A sloppy education is a kind of bringing up, that I think I can thoroughly understand – though I don't remember to have ever heard it so expressively described. In case Mrs Clayton should turn out sloppy in other respects, don't you think it would be well to put her working abilities to the test, and to give her something difficult to do with her needle, and see how she does it?

Whether Eliza Clayton's needlework was up to it or not, we will never know. She is one of the many young women who passed under Dickens's watchful eye and into an unknown future.

The whole educational enterprise spurred his zeal from the outset. 'I wish you could have seen them at work,' he wrote to Miss Coutts the day after Urania opened, 'the two girls deep in my account of the lesson books, and all the knowledge that was to be got out of them, as we were putting them away on the shelves.' He was engrossed by the topic, could 'sacrifice a quire of paper' on it. 'Divers schemes' filled his mind, 'including a series of small evening lectures which I should like to deliver to them in April when Dombey is done.' He kept a close eye on books for the Urania 'library' as he called it, which contained poetry and novels for the matrons to read aloud to the girls. He welcomed Miss Cunliffe's suggestion to add selections from Wordsworth and Crabbe, explaining why to a doubtful Miss Coutts. 'If their imaginations are not filled with good things, they will choke them, for themselves, with bad ones.'

Filling the imagination with good things: Urania could sound at times more liberal arts college than refuge for down-and-outs. Dickens's words also echo the preoccupations of *Hard Times*, which he wrote in 1854, during the Urania years. Its louche nomadic circus is a colourful version of the Victorian underworld. And in some ways Sissy Jupe, the 'stroller's daughter', is a Urania girl. When Mr Gradgrind offers to take her into his house she must first promise to 'communicate no more' with anyone from her past life. '"You will be reclaimed and formed,"' Mr Gradgrind tells her; that's one way of looking at the Urania project. Mr Gradgrind's own daughter Louisa, who has been indoctrinated according to his utilitarian fact-based philosophy, reminds him of her deficiencies. '"What do *I* know, father," said Louisa in her quiet manner, "of tastes, and fancies; of aspirations and affections; of all that part of my nature in which such light things might have been nourished?"'

Urania girls would not lack for such nourishment. Gratified when Miss Coutts yielded to his faith in the 'imaginative faculty', Dickens ordered catalogues of children's books for her to make selections for the Home. His own favourite was 'a charming collection of stories called *The Child's Fairy Library*.'

On his wild island off the coast of Australia, Alexander Maconochie had tamed his savage criminals with the civilising powers of music. Every Sunday and Thursday the prison orchestra played selections of patriotic, naval and religious melodies. Maconochie believed that these concerts promoted the 'general softening of manners among us'. Furthermore, orchestra members would have to learn the useful social skills of co-operation and perseverance.

Music would likewise harmonise the Uranian family. As he hunted 'high and low' for a cheap second-hand piano, Dickens expounded his philosophy to Miss Coutts. 'The fondness for music among these people generally, is most remarkable; and I can imagine nothing more likely to impress or soften a new comer, than finding them with this art among them, and hearing them sing their Evening Hymn before they go to bed.'

He proposed bringing his old friend John Hullah to teach the girls to sing. Hullah had studied at the Royal Academy of Music with Dickens's sister Fanny; he and Dickens collaborated on an operetta way back in the 1830s. Now he was reaching huge audiences with his 'singing school' for school-teachers in London, where he introduced continental teaching methods into England. He and his disciples also taught at Eton, Winchester and Charterhouse; he was a professor at King's College London and gave lessons to the young ladies at Queen's College in Harley Street.

Telling Hullah he attached 'immense importance to the refining influences of his instruction', Dickens urged him to begin without delay. The girls would learn to sing in parts according to Hullah's system, which interested Dickens so much that he resolved to attend one of the lessons himself. Would one class a week be enough? They started with two. It was all rather high-end for Miss Coutts. Sensing this, Dickens reminded her of the benefits. This was 'so much the kind of ingredient we want' – though his nicknaming Hullah 'the Dragon' did not bode well.

Miss Coutts paid the bills for a few months and then called a halt. 'Our young ladies have made sufficient advancement,' she thought. Hullah's methods were fine for a finishing school and 'the wants of a superior class of pupils who have not so much work to attend to.' At Urania Cottage a female teacher who could teach the girls a few hymns would be enough. Dickens sulkily relayed her words to Hullah: 'I state her views, of course, without any admixture of my own.' At least the piano stayed. It was popular, and rumours duly circulated. In 1850 the emigration expert Caroline Chisholm asked Dickens 'if it were true that the girls at Shepherd's Bush "*had Pianos*". I shall always regret,' he told Miss Coutts, 'that I didn't answer yes – each girl a grand, down stairs – and a cottage in her bedroom – besides a small guitar in the wash-house.'

Between visits to Shepherd's Bush Dickens mulled over the welfare of his girls. In 1852, five years into the life of the Home, he outlined a 'plan [which] I have had in my mind a good deal since I was last there'. Susan Matcham was ill in bed and needed nursing. While Dickens understood his girls to be 'generally extremely compassionate . . . in their lives outside', he was dismayed to see how callously they behaved towards Susan. They were not soft-hearted enough for Dickens. He wanted them to feel more for each other. Time to launch a new experiment. He told Mrs Morson to do less of the nursing herself, and make the inmates take turns to sit by the bedside of the sick girl.

They seem to have done a good job. Dickens described Susan as 'most tenderly nursed and restored' after her long illness. It was disappointing then, that she subsequently had to be discharged 'under very flagrant circumstances indeed'. She had interested Dickens 'as much as any girl we have ever had' and he felt 'very sorry for her'. Because she was not fully recovered the committee gave her five shillings for her cab fare and sent her off to St Thomas's Hospital, but 'handsome' Susan did a bunk, probably with the young man who had been hanging round the Home.

Dickens reckoned that an inmate should be fully trained and ready to emigrate after about a year. It was a year of miraculous metamorphosis for the grubby outcasts. They blossomed under the attention of their carers: sometimes they would be literally unrecognisable. A police magistrate coming to bid farewell to 'a girl before her emigration who had been taken from his bar' said he could 'detect no likeness in her to the girl he remembered'. At the Home, starved youngsters ate properly for the first time in their lives. They put on weight, their figures rounded out, their complexions improved. Backs were straighter, hair shinier, cheeks rosier. Anxious faces relaxed into smiles; youthful voices sang cheerfully together round the piano. Their old companions, Dickens claimed, would not know 'the majority of the worst cases . . . again at a year's end'.

Although he was adamant about abroad and the clean break with old ways, he did once make an exception and offer a Urania girl a job in his own house. He suggested that if Miss Coutts agreed, Mary Essam could be employed by Mrs Dickens's mother at Tavistock House during the summer of 1855 while the rest of the family was away. 'If she goes on well, we shall be willing to take her ourselves when we come back.' Mary was still in service in 1861: the census lists her as working for a baker in Leadenhall Market.

Today you too can skivvy for Dickens. The Friends of the Charles Dickens Museum organise volunteers to give his house in Doughty Street an annual spring cleaning. Dusting the furniture of the Inimitable is a memorable experience. And seventy years after his death, his own great-granddaughter Monica was one of the first to exploit the comic potential of housework. *One Pair of Hands* was published in May 1939, the twilight of an era for domestic service. Monica attacked her labours with true Dickensian vigour; she was a servant who certainly knew best.

Before we parted I asked Mrs Randall to give me a reference, and she did not know what to put, so I offered to help her, and between us we concocted the following flight of fancy:

'This is to say that M. Dickens has worked for me for several weeks in the capacity of working cook-housekeeper. I found her sober, honest, and most refined, a very well-spoken girl. Her cooking, both plain and fancy, is excellent; she is scrupulously clean in her methods and her person, and has no eccentricities of religion.'

CHAPTER SEVEN

Toiling Dowagers

'No, sir,' returned Mrs Sparsit. 'It was once my good or ill
fortune, as it may be – before I became a widow – to move
in a very different sphere. My husband was a Powler.' 'Beg
your pardon, really!' said the stranger. 'Was –?' Mrs Sparsit
repeated, 'A Powler.' 'Powler Family,' said the stranger, after
reflecting a few moments. Mrs Sparsit signified assent.
Hard Times, Part II chapter 1

'I AM SORRY to say that I have been brooding very gloomily over our
Shepherd's Bush prospects' wrote Dickens in 1849. It was not the
girls who were giving him grief, it was the staff. Generalissimo Dickens
cannot have been the easiest man to work for, and the women who ran
his little colony should be given credit for much of its success. They
were pioneers in their field, members of a new breed of professional
working women.

One of the first appointments led to a rare falling out. It had taken
much time and effort to secure young Mrs Fisher for the post of assistant matron. Dickens had known her late husband slightly, and readily
approved her 'mild sweet manners'. She quickly made the job hers.
She had just the sympathy for the girls which Dickens was looking
for, as well as the tact and ability to take directions from him. He was
furious when she was forced out after only a month. This was because
Miss Coutts had just discovered that Mrs Fisher was a Dissenter. The
matrons were to be entrusted with teaching the inmates: Miss Coutts
would tolerate no deviation from straight down the line Church of

England. Although Dickens himself did not care for such exclusiveness, he knew that Miss Coutts did, and Urania Cottage was after all her money and her project.

It was a sword-crossing moment. Had Mrs Fisher told Dickens about her religious affiliation during her interview, he might have been able to finesse it with Miss Coutts. He had not known, he should have, and now he could not do anything about it. While he did not concur with Mrs Fisher's 'private opinions', he did object to the Coutts inflexibility, and the loss of his bright young widow. He gave way with poor grace and Mrs Fisher was replaced within a week.

She was followed by a series of flops. Despite some sporadic altercations, Mrs Holdsworth hung on as matron for the first eighteen months. Dickens learned to appreciate how lucky they were with her. Assistant matrons came and went. The problem was that there was no pool of expertise to draw on. Dickens's exacting job specification did not help: 'To improve them [the girls] by education and example – establish habits of the most rigid order, punctuality, and neatness – but to make as great a variety in their daily lives as their daily lives will admit of – and to render them an innocently cheerful Family while they live together there.' Rigid order plus jolly variety made for a difficult balance.

One source for staff might be from prisons, but women who worked there could be quite tough. George Chesterton characterised Mrs Meriton, who was on his own staff at Coldbath Fields, as 'A stern functionary, little given to tears'. Then as now, tales of life in women's prisons could sell books, as the hack novelist Frederick Robinson realised in the 1860s when he ghosted his way to a steady seller with *Female Life in Prison* by A Prison Matron. Robinson's prison officer starts briskly: 'I wish it to be clearly understood that these are the honest reminiscences of one retired from Government service.' She is a no-nonsense type, with no time for 'the flighty women; the half mad or the wholly mad, who require some careful observation to make sure that they are not acting, and who are at last taken away to Fisherton Asylum, and are heard of no more.'

Robinson's officers bicker among themselves and foster favourites among the prisoners. Too rough for Dickens, their reign would grimly recreate 'the extraordinary monotony of the Refuges and Asylums now existing'. On the other hand, the lady who applied for what she called the 'horrible task' at Urania Cottage was just as ill suited. So were the sprightly candidates presenting themselves via classier routes; they were too green and innocent. 'I have seen your pretty protégée and like her extremely', Dickens wrote to the society hostess Mrs Milner Gibson in the autumn of 1847. But 'there is a great difficulty, without distressing her – or I fancy so – in exactly stating to her what the object of this Institution is. For she is so young, and (necessarily) inexperienced, that I hardly know how to come at her with such notions.'

While the pretty protégée seems to have fallen at the first hurdle, the early months of the Home were dogged by a succession of the overly genteel. Dickens raged at the airs they gave themselves, the 'mincing nonsense' of those 'toiling and all-enduring dowagers'. This was Mrs Graves and Mrs Holdsworth considering themselves too posh to wash. 'Intolerable' thundered Dickens, as Graves ('sombre') made way for Coombs ('grim') and Furze ('vinegary'). He was reduced to making jokes about their names – Mrs Furze was predictably 'rather thorny and irritating' – and calling them after unpleasant employers in his novels. *The Old Curiosity Shop*'s Sally Brass had her uses. Perhaps he was venting his spleen on some of them with Mrs Sparsit (Mr Bounderby's snobbish housekeeper in *Hard Times*), 'making her nose more Roman and her eyebrows more Coriolanian in the strength of her severity'.

The worst arrangement was when Mrs Holdsworth had two assistants. Even the experienced prison governor George Chesterton was taken aback by the fireworks. 'A blaze of discord was this morning lighted up by Mrs Furze (a very combustible material)' he reported to Dickens, with more feeble name jokes to mask his unease as he waded into the foray. By this time the first intake of inmates had been at Urania nearly a year and they had their own views on how it should be run. 'Rubina Waller was the principal belligerent, and she was supported by others, and amongst them by Jane Westaway, in whose temper and discretion I confide.'

Chesterton should not have listened to the girls' gossip, but he knew them well by now, and decided to sound out the responsible Jane. She intimated that Mrs Furze was 'harsh, unreasonable and "fidgetty" (Jane's own word)'. It is probably the only one of hers we will ever hear. Chesterton's next heroic move was to tackle Mrs Furze herself. 'I found her ignorant, ill-tempered manifestly, and presumptuous.' Miss Coutts had appointed her, she said, to the same rank as Mrs Holdsworth rather than as her assistant. Chesterton's report could not have been more scathing. 'She is . . . a bad house-wife, utterly ignorant of cookery, and no great adept at the needle. Without method or judgement: detractive of her superiors, jealous of any mention of her own name, exclaiming *shrewly*, when she hears it, "well, what have you got to say about Mrs Furze, now?"' But neither he nor Dickens could handle the situation. It was left to Miss Coutts to get rid of her, which she accomplished with a subtle 'master-stroke'. 'I think', Dickens told her, 'you would, after that, make a brilliant figure as a Diplomatist.'

Miss Cunliffe started well and lasted longer. 'I like her very much,' Dickens decided. 'There is something in her face, exceedingly agreeable and promising, and she improves greatly on being talked to.' He was charmed by her air of 'conscientious timidity' and her ideas about reading poetry to the girls. But then she exhibited symptoms of the insupportable presumption of thinking she knew better than Dickens. She made the mistake of questioning his wisdom in brandishing marriage as an incentive to the inmates. There had also been talk of her taking sole charge. This threw Dickens into despair.

> All possible deductions and allowances made, it is quite clear to me that Miss Cunliffe is a woman of an atrocious temper, and that she violently mistakes her office and its functions. . . . The idea of hectoring and driving them [the young women] is the most ignorant and the most fatal that could be possibly entertained. I am quite confident she will bring about such an outbreak as we have not had there.

He was right. Within a week there was indeed an outbreak, which involved Miss Cunliffe 'looking like a Stage Maniac in a domestic drama, or an illustration of "The Bottle" on very bad paper.' 'The Bottle' was a series of engravings by Dickens's early illustrator George Cruikshank about the evils of drink. It sounds like drink in this case, and Miss C got her marching orders. By the next week all was 'quiet and comfortable . . . Miss Cunliffe rigidly secluded in her own chamber – making a perfect Brougham of herself in point of Oratory, I have no doubt'. The last we hear of her is her exit, 'very solemnly, in a fly.'

Dickens's spirits soon recovered. Georgiana Morson arrived in the spring of 1849 and looked '*very promising*'; she '*certainly* begins well'; 'I have a strong hope that she is exactly the person we have always wanted.' This time he was not disappointed. Over the next five years Georgiana Morson proved herself the best matron Urania ever had. She is a new variant of Victorian womanhood: a middle-class single parent supporting her family by means of a satisfying career.

Georgiana Collin came from what was known as a 'good family' who lived at Merton Abbey in Surrey and included Isaac Newton among their forebears. It was a world which lively Georgiana left far behind on her marriage to James Morson. He had trained as a doctor at St George's Hospital in London before enrolling as Chief Medical Officer for the Brazilian National Mining Association. Back on leave in England, he met Georgiana and wooed her with tales of adventure. When he returned to Brazil in 1838 he had with him his new wife and baby daughter Georgina.

The Morsons were posted to Cuyaba, a small town of earth and clay houses in the Matto Grosso, buried deep in Brazil's rainforest. Even today Cuyaba is accessible only by air or river, and trades on its remoteness. It features in travel literature as Brazil's wild west, the staging post for eco-tourists visiting the Pantenal, the world's largest wetlands with a stunning array of wildlife. In the Morsons' day *The Modern Traveller* warned that the area 'must be considered as *terra incognita*, being still, for the most part, in the possession of native tribes'. By the time the famous English explorer and writer Richard Burton visited Cuyaba in the 1860s, the silver mine which had employed James Morson was bankrupt. A tiny outpost, it had never covered its costs – even in its heyday when it employed thirty English miners, thirty free Brazilians, and three hundred of the mining company's black slaves. The Morsons were among the very few Victorians to witness slavery at first hand.

James Morson died in 1844, leaving Georgiana with Georgina, Nina, and another child on the way. Her only option was to return to England, where she could draw on the funds which James had provided for her. It was an epic journey. First of all she and her two small daughters had to travel hundreds of miles by mule, then they had to find a ship sailing for England. The only one available was a Man-of-War, a men-only vessel sent by the British Navy to police the abolition of the slave trade. When the pregnant Georgiana was taken ill, no one could have nursed her back to health more attentively than the captain and chief officer.

Once in England her troubles were far from over. The funds James had left her had been embezzled by his brother. Georgiana possessed nothing but her address book and a testimonial commending her as 'A wonderful woman in every way'. Luckily her contacts included Miss Coutts: James had treated Angela's father years ago at St George's Hospital. So Georgiana settled the two girls and little baby James with their grandparents in Surrey; then she wrote to ask Miss Coutts if she knew of a job which might suit.

Dickens's approval may have had a class bias. He was weary of 'Coombses and Cunliffes' and their parades of false gentility. Above all he liked Mrs Morson's approach. She had the warmth he wanted so much at Urania and had missed in the staff up till now. Even Mrs Holdsworth, who had lasted unexpectedly well, 'seems to me to have a secret idea that her charges are her natural enemies'. Georgiana was just the opposite. She was kind, friendly, motherly. She immediately took to the girls and they took to her in return.

She was also intelligent. Within weeks of arriving she had used ingenious tactics to calm the row between Isabella Gordon and Rachael Bradley. She had the knack of getting the best out of the inmates, partly by appealing to them to help each other. Noticing the low spirits of Eliza Clayton – this was the upmarket widow whose education Miss Coutts considered 'sloppy' – Mrs Morson 'discreetly told Matilda Thompson (as the most civilised of our young friends) to give her any little help and support that she could'.

One of her first tasks was learning how to work in harness with Dickens. She was stepping on his toes when she asked for more leeway with her charges. Eager to stand between her and the girls, Dickens bristled predictably. 'I think in reference to Mrs Morson's knowing about the girls, that her information ought to be strictly confined to such general ideas of their several characters as I can give her for her guidance, founded on some broad explanation of their several histories.'

In his turn Dickens learnt to trust Georgiana Morson as he hadn't her predecessors. Consultations about day-to-day details brought them into constant contact. He enjoyed long conferences with her during his visits to the Home. And what a relief to be able to delegate the tedious paperwork for rent and rates, relying on her to 'go on zealously, and in a business-like way'. In his letters we can see her as a competent, self-assured woman moving freely around London: collecting new inmates from the police courts, calling on Dickens and Miss Coutts to update them on the latest developments.

At Urania she taught the girls to read and write, as well as all the household skills a servant needed. She presided over the dining table, and made mealtimes a social occasion the girls had not known before. They ate the good food she had taught them to cook and chattered about their future prospects. 'Senior' girls about to emigrate sat at her end of the table, listening with amazement to her traveller's tales. They were both excited and reassured. If she could cope on her own, perhaps they could too.

She also knew how to handle a crisis. Beer was kept on the premises under lock and key, as a special bonus for the girls working with the heavy laundry. While Mrs Morson was out one evening 'that very bad and false subject, Jemima Hiscock, forced open the door of the little beer cellar with knives, and drank until she was dead drunk; when she used the most horrible language and made a very repulsive exhibition of herself.' That was not all. 'She induced *Mary Joynes* (!) to drink the beer with her; and that young lady was also drunk, but stupidly and drowsily.' Next morning Mrs Morson arrived to tell Dickens about it. He was relieved to hear that she had 'wisely abstained from calling in the Police'; instead she had managed, with assistance from the gardener, to get them both to bed and locked up.

Dickens was not a fan of Jemima's. He reckoned she must have shipped in some spirits from outside. 'I am perfectly sure that no woman of [her] habits, could get so madly intoxicated with that weak beer.' He suspected her of plotting to steal the house linen after it was freshly washed and ironed. She should, he instructed Mrs Morson, be stripped of her Urania dress, put in 'her own clothes, however bad', and expelled instantly with absolutely no money in her pocket.

'And now,' he ended his letter to Miss Coutts, 'what on earth is to be done with Mary Joynes?' The Home Secretary himself had expressed an interest in her case and Dickens had jumped to attention. 'I have not the least doubt of the expediency of immediately taking it. His interest in it is very agreeable to observe.' Now Mary's days at Urania were over, she had let them all down. 'I am more indignant with that Mary Joynes, than I have ever been with any of them.'

New arrivals were the most likely to cause trouble; Mrs Morson learned to keep an eye out for them. In 1853, after only a fortnight at the Home, Mary Ann Shadwell was back in the dock at Hammersmith Police Court. The 'pretty-looking young girl' gave her age as sixteen, though the reporter from *Lloyd's Weekly Newspaper* thought she 'had the appearance of being much more than that', which she probably was. Mary Ann's word was not to be trusted. She had previously stolen only a bonnet and shawl, she had confided to Mrs Morson; now the court heard that Mary Ann had in fact stolen three expensive silk dresses.

At Urania Mary Ann and her accomplice, who evaded capture, wriggled out of the larder window with five cotton dresses, two merino dresses, some underclothes and two shawls. They also ransacked the parlour, bagging seven spoons, two silver-topped scent bottles, assorted thimbles and scissors, and even the crimson tablecloth from the parlour table. Mary Ann was wearing three of the dresses and one of the shawls when she was caught a few days later, rather warmly clad for August.

Reconciled to girls lying to her, Mrs Morson was disheartened this time by the 'shocking state of confusion' which the thieves left in the parlour. She wanted the court to know about the books thrown all over the floor, and 'the ornaments removed from their places. Everything in the room appeared to have been upset.' As a consequence, she said, she thought that Mary Ann 'should be punished for the purpose of making an example to the other young women of the establishment.' Taking the hint, the judge sentenced Mary Ann to one year's hard labour.

To Mrs Morson Dickens could be an uncompromising task-master. He would not budge on the principle that all the washing and baking should be done in-house, however much work it made for Mrs Morson and her assistant. He continued to meddle and nag – 'I have repeatedly cautioned her' – and to all of it she responded with good humour. She patiently tolerated the thefts of clothes and personal possessions, as well as the inevitable courtroom sequels. Summoned on another occasion as a witness before a Grand Jury at the Old Bailey, she 'acted very steadily', observed Dickens's solicitor William Loaden, 'and very much like a lady in every stage of the business'.

Eventually Dickens recognised what an asset she was. He deputed her to visit prospective inmates and carry out the follow-up enquiries he insisted on. 'I should like to know – must indeed, before it is possible to admit her – that her story is so far true,' he wrote to Mrs Morson about an applicant in 1852. He asked her to enquire 'at Mrs Crouch's at the Turnham Green Hall – and at the place where she lodged' to see if the girl is telling the truth. If not, 'no more can be done for her.' If she is, Mrs Morson is to give her 'a shilling or two today' and report back to Dickens tomorrow.

Her errands sent her right into Dickens's own study. It was her job to take the ailing Maria Cridge to St Bartholomew's Hospital '*directly you receive this*'; then 'call here on your way back, and leave word (in case Mrs Dickens should not be at home, write a line in my room) stating whether you have got her in, or whether she will have to wait another week' (Bart's had only one 'receiving day' a week). And while Maria was in hospital, Mrs Morson must make 'particular enquiries' about her behaviour there. She would need all the briskness Dickens commended in her to keep up with her demanding schedule.

She also managed to build a friendly relationship with the reserved Miss Coutts. When Hannah Brown was ill she offered her own services as a nurse. 'Thinking of you both,' she dashed off in a quick letter in 1852; 'let me know if I could be of any use.' Understanding that they liked to be kept abreast of life at the Home, she added: 'I am happy to say the family are all going on well. Last Tuesday I had some trouble with Sarah Youngman, she was exceptionally impertinent but in a little time she expressed her sorrow and has behaved well since.'

Mrs Morson entered into the spirit of Urania with all her heart and soul. 'I felt it was so good, so very very good of you to save that poor little orphan,' she wrote to Miss Coutts about her offer to shelter Anne Johnson's undersized little sister. Mrs Morson had taken Anne from Urania Cottage to see her dying mother: 'it was a most distressing meeting – that poor forsaken woman seemingly in the last stage of consumption and quite blind.' She wanted Miss Coutts to know that the dying woman had 'prayed for blessings to descend upon your head'.

For Mrs Morson Dickens finally relaxed his golden rule and shared some of the secret histories he guarded so jealously, though the evidence from the Mary Ann Shadwell case suggests that she already knew much more than Dickens supposed. After all, it was she who made Urania the family he wanted it to be. The girls wept with her when they left; and Dickens laughed with her at the sight of her small son home for Christmas from Christ's Hospital School, 'such a small son in blue-coat boy's clothes, that he looks like a toy. He ought to have a little wire handle just below his shoes, to make dismal music when turned round.'

By 1852 Urania was running so peaceably under her care that Dickens and Miss Coutts could incubate more philanthropic schemes, this time a plan for Model Dwellings in the East End of London. Mrs Morson also thought she would like a change. She went for the bigger challenge and increased salary of the top job at Thomas Coram's Foundling Hospital. Dickens rejoiced when she did not get it. She was now his proxy, inasmuch as anyone could be. He was planning building works to expand Urania Cottage, and Mrs Morson was deputed to relocate the girls to Broadstairs while the alterations were made. All seemed to be going smoothly.

Two years later he was dismayed when she handed in her resignation. She was going to be married, and told Dickens all 'the circumstances'. Her fiancé, George Wade Harrison, was a comfortably-off printer and bookseller; the couple planned to settle in Sevenoaks. She offered to stay until they found a replacement but '"would rather not put him off, if she can help it"'. In later years she treasured her time at Urania, preserving even the briefest of notes from the great man. In return Dickens played games with her name. 'Also Georgiana Wife of the Above' appears on the first page of *Great Expectations* in 1860. And in 1864 Miss Podsnap's name provokes a long discussion between Fascination Fledgeby and Alfred Lammle in *Our Mutual Friend*:

> 'Is the right name Georgina or Georgiana?'
> 'Georgiana.'
> 'I was thinking yesterday, I didn't know there was such a name. I thought it must end in ina.'

'Why?'

'Why, you play – if you can – the Concertina, you know,' replied Fledgeby, meditating very slowly. 'And you have – when you catch it – the Scarlatina. And you can come down from a balloon in a parach – no you can't though. Well, say Georgeute – I mean Georgiana.'

Mrs Morson was succeeded by Lucy Marchmont, a widow in her early forties. She had been working at Tothill Fields prison, where governor Augustus Tracey thought highly of her. At first Dickens could not see past her appearance. She was large, 'flabbier than I could wish', and compared poorly with Mrs Morson. She had none of her brightness, was 'common looking, and lumpish'. Expect to be disappointed, he told Miss Coutts. 'Tracey is so certain of her that he staggers me.' But her quiet confidence told in her favour, so 'May Marchmont prosper!'

Initially wrong-footed by Urania etiquette, she did not acclimatise as quickly as Mrs Morson had done. It was so different from Tothill Fields. Take the ceremony of arrival for instance. New inmates should, Dickens ordered, be fetched by the head matron herself in a private coach. The journey was a rite of passage, a gesture to show these down-and-outs that they were on their way up in the world. To this effect Dickens considered public transport 'very objectionable'. Mrs Marchmont had broken all the protocols by sending her second-in-command Mrs Macartney to collect a new girl from the railway station and bring her to Urania Cottage by bus.

To begin with some of the girls gave her a rough ride. The better-behaved ones took it upon themselves to explain it all to Dickens. They 'praised Mrs Marchmont's kind conduct highly, and said that, being new, she had more to bear than she ought to bear, or than Mrs Morson ever would have borne, from "some of 'em"'. When Dickens pressed them to be more specific, they spilled the beans about the night before.

Mrs Marchmont had ticked off new girl Ellen Stanley 'for general defiance', to which Ellen retorted that she had had enough of the place and was on the point of leaving. Hesitating not an instant in their support of Mrs Marchmont, Dickens and the committee summoned her and Ellen in together.

> Stanley beginning a long story about 'Which blessed will be the day when justice is a-done in this house,' I said that the only thing we had to do with, was whether she had said she meant to go. To which she rejoined that she had, and that she could turn her hand to anything, she thanked the Heavenly Powers! I remarked that the only thing she had to turn her hand to, at present, was to going; and that she would understand she was to withdraw before tomorrow evening.

Once settled in, Mrs Marchmont vindicated Tracey's high opinion. She was steady, capable and kind. Her prison background did not pre-dispose her to severity, as Dickens feared, unlike the strong-willed Mrs Harries who came from governing Exeter Penitentiary to terrorise the students at Whitelands College with her regime of silence and religious fervour. 'No coloured bonnets', stipulated her minutely detailed dress code, 'unless of a very dark colour, and they are to be trimmed *neatly* with ribbons of one colour and *no* flowers, feathers and bead trimmings. Neither Pink nor Red ribbon of any shade.'

If Dickens never warmed to Mrs Marchmont as he had to Mrs Morson, he did get into the habit of 'consulting' with her. And when she needed a boost he was on hand to intercede tactfully. Both Mrs Marchmont and her assistant had been 'tremendously cast down by your having had occasion to blame', he wrote to Miss Coutts, who could be brusque. 'They really seem so sorry and depressed, and it is so necessary that they should have self-reliance and a sustaining pride in what they do, that I comforted them with what majestic consolation I felt it Ministerial to impart.' Mrs Marchmont's assistant, Jane Macartney, worked at Urania for about twelve years. She is mentioned infrequently in Dickens's letters, the 'useful' figure in the wings contributing to the smooth running of the Home. By 1861 Clara Bannister has joined the staff, to be listed after Mrs Marchmont and Mrs Macartney as 'House-keeper' in the census. This was after Dickens's time; he would have vetoed taking on extra staff.

The matrons at Urania all knew they must work precisely to Dickens's orders, and sometimes literally to his script. The first words a new girl heard would be his. 'I am writing a little address,' Dickens told Miss Coutts as the Home opened in 1847, 'which Mrs Holdsworth shall read to each, alone, when she comes in'. When anything out of the ordinary cropped up his instruction was often 'wait till I get there'.

Chaplains, naturally, had more autonomy. From the first Miss Coutts was adamant that the young women must have religious instruction. Nor could Dickens disagree, so his influence over the choice was vital. What he did not want he knew only too well, and drew in the savage portrait of *Bleak House*'s Mr Chadband. He is a greedy hypocrite 'with a fat smile, and a general appearance of having a good deal of train oil in his system'. The sermon he gives on 'Terewth', perfectly illustrated by Phiz, is a masterpiece of idiocy, hectoring and wilful blindness. Jo, the crossing-sweeper boy to whom it is addressed, cannot understand a word of it. It is left to Guster, the put-upon servant who comes from the infamous Tooting orphanage and suffers from fits, to share her bread and cheese supper with Jo and pat him kindly on the shoulder. 'It is the first time in his life that any decent hand has been so laid upon him.'

For the chaplain who would teach at Urania, Dickens favoured men recommended by Chesterton or Tracey. The job went to Edward Illingworth. A slightly older man than Dickens, he worked as chaplain at Coldbath Fields prison for over thirty years, not the easiest clerical posting. Prison chaplains were often the only sympathetic person a convict would come across: Illingworth was one such chaplain.

In Dickens's opinion he could be naive. He should never have trusted the 'false' Jemima Hiscock and her 'pious pretences'. Illingworth had believed Jemima when she pretended to recognise a friend at church on Sunday and asked permission to spend time with her. Dickens judged it '(knowing the girl's antecedents) a piece of unmitigated falsehood' and was proved right.

If Illingworth was a soft touch, he was also conscientious. Keen for candidates from his prison to do well, he followed their progress optimistically. He must have tolerated the Dickens line, omnipresent as it was on the very walls of the Home. Inscriptions, some from sermons chosen by Dickens, others he had written himself, adorned the living room. His own precepts nagged the girls about order, punctuality and good temper. Not content with this, he pursued them to their bedrooms with notices 'admonishing them against ever lying down to rest, without being affectionate and reconciled among themselves'.

Illingworth served on the Urania committee, alongside other churchmen corralled by Miss Coutts. William Tennant came on the recommendation of the Bishop of London, and was described as 'one of the best parish priests in all England'. Archdeacon John Sinclair was an emigration enthusiast: his pet notion was Colonial Schools of Industry for poor children sent overseas. Miss Coutts also roped in the educational reformer and bureaucrat James Kay-Shuttleworth. Dickens was initially polite and finally exasperated. 'I am so dreadfully jaded this morning by the supernatural dreariness of Kaye Shuttleworth', he wrote to Miss Coutts in 1853 after dutifully reading his new book *Public Education*, 'that I feel as if I had just come out of the Great Desert of Sahara where my Camel died a fortnight ago'.

Dickens chaired the Urania committee, but he was not a committee man. He preferred operating through his private networks, and playing any troublesome cards close to his chest. When Mrs Morson paid one of her visits to Tavistock House to consult him about Martha Williamson he gladly took command. A good bonnet and gown had been removed from the wardrobe room and found hidden in the dirty washing. Mrs Morson – whose 'penetration does her great credit' – suspected Martha of taking the clothes 'with a view to decamping'. Martha had only been at the Home five weeks. She confessed to the theft but begged for mercy 'as she was utterly destitute'. What should Mrs Morson do?

Bustling over to Shepherd's Bush, Dickens immediately summoned Martha into the parlour 'the instant I arrived at the Home, in order that she might have no time for preparation'. She put up a poor show. Although Dickens felt sorry for her, there were no extenuating circumstances. He told her she must put on her old clothes and leave by noon tomorrow. But before he left Shepherd's Bush he sent a note to Augustus Tracey. Martha had come from his prison, did he want to give her a second chance? 'You may have an interest in her, or that knowledge of her, or that kind-heartedness about her, that you would like to give the destitute wretch another trial. I would like to do so, but I am afraid the circumstances are very bad.'

Since Tracey offered no objections, that should have been the last they heard of Martha; but she was determined not to go empty-handed.

Next day Mrs Morson appeared once again at Tavistock House. Martha had robbed the house at six o'clock that morning, jumped out of the window and over the gates, only to be caught in the lane by a policeman who brought her back. She was now locked up in one of the bedrooms. What should they do with her now?

Dickens's main concern was to prevent the affair reaching the newspapers. He had Martha frogmarched to his solicitor William Loaden, with instructions to take her to the local magistrate at Hammersmith, and 'beg the Magistrate, quietly, to convict her summarily and so prevent trouble and noise at the Old Bailey'. So smoothly was this process handled that Martha was soon back for 'two months of Mr Tracey's severest discipline'. Unfortunately, a *Times* reporter was hanging round Hammersmith and gave Martha and 'Ooranio-house' a couple of column inches. Miss Coutts was then on holiday in Germany; Dickens anxiously predicted her reaction on reading about what he called the 'little trouble'. Accordingly he wrote at length to forestall any criticism: 'I hope you approve of these proceedings?' How much trouble for one short-stay girl. And how much easier it was to deal with Urania on his own. He was happiest on his visits there 'alone in my glory', 'a Committee of One' dispensing justice, order and mercy to his pocket-sized Utopia in west London.

CHAPTER EIGHT

Audacious Rhena Pollard

However at this forgiving Christmas time
Dickens to Georgiana Morson, 4 January 1854

RHENA POLLARD IS the Urania cliffhanger. She is one of the young women we know most about, as she scraped herself in and out of trouble. Did Urania do right by its girls? Rhena's story gives us some answers.

Born in 1836, Rhena came from the rural area of West Sussex. Her father was a farm worker and 'Reney', as she appears in the 1841 census, was the youngest of four children. Life does not sound too easy: the Pollards shared their house with another family of agricultural labourers. In 1845, when Rhena was nine, her mother was sentenced to fourteen days' hard labour for stealing a dress worth four shillings. By the 1851 census the Pollards have dispersed. Fifteen-year-old Rhena is living in the local workhouse, Thakeham Union, where she is listed as a 'scholar'.

By the next year she has graduated to Petworth prison. She has also managed to find friends in high places. At Goodwood, the grand house nearby, the Duchess of Richmond interested herself in the case. Could something be done for the girl? The Duke was a governor of Pentonville prison, and had heard about Urania Cottage through his contacts there. So the Duchess wrote to Dickens and he duly forwarded the letter to Miss Coutts. Then he left on a whistle-stop theatrical tour with his band of amateur players. They performed in seven northern towns in ten days and dazzled appropriately. 'Seldom has Nottingham witnessed a more brilliant and fashionable assembly' reported the *Nottinghamshire Guardian*. Even so Dickens found time for Rhena. Miss Coutts's reply to his letter caught up with him in Derby and he responded instantly to say he was writing 'by this post' to the chaplain of the Petworth House of Correction, 'making all needful enquiries into the girl's case'.

Enquiries, in Dickens's view, were always needful. He never took a girl into the Home without rigorous investigation throughout his extensive networks. It was the kind of detective work he relished. No girl came into the Home without his approval. If possible he would go to the police courts, workhouses, ragged schools and prisons to see them. He prided himself on his ability to read faces. 'He was reading your character,' explained one of his servants to a newly arrived parlour maid, disconcerted by the man scrutinising her so intently; 'he now knows you thoroughly'.

The chaplain made encouraging noises and the Duchess packed Rhena off to Shepherd's Bush, where she stayed for longer than the usual year. Rhena seems to have been a slow settler; she was also a trouble-maker. At sixteen, she was small, noisy and wilful, and enjoyed putting herself forward. She had quite a tongue, quite a temper. Dickens did not like her any the less for that, but she did need watching. She crops up in his letters more than other inmates. 'The little girl from Petworth is an extraordinary case of restless imposture and seeking after notoriety; but there are chances (not desperate chances, I think) of something better being made of it.' This was in August 1853. Rhena was still at Urania nearly eighteen months after her arrival, at the beginning of January 1854.

During those months the Home had flourished. To its benefactor, Miss Coutts, Dickens often reported 'all quiet'. The idea of expanding the operation came up; they discussed taking over the lease of the neighbouring house. In the event they decided on an extension to the existing house. There is an air of stability about the place: this is a success. A modest one, with some failures of course; but nevertheless satisfaction is in order.

From the very beginning, 1854 looked like being a different sort of year. In the freezing early morning of a snow-bound January Mrs Morson appeared at Tavistock House to report a break-out the previous day. The girl had chosen her moment well, just as they were all coming back from church. Smartly dressed in her Sunday 'cloak and bonnet and best gown', she had 'bodily vanished' over the garden wall.

Dickens wasted no regrets on the absconder, although he was annoyed to lose the clothes. What worried him more was the effect the break-out might have on the others, especially on the absconder's best friend. This was Rhena, and she was now threatening to be off too. She was only waiting for the committee day to make her announcement, she confided condescendingly to Mrs Morson, 'as a kind of obliging favour on her part'.

This was a mistake. If there was to be any threatening, Dickens had to be the one doing it. Rhena's 'most inveterately audacious manner' could not go unnoticed. On the other hand, he had come to know her well over the last year and a half. He recognised a kindred spirit in her restlessness, and a not unlikeable bravado in her threats. She had, after all, absolutely nowhere else to go. Usually, the moment a girl talked about leaving, out she went. This time, Mrs Morson was on her side and pleading for mercy. And it was Christmas. So he cooked up a drama for Mrs Morson to act out with him, a benefit performance in aid of the reclamation of Rhena and the edification of all the other inmates. This would be a Christmas story for real.

The ensuing episode features in two long letters, one to Mrs Morson and the other to Miss Coutts. It is the first letter which shows up the staginess of the event so clearly, with Dickens's elaborate set-up and working of the whole thing with Mrs Morson. The second letter to Miss Coutts described how it went. The letter to Mrs Morson is part of the show. It came to light only recently; how it did so is a story in itself.

Norstead is a large house in Devon. For seventy years it was the home of the celebrated cabinetmaker Judith Hughes, 'Miss Chippendale of Tavistock' Sir Basil Spence called her. In her nineties she was persuaded into a nursing home, and the local auctioneer, Robin Fenner, was called in. He knew about Judith Hughes and was impressed by her art collection, which included vases from Ancient Greece and pots by Lucie Rie.

He did not know about the Dickens connection, but in one of the bookcases he spotted a complete early edition of the novels in first-class condition. What he called the auctioneer's third sense drew him to the bookcase; special affection drew him to open the copy of *David Copperfield*. Out of it fell a letter in Dickens's writing. A direct descendant of Georgiana Morson, Judith Hughes had inherited a cache of notes and letters from Dickens, which take us to the heart of daily life at Urania Cottage. Fearful of burglars, the elderly Miss Hughes had squirreled the letters in hiding places round the house. Some she rolled into a batch of architects' plans, others into a bundle of old silk stockings.

If we put the newly discovered letter to Mrs Morson alongside the letter to Miss Coutts, we can see it for what it is: a stage prop for the Rhena Pollard show. Dickens has written and assigned parts for Rhena and Mrs Morson, plus full supporting chorus of all the inmates. This will be a morality play for one performance only. Dickens had the knack of casting real people in fictional parts, as his friend Arthur Helps remembered: 'he looked at all things and people dramatically. He assigned to all of us characters; and in his company we could not help playing our parts.' So it would be at Urania. Events moved swiftly. It happened that the next committee day was fixed for 3 January, the day after Mrs Morson's visit to Dickens with the news of the absconder. So much the better. Dickens always was a striker of hot irons.

An important element of the monthly committee meeting was the interview with each girl on her own, to check that she was making progress and had no complaints. Dickens described one of these meetings for Miss Coutts in the summer of 1851, after he had come up from Broadstairs to 'preside at that great Tribunal': 'Our charges were one and all the most innocent and deferential of girls. The first one (Rupkin) spoke very low, with her arms hooked behind her, and her eyes on the ground – and all the others, one after another, did exactly the same.'

At the 'Tribunal' three years later, in the freezing January of 1854, Dickens waited for Rhena to make her entrance. Then he summoned Mrs Morson: the whole incident is recreated at great length in the letter to Miss Coutts the next day. '"Mrs Morson"', says Dickens, '"this is the girl who wants to go, I believe" – "Yes." – "Take her at her word. It is getting dark now, but, immediately after breakfast tomorrow morning, shut the gate upon her for ever."'

This was shock tactics. Dickens's original philosophy for the Home had built in a generous array of second chances. He had foreseen mood-swings and jitters, and legislated accordingly. 'I would have some rule to the effect that no request to be allowed to go away would be received for at least four and twenty hours, and that in the interval the person should be kindly reasoned with, if possible, and implored to consider well what she was doing.' In addition to the twenty-four-hour time lock, he suggested the radical idea of readmitting anyone who left and then regretted it. He underlined his words for greater emphasis. '*I would not make one, or two, or three, or four, or six departures from the Establishment a binding reason against the re-admission of that person being again penitent.*' But that was seven years ago, before any girls had even arrived, let alone threatened to leave.

Over the years the Urania team discovered what worked and what did not. Early on they learned to be wary of the borderline between volatile and violent. Dickens rejected a candidate offered to him by a Unitarian minister from Banbury. 'A violent temper would be an immense objection', especially in a home as small as Urania. 'Experience shews us that of all things it is the most difficult to combat. It is certain to break out, like a madness.'

Restless Rhena had managed to keep herself more or less under control for eighteen months, and Dickens did not want to throw away all that time and effort. So he called her bluff with his order of release. The risk paid off as he hoped: Rhena did not really want to leave tomorrow at all. She may have realised this herself only when she heard Dickens tell her she would be out on her ear after breakfast. Or maybe she was trying to provoke Dickens and Mrs Morson into supplicating her to stay. At any rate, when Dickens issued her marching orders, 'the girl was more taken by surprise, and more seized with consternation, than anybody I have ever seen in that place.'

Faced with ejection on to the icy streets, Rhena fell plumb into role, acting up – and out – with all the emotion Dickens premeditated for her. The committee could not handle her. 'She begged and prayed – was obliged to be taken out of the room – went into the long room, and, *before all the rest*, entreated and besought Mrs Morson to intercede for her – and broke into the most forlorn and dismal lamentations.' 'Before all the rest': the other girls must witness Rhena's distress. She was producing exactly the kind of public show Dickens had choreographed for her.

Next into the spotlight was Mrs Morson, to be given her directions for the ensuing scene. She must 'have the rough dress down and air it in the long room.' Stage manager Dickens was marshalling all his props. This rough dress shadowed the attractive clothes which certified the initiation into the Urania life. Meanwhile a set of nasty old clothes were biding their time in a cupboard upstairs. If you were expelled, that is how you would leave, marked out in the garments of disgrace.

In the early days the sight of a smart dress walking off on the back of a girl he had discharged annoyed Dickens; but what could he do when she claimed she had no clothes of her own? To prevent this he gave Mrs Morson instructions 'to buy at a slopseller's, the commonest and ugliest and coarsest (but still clean and whole) woman's dress that she could possibly purchase, and invariably to keep such a thing by her.' Mrs Morson's ostentatious airing of the rough dress in the long room was a public warning, with Rhena being held up as a lesson for them all. It was like showing a heretic the instruments of torture.

The committee meeting ended, its members pulled on their thick overcoats and sallied out into the snowy evening. Dickens left issuing Mrs Morson with yet more commands. The drama he was drafting for Rhena to star in was to be a marathon all-nighter. Until now Mrs Morson had comforted and defended Rhena. Dickens deliberately removed this support, telling Mrs Morson to give the girl 'no hope or relief all night'. Rhena's spirits must be utterly crushed. Further, she must again display herself publicly in the pose of prostrate supplicant. She must repeat her pleas to be allowed to stay, once more in the long room '*before all the others*'. Only then would Dickens be prepared to reconsider.

He was already lining up his props for the next scene. As he said goodbye to Mrs Morson he finalised the arrangements for the following morning. If Rhena stuck to his script of total humiliation, Mrs Morson should send him word. He would then write a letter for the messenger to bring back to Shepherd's Bush by return. This letter Mrs Morson would then read aloud to Rhena in front of the assembled inmates. What a disruption to the careful routines of the day all this would make.

As he expected, Mrs Morson did indeed send word to him that Rhena had begged to stay and, yes, in front of all the others. The letter he sent back for Mrs Morson to read out – the one which has just surfaced – looks like a private letter but is designed for public broadcast and consumption. It is long, heavily embellished with oratorical ribbons and bows. Dickens appears at his least sympathetic. This was intentional. He casts himself as the stony-hearted one, entreated by Rhena's champion Mrs Morson, to give 'the unhappy girl one more trial'. I shouldn't listen to you, he tells the matron. What about my duty to Miss Coutts, and Rhena's 'ingratitude' to the 'benefactress who has tried so hard to rescue her from ruin'? What a bad girl Rhena must be, 'so extraordinarily wicked' to reject the refuge offered her and 'audaciously pretend that she desires to leave it!'

The letter has Dickens sounding like the tub-thumper he detested, but he wants to rub in the point to all the Urania girls that really they have no alternative. So he invents a conversation between himself and Mrs Morson, to spell out the inevitable scenario. This is what Mrs Morson had to read aloud: 'You say that she has no friend in the world, no place to go to in this bitter weather, no chance before her but a jail, a hospital, disgrace, misery, despair, Death. I know all this as well as you do, and we both know it far better than she does.'

Rhena must listen to the story of her own future, written by Dickens in the dialogue between himself and Mrs Morson.

> You say that if she left [the Home], she would almost yield up her life to come back, the moment she passed the gate. I know she would. You know as well as I, that there never has been one case of a girl quitting the Home or sent away from the Home, in which this has not been proved to us.

The next move is pure Dickens. This is all going on at the beginning of January; he has just returned from Birmingham where, at the end of December, he too had been reading aloud. One of his first public readings, it affected him deeply. 'If you could have seen the two thousand five hundred work-people on Friday night,' he told Miss Coutts, 'I think you would have been delighted.' In keeping with the season, he read two of his Christmas stories, 'The Cricket on the Hearth' and 'A Christmas Carol' (twice).

Back in London, Rhena Pollard will be Christmas story for real. Having dwelt on misery, disgrace and Death, the histrionic letter which

Mrs Morson was reading to Rhena in front of the assembled inmates now shifts its attention to the matron herself. She found herself singing her own praises. 'It is natural and womanly in you', Dickens writes, 'to pity this deluded Rhena Pollard or any other girl in the same tremendous danger.' Finally, her intercession on the part of the impetuous girl is successful. 'However, at this forgiving Christmas time, and at your request,' he tells Mrs Morson; the austere dispenser of justice is swayed by her pleas and softens into mercy. Rhena will be offered a second chance. 'The unfortunate creature,' as Dickens paints Rhena to herself, 'so young and so forlorn,' can be brought back into the fold.

The 'great forgiving Christmas time': Dickens loved the phrase and used it again, adding the 'great' for sentimental emphasis, when he wrote to Miss Coutts later that day. At this point he does not yet know the outcome. Rhena has been given her role in his Christmas tale, as the Forgiven. Will she take it? Will she, Mrs Morson and the Urania ensemble act his script as planned?

The word he often uses about Rhena, 'restless', is the word he applies to himself at this period of his life. That is partly why she got her second chance, which Dickens feels he must justify to Miss Coutts because it is such a reversal of his current thinking of 'one strike and you're out'. 'This bitter weather' had its part to play too. So did Rhena's plight as 'a stranger in London, and an utterly friendless speck in the world' – what an image. With his next sentence, 'Snow two feet deep in the streets today!' he ends his letter to Miss Coutts, waiting impatiently to see what will happen next.

It was a lot of time and emotional energy to spend on one girl, and make him 'as emphatic as I could possibly be'. As well as the undoubted sympathy with Rhena, there is another recognisable pattern of thought at work. In his mind, the girl who comes into Urania Cottage always leaves another girl outside on the streets. She first appears in the letter Dickens wrote for his prison governor friends to read aloud to likely candidates in their cells. This appeal ended with stern words. 'You must resolve to set a watch upon yourself, and be firm in your control over yourself, and restrain yourself.' And finally, 'you must solemnly remember that if you enter this Home without such constant resolutions, you will occupy, unworthily and uselessly, the place of some other unhappy girl, now wandering and lost; and that her ruin, no less than your own, will be upon your head, before Almighty God.'

This girl reappears seven years later in the two Rhena Pollard letters. Rhena must keep in her mind 'the miserable girl in the streets who really would try hard to do well if she could get into the Home', 'the other girl' whom Rhena 'keeps out'. Dickens asks himself rhetorically 'how *can* I reconcile it to myself to allow her to occupy in Miss Coutts's home, the place which a grateful girl sincerely trying to reform herself – one of the hundreds I could take out of the streets at this moment – would be glad and happy to fill?' The dozen young women listening to Mrs Morson read out these words had been such girls themselves, had friends and sisters out there still.

Down-and-out boys and girls throng the streets of *Bleak House*, the novel Dickens completed in August 1853, five months before the Rhena Pollard affair. A five-year-old boy and a baby of eighteen months have been locked into a cold bare garret for safety, where Esther Summerson and her guardian Mr Jarndyce find them.

> We were looking at one another, and at these two children, when there came into the room a very little girl, childish in figure but shrewd and older-looking in the face – pretty-faced too – wearing a womanly sort of bonnet much too large for her, and drying her bare arms on a womanly sort of apron. Her fingers were white and wrinkled with washing, and the soap-suds were yet smoking which she wiped off her arms. But for this, she might have been a child, playing at washing, and imitating a poor working-woman with a quick observation of the truth. . .
>
> 'O, here's Charley!' said the boy. . . .
>
> 'Charley, Charley!' said my guardian. 'How old are you?'
>
> 'Over thirteen, sir,' replied the child.
>
> 'O! What a great age,' said my guardian. 'What a great age, Charley!'

Dickens has softened the edges for these orphan children. Charley would more likely have been a child prostitute than a child laundress, as Andrew Davies suggests in the glimpse of her bedizened face in the streets of the 2005 BBC adaptation. Fifteen years after *Bleak House* Dickens himself would tackle the issue more openly.

In 1868 he welcomed an article which the novelist Geraldine Jewsbury submitted to *All The Year Round*, the successor magazine to *Household Words*. He was glad to lend a 'helping hand' to the good cause of the Children's Home and Laundry in Leytonstone. Jewsbury's piece is hard-hitting and unambiguous, scarcely suitable for the family readership Dickens courted. The children she describes have been living a 'life of pollution'. They are all girls aged between eight and fifteen: too young for the penitentiaries and 'too deeply tainted with evil to be admitted into ordinary industrial schools and orphanages'. They come from brothels and police courts, some are already alcoholics. 'One little girl there distinctly remembers her mother taking her to one of the London bridges, and telling her she would throw her over.' Without the backing of a Burdett Coutts, the Leytonstone Home was strapped for funds. The children took in washing, much as Dickens's fictional Charley had done.

He made sure that his child laundress was emancipated from her treadmill. Domestic service is, as ever, the solution. Charley will maid for Esther, another vulnerable child saved from harm. And that utterly friendless speck Rhena Pollard got her second chance too. At seventeen she was older than Charley but just as much at risk. That did not cow her spirits though. Six weeks later, in mid-February, she is making trouble again, 'persisting in telling me the most audacious lie', Dickens grumbled to Miss Coutts, and getting 'the better of the establishment'. He determined that she 'must be brought to book somehow'.

Rhena weathered the battle of wills and clung on. She seems to have liked living dangerously. Three months later Dickens reports yet again that she 'had been troublesome, but was recommended to mercy'. By this time Mrs Morson has left, and Rhena seems to have found another ally in the new matron, Mrs Marchmont. Eventually she simmered down, grew up. The next we hear is in the following year, when she is 'the subject of a specially good report'.

This was February 1855, when Dickens was describing himself as 'altogether in a dishevelled state of mind – motes of new books in the dirty air'. *Little Dorrit* is beginning to take shape, a novel with a very angry girl in its second chapter. Kindly Mr and Mrs Meagles want to rescue a child from the Foundling Hospital; she will be a 'little maid' for their daughter Pet. They choose Harriet Beadle and change her name to Tattycoram, for the reason Mr Meagles explains to Arthur Clennam. "'Now, Harriet we changed into Hattey, and then into Tatty, because, as practical people, we thought even a playful name might be a new thing to her, and might have a softening and affectionate kind of effect, don't you see?'" Coram came from the name of the Foundling Hospital: Tatty would not forget her provenance.

Salvage work like this is not easy, as Dickens knows only too well. Tattycoram resents her benefactors and rages against her lot.

> A sullen, passionate girl! Her rich black hair was all about her face, her face was flushed and hot, and as she sobbed and raged, she plucked at her lips with an unsparing hand.
> 'Selfish brutes!' said the girl, sobbing and heaving between whiles. 'Not caring what becomes of me! Leaving me here hungry and thirsty and tired, to starve, for anything they care! Beasts! Devils! Wretches!'

It is a brilliantly observed scene of self-harm and self-loathing – Tatty disfigures her neck 'with great scarlet blots' – made all the more powerful because it is seen through the eyes of Miss Wade, a woman we cannot at all fathom at this point. Tatty finally sobs her hysterics out in a scene Dickens chose for illustration, collapsed on her bed cuddling her blanket, 'half to hide her shamed head and wet hair in it, and half, as it seemed, to embrace it, rather than have nothing to take to her repentant breast'.

Later in the novel Tattycoram is persuaded (or seduced) to run away from the Meagleses by Miss Wade. Subsequently she regrets it, and they take her back. We last see her at the end of the book promising to count not to five and twenty (Mr Meagles's remedy for her bad temper) but to "five-and-twenty hundred, five-and-twenty thousand!" She sounds like a Urania girl totting up her reward marks.

What about Rhena's story? Could there be a happy ending for the friendless speck? There is one last reference to her in Dickens's letters. In June 1856 he returns a letter from Rhena to Miss Coutts without mentioning its contents. Girls usually wrote back when they had good news to pass on, so where was Rhena now? Australia was the destination for most of the Urania emigrants, with South Africa as second choice; but Rhena left no trace in any records I could find. Finally she did turn up, but in Canada. Trust Rhena to go in the opposite direction.

The good news she was dispatching to Urania was about her wedding that month to Oris Cole. He was twenty-six years old; his family had moved to Canada from Vermont. According to an account written towards the end of his life, Oris 'started out for himself in the only way open for young men in Canada, and began as a lumberman'. He and his new wife Rhena became homesteaders in south-central Ontario. To make their farm the large trees had to be cut by hand and the ground tilled with oxen. The men usually spent the winter in lumber camps, so Rhena would have to be self-reliant in the home they had built for themselves of logs, with the cracks between them 'chinked' with moss.

It was a good marriage for Rhena. Her father-in-law was a school trustee and commissioner at the local court. Here in Ontario the Coles put down their roots and had seven children, including twin girls. The eldest son Frederick grew up, in the words of his grand-daughter, to be 'religious to the extreme, not even allowing his children to play at sleighing or card games on a Sunday, that day was reserved for Bible study.' Oris and his family were Wesleyan Methodists. Rhena, to be different, joined the Salvation Army. When she died at the age of sixty-three the family were flourishing; she and Oris were living in comfort. They have many descendants alive today.

And at last, with Rhena, I had in front of me my first photograph of a Urania girl. It was an extraordinary moment. Early in Dickens's career an appreciative critic remarked on the way his characters live for us, and the ensuing 'ridiculous confusion in the brain' which muddles fictional and real:

> The literary and the social have become the same. The imagination seizes on some of the favourite characters, and regards them with the same force and entireness of identity with which it recognises the persons we met at Bloomsbury, or in Buckinghamshire, last spring or autumn.

My own brain, I now realised, was confusing fictional with real. I had been chasing these elusive Urania women for so long, at the same time as reading about their fictional counterparts in Dickens's novels. When a member of the Cole family sent me a photograph labelled 'Oris and Phena Cole', I was transfixed. This is surely Rhena, and it is as if one of Dickens's characters had got herself a real body and come, almost, to life. A small woman, Rhena has dark hair and eyes just like Tattycoram. She has a determined look about her as she sits with hands clasped and chin forward. She and Oris called one of their daughters Harriet, Hattie for short. It would be nice, if improbable, to imagine that Rhena recognised herself in Tatty, formerly Harriet Beadle.

PART THREE

WRITING URANIA

CHAPTER NINE

Case Book

> The conference was a long one. Oliver told them all
> his simple history, and was often compelled to stop,
> by pain and want of strength. It was a solemn thing,
> to hear, in the darkened room, the feeble voice of the
> sick child recounting a weary catalogue of the evils and
> calamities which hard men had brought upon him.
>
> *Oliver Twist, Chapter 30*

URANIA COTTAGE WAS good theatre. It was an even better data-
base. From the streets, from the prisons, from the lowest of the
below-stairs servants' quarters, from the crowded tenements and from
the sweat-shops of the rag trade, the young women brought with them
a whole other world. They were to have a huge impact on Dickens's
fiction, as he knew they would. Hearing the girls' life-stories was part
of the enterprise, the deal he had had in mind from the beginning.
But they were to be for Dickens alone. Secrecy was the other half
of the deal.

Other asylums and refuges were happy to advertise themselves. They
wanted to attract funds from the well-disposed and well-off, and to tell
those who needed them about their services. Indeed, by 1850 Sampson
Low was selling a gazetteer of *The Charities of London*. Urania Cottage
was not there. It did not need the money; Angela Burdett Coutts had
seen to that. And she did not like the publicity. Dickens had his own
reasons for preferring low profile.

Urania was always to be a secret place. Dickens soon planned to heighten the fence he had initially ordered by another three or four feet. He was irritated when the owner's son resisted the prison-camp effect. 'Mr Scott, after much pondering, has arrived at the conclusion that he can just bear the addition of a lattice-work, *two feet high*, to the present fence. How, or by what process, he got to that express measurement, I don't know. But he intimates that one additional inch would be the death of him.'

The high fence was to keep out as well as in. Dickens was sensitive to institutional stigma. Even the census enumerators would be fobbed off. The 1851 census describes the young women as visitors 'of no occupation'. The 1861 enumerators got nearer the mark by calling them 'inmates' and listing their occupation as 'domestic servants'. In what looks like a later hand somebody has written in the word 'Reformatory'; but by this time Dickens was no longer involved.

If there was to be silence towards the outside world, there was to be secrecy inside the house too. Urania was the house of unspoken stories. The young women were absolutely forbidden to confide in each other about their past lives, or even to tell the women who were looking after them. A clean slate was what Dickens was after; the past must be a closed book. 'That their past lives should never be referred to, at the Home, there can be no doubt. I should say that any such reference on the part of the Superintendent would be an instance of blind mistake that in itself would render her dismissal necessary.' This would have been Miss Cunliffe's fate for noseying into Isabella Gordon's past life, but for the fact she was leaving anyway.

The one exception was Dickens himself. The painstaking preparations he made before the Home opened included getting a special book printed up, 'in which we shall keep the history of each case, and which has certain printed enquiries to be filled up by us, before each comes in.' It would also, such was his optimism, have 'a final blank headed its "Subsequent History", which will remain to be filled up, by degrees, as we shall hear of them, and from them, abroad.'

Over the Urania years there are frequent references to 'the Case Book' in Dickens's letters. He devoted much time and trouble to keeping it up to date. At the end of 1851, for example, he writes to Miss Coutts:

I considered it necessary to caution Mrs Morson respecting Mary Anne Church, whose pilfering propensities (I find on her own shewing) to have been very strong, and exercised under no pressure of necessity; and whom I greatly doubt. Little Elizabeth Hogg is quite a phaenomonon of slyness, I think. I was there some hours making up the Case Book which I want to leave in no arrear at the close of the year – and made these remarks in the course of that operation which is still unfinished.

He could be a bore about it too, using it to prove he had been right all along about one of the inmates. 'It is remarkable that on the day when [Ellen] Walsh was discharged, I shewed the Committee two entries I had made in her case,' he told Miss Coutts. He often mentions being at Shepherd's Bush 'for some hours making up the book'.

To begin with it shuttled between him and Miss Coutts, as they shared their absorbing interest in this new world. 'I send you the Case Book, which you will perhaps return to me . . . in order that I may fill up Emma Lea's history.' This was within a month of the Home's opening, and as he jogs Miss Coutts's powers of discretion, we can see he dislikes the arrangement. '*The sequel of Sarah Wood's history is stated in the book.* I mention this, to prevent your accidentally putting any one in possession of it, to whom you have not mentioned the circumstance.' At this point Miss Coutts is allowed in the loop, but the two women in charge, Mrs Holdsworth and Mrs Fisher, are kept explicitly at arm's length. 'Neither of those ladies are acquainted with the circumstances of each case, otherwise than very generally indeed. If I feel it necessary to give them any particular caution or piece of advice in reference to any Individual, I give them the immediate reason I have for so doing – but nothing more.'

Soon Miss Coutts was cut out of the Case Book loop too. She kept in regular contact with the matrons, knew each girl by name, and was the person they recognised as head of the Home. The few surviving letters that ex-Uranians wrote back are addressed to her. One, from star student Louisa Cooper, gives a little glimpse into the relationship between benefactress and inmate. 'I often think of your kind and gentle words . . . I never can forget how much I dreaded her [Miss Coutts's] coming or how soon I learned to love and respect her she has been so very kind in writing to me and given me good advice.'

Kindness and advice notwithstanding, Dickens put a damper on too much input. In an article he wrote about Urania Cottage for *Household Words* in 1853 he claimed that 'The ladies who established the Home' – Miss Coutts goes into the plural for the purposes of disguise, and Urania is not referred to by name – 'hold little confidential communication with the inmates, thinking the system better administered when it is undisturbed by individuals.' Miss Coutts could see the Committee Minutes Book and the Accounts Book, but by this stage Dickens was sole keeper of the Case Book.

Over the years he fine-tuned his methods. First he would meet a prospective candidate, perhaps in jail or police court, or the room beside the Magdalen Hospital. He would question her, and then have her story checked. If he decided to go ahead, and only after she had agreed to the emigration clause, he would give her a couple of days to settle in at Shepherd's Bush. The *Household Words* article describes what faced her next:

> The history of every inmate, taken down from her own mouth – usually after she has been some little time in the Home – is preserved in a book. She is shown that what she relates of herself she relates in confidence, and does not even communicate to the Superintendents. She is particularly admonished by no means to communicate her history to any of the other inmates: all of whom have in their turns received a similar admonition.

Dickens was the one doing the interviewing, and as the process evolved its confidentiality appealed to him. What started as a formal questionnaire with 'printed enquiries' transformed itself under his pen. No longer a matter of forms to be filled in by 'us', the Case Book was to be for him alone. The secret book would bulge with the life stories of the Urania women ghost-written by Dickens. Their back stories would be his great dividend. The Urania Case Book is Dickens's *ur*-text, the book behind his other books.

'Here is a prize,' boasted Wilkie Collins to Dickens on one of their trips to Paris in the mid 1850s. He had unearthed 'some dilapidated volumes of records of French crimes, a sort of French *Newgate Calendar*.' In its dirty pages Collins found 'some of my best plots. *The Woman in White* was one.' The Urania Case Book was just such a prize for Dickens. 'A most extraordinary and mysterious study it is, but interesting and touching in the extreme,' he reflected as he launched his daring experiment in imaginative invasion during the autumn of 1847.

From his earliest writing life the voices of the damaged, the victimised and the oppressed had pulsed through his fiction. But they are filtered. We do not hear word-for-word the 'weary catalogue' of Oliver Twist's history of abuse, which he recounts to his appalled middle-class listeners. The language would be too shocking in the mouth of the child who must be protected from his own knowledge. And so must his respectable readership. As Dickens questioned the young women at Shepherd's Bush and transcribed their 'deep testimony' of 'suffering, misery, cruelty and wrong' (his description of stories like Oliver's), he was writing his sixteenth novel, but one he knew he could never publish.

He prided himself on his interviewing technique. Non-directive was the way: 'Nothing is so likely to elicit the truth as a perfectly imperturbable face.' He set himself the task of winkling out the facts and relished the challenge of 'the more artful cases'. 'An avoidance of any leading question or expression of opinion' would yield best results. 'Give the narrator the least idea what tone will make her an object of interest, and she will take it directly.' The tone he most feared was 'stock religious', and yet one more reason for resisting the infiltration of clergymen whom he had not personally vetted. If you give your interviewee no steer about what you want to hear and how you want to hear it, he realised, 'she will be driven on the truth, and in most cases will tell it'. There was the added incentive that anyone caught out in a lie would risk being thrown out. Nothing else in their histories, however vile, could jeopardise their place at Urania.

These interviews were to become one of the most absorbing aspects of the Home for Dickens. 'I was there on Friday afternoon,' he tells Miss Coutts in 1848, 'and wrote Martha Goldsmith's history into the book. Her manner pleased me greatly. She answered all I asked her, very well indeed, and (I have no doubt), truly.' This was a big factor in Martha's favour. There would be, it was understood, no shying away or false modesty. This meant asking the young women about their sexual experience, and Martha must have been frank. This might not have been so difficult for her: she had after all put herself through the London Magdalen Hospital 'for the reception of penitent prostitutes'. But Dickens had no qualms about questioning all his subjects. Well, occasionally he did, as with the thirteen-year-old Charlotte Glyn. This was the girl whose age he mistrusted, but the census the following year lists her as fourteen, so if it was a lie at least it was a consistent one. Charlotte was nursing her dying mother, and 'I did not think it well to ask this girl the question I usually put. It is probably that what I doubt in the other cases, may be true in hers.'

For these encounters with the truth, these intimate and potentially painful interviews, Dickens knew he had the right skills. To begin with he had, said his friend Mary Boyle, a 'remarkable gift for setting others at ease when in his company'. Then there was his flair for invariably drawing 'out what was best and most characteristic in others'. He was a good listener; he had the motive for it. Hearing these young women's histories was a great privilege. How else could he hear out of their own mouths and at first hand these autobiographies from the underworld? What a window on to some of the rawest aspects of London life, and what stories would take shape on the Case Book's pages, as he updated the 'Subsequent History'.

Busy though he invariably was, Dickens dedicated hours to interviewing, listening, writing down, updating. 'I was out at Shepherd's Bush on Saturday all day, making up the book', he wrote in 1854. Seven years into the life of the Home, his investment in the written record of Urania was still firing on all cylinders. When he was on holiday he deputed others to collect information on his behalf. In July 1853 his sister-in-law Georgina Hogarth wrote to Mrs Morson: 'Mr Dickens begs me to write you a line to ask you, if any of the other girls leave, to *take notes of their case* before they go with a view to his book.' What a treasure trove for the novelist this Case Book must have been, and what riveting reading it would make.

So where is it now? Nowhere obvious, that is for sure. It is not in any of the collections of Dickens's papers or manuscripts that we know about. His will bequeathed all his 'private papers whatsoever and wheresoever' to 'my dear sister-in-law Georgina . . . the best and truest friend man ever had.' Perhaps she inherited it and sold it. She survived Dickens by forty-seven years, outlived all but two of the nine children she had taught to read, and ran through the legacy which Dickens left her. In her latter years she was befriended by a bookseller who guessed she was living beyond her means. Noticing that she was spending 'a great deal of money on cut flowers for the decoration of her rooms', he made her offers she could not refuse. Her prized possessions slipped out of the house a few at a time: 'some of Dickens's less private letters, his New Testament, a lock of his hair'. Sometimes her maid would be dispatched once or twice each week, and sometimes less scrupulous dealers came sniffing round. Georgina's biographer, Arthur Adrian, was told that 'Once Harry [Dickens's surviving son] arrived just in time to rescue some valuable material that was being carted off without the family's knowledge.' If the Case Book did fund Georgina's cut flowers habit it hasn't reappeared yet.

Angela Burdett Coutts might have rescued it from the Home after Dickens's departure, but it has not survived in the carefully tended archive at Sandon Hall, family seat of the earls of Harrowby (Angela was a cousin). In the quiet muniment room at the top of a tightly winding staircase you can read the fulsome obituary to Angela in *The Times* of 1906. The Home at Shepherd's Bush earns a mention as one of her various 'schemes' which were all 'marked by a certain individuality'. Her letters show a life dogged by family money squabbles; there was also the scandal of her father's affair with Lady Oxford. Angela always meant well but was shy and could be difficult company. The sixth earl recorded the reminiscences of an old man of ninety-one who had been a clerk at Coutts Bank. He remembered that when he was a lad and Angela called at the Bank, word would go round the senior staff. They would melt away, leaving him alone with her for half hours at a time. But neither at Sandon nor anywhere else can the Case Book be found, according to the editors of the monumental twelve-volume edition of Dickens's *Letters*. No more diligent or thorough editors could there be, and they have clearly done their Home-work. 'It has not been traced', they conclude in a regretful footnote.

Is there anyone else Dickens could have given it to? At the end of 1855 Miss Coutts asked Dickens if he knew someone she could employ as a 'confidential Secretary'. William Brown, who had been shouldering much of the business relating to her charitable interests, had died that autumn. Dickens instantly wrote from Paris to lay his own services at Angela's feet. 'Consider whether a daily messenger with a Dispatch Box could not put me in possession of all such business.' On second thoughts, the first instalment of *Little Dorrit* was about to hit the bookstalls. Writing the novel must be Dickens's priority for the next year and a half. Nor could he forsake *Household Words*, the weekly magazine he had founded in 1850 and edited ever since. But if he did not have the time, he must know a man who did. How about his second-in-command at *Household Words*, Harry Wills? 'My Sub Editor and Factotum', Dickens had earlier rather pompously described him to Miss Coutts. Now he characterised him more enthusiastically: 'It is impossible to find a more zealous, honourable, or reliable man.' Knowing that Wills could do with the money, he wrote to him that same day about his brainwave, warning him not to be 'amazed by the suddenness of this note'.

As it happened, Dickens and Wills had much in common. Harry was two years older, born in Plymouth down the coast from Dickens in Portsmouth. His father was, like Charles's, attached to the navy; like Charles's father he too came down in the world and decided to try the family's fortunes in London. Harry vividly recalled the momentous week-long stagecoach journey. They migrated to North London, as the Dickenses did, and Harry began a career as a wood-engraver. But journalism and theatre were, as for Dickens, his first loves. He did quite well. A couple of plays were performed; *The Law of the Land* ran for fifty-three nights at the Surrey Theatre. Dickens accepted some articles for *Bentley's Miscellany*.

This was in the 1830s. In the early 1840s Wills left London for Edinburgh, to work for William and Robert Chambers and edit their famous journal. He had the luck to be there during one of the great publishing sensations of Victorian times, the anonymous publication of *Vestiges of the Natural History of Creation*. This was a controversial 'evolutionary epic' covering everything in the solar system. For the next forty years its authorship would be hotly debated: Thackeray, Darwin, Harriet Martineau and Prince Albert were all in the frame. Only after the author's death did his identity emerge. It was Robert Chambers himself, prudently hiding his tracks by having his wife copy out the manuscript before it went to the printers via a third party. Most of his family and friends he kept well in the dark. Wills, though, who loved a good secret, knew about it. Maybe this was not surprising: he was about to marry Robert's sister Janet. Two decades later he let the cat out of the bag to Dickens and then panicked. Dickens reassured him. 'The secret concerning our Vestiges friend, remains a secret.'

Household Words would have been impossible without Wills. Dickens's letters to him show complete trust and growing affection. Over at the *Cornhill* Thackeray was envious. 'If there were only another Wills, my fortune would be made!' There could be friction sometimes, and Wills still had literary ambitions of his own. He once had the temerity to show Dickens a novel he was writing. Dickens stamped on it mercilessly: 'all working machinery, and the people are not alive'. The extracts in the auctioneer's catalogue do look rather laboured. It is a historical novel and the history is laid on with a trowel. Anyway, Wills was more useful as assistant editor, right-hand man, Dickens's alter ego even, in the judgement of one biographer. He would act as confidant and go-between during the Nelly Ternan years. In John Forster's opinion, 'Dickens's later life had no more intimate friend.'

'Dear kind Harry' was universally beloved. A childless couple, he and his wife Janet were hospitable and popular. Their Chambers nieces adored them. Nina Chambers nicknamed him 'The Dodger' and described him as 'very spry'. In later years he would entertain his great-nieces and -nephews with games of tally-ho through the nursery. That was after Dick, as Wills called Dickens, had died. Wills lost interest in editing magazines, gave up business and embraced the life of a country gent in Hertfordshire. As thin as a rake and weighing barely nine stone, he learned to ride, and took to large horses and reckless hunting. He was repeatedly thrown; locals referred to him as the Welwyn Demon.

He took the job with Miss Coutts, which included some Urania Cottage business, and worked for her over many years. On his death-bed (from a riding accident; he was thrown while leaning over to open a gate for one of his nieces) he was invigorated by the gossip about her engagement to the much younger Ashmead Bartlett. Wills's friend, the local historian John Edwin Cussans, witnessed his reaction: 'He furiously refused to believe it, and during his conscious hours lashed himself into a perfect rage on the subject. "I won't believe it, until I see it" was nearly all he said, consciously and unconsciously.'

Might Dickens have passed the Case Book on to Wills along with the responsibilities? The County Archive at Hertford has some of Wills's papers, including the full account of his funeral in the local paper. Scores of mourners attended. 'The last offices were performed not by undertakers' men, but by labourers, who were at once servants and friends. Never before did we see, as we saw on Monday, tears fall on the coffin from the eyes of those whose duty it was to lower it into the earth.' Also in the archive are some letters from Wills, mostly on *Household Words* business. But no Case Book. Perhaps it passed on to his wife Janet, along with the rest of his effects.

Janet was herself quite a pet of Dickens. He gave her prominent parts in his theatricals, such as the Scottish nurse who opens the show in *The Frozen Deep*, the play he co-wrote with Wilkie Collins. The role was created especially for her, he told Wills. 'If she says No (but she won't), no Scotch Housekeeper can be. The Tavistock House Season of 4 nights pauses for a reply. Scotch song (new and original) of Scotch House-keeper, would pervade the piece.' Janet said yes of course. A lively and witty woman, she seems to have known everyone in the literary world. Like her husband, she was an inveterate gossip: she was first with the news about the Lewes/Eliot elopement after she had had tea with Marian Evans, soon to be known as George Eliot. She wrote verse too. Some of it was set to music and appeared frequently on Queen Victoria's request list, doubtless for its chorus about 'no bring[ing] *him* back that looked kindly on me'.

Janet Wills bequeathed her library and all her papers to her niece Eliza, wife of the eminent doctor William Priestley. In her memoir, *The Story of a Lifetime*, Eliza refers to 'turning over a little rubbish-heap of my uncle Harry Wills's old MSS' and coming 'across a dirty-looking brown paper pamphlet pocked over with drippings of wax candle, almost too dirty to touch.' Not, alas, the Case Book. But perhaps it was inside that 'large tin box' which Eliza inherited, containing 'nearly five hundred of Charles Dickens's letters to my uncle, with other relics'.

Eliza passed all the Dickens stuff on to her nephew Rudolf Chambers Lehmann and from him it went via John Lehmann to Princeton University Library. Might a trawl through them do any good? There are certainly some oddities in the collection, including a box full of Lehmann family hair-clippings. But no Case Book.

If it did not go the Coutts or the Wills route, where else might it be? 'I was out at Shepherd's Bush on Saturday all day, making up the book' sounds as though the book usually lived at the Home. Perhaps Mrs Morson picked it up. But it was not with the haul of letters which the auctioneer found at Norstead, the house of her descendant. And anyway Dickens was still making his entries when Mrs Morson left in 1854. Perhaps the book remained at Shepherd's Bush when Urania Cottage closed its doors in 1862. Might Lucy Marchmont, who was the matron at that time, have pocketed it as she cleared the house for its next tenants? She stayed in the area and died in Brentford nearly twenty years later in 1881. But she did not leave a will, and none of her possessions can be traced.

In September 1860 Dickens lit a colossal bonfire. His marriage was over, his children were leaving home, he was giving up the London house in Tavistock Square. It was the end of an era, and Dickens painted it for Wills in apocalyptic terms. 'Yesterday I burnt, in the field at Gad's Hill, the accumulated letters and papers of twenty years. They sent up a smoke like the Genie when he got out of the casket on the seashore, and as it was an exquisite day when I began, and rained very heavily when I finished, I suspect my correspondence of having overcast the face of the Heavens.'

It may well have done. Scholars reckon it was 'probably the most valuable bonfire on record'. Destruction would be Dickens's way from now on. He professed himself horrified by the 'improper uses made of confidential letters'. With what might have been an eye to his own fate in posterity, he declined an article on Charlotte Brontë for *Household Words* shortly after her death: 'I have no sympathy whatever with the staring curiosity that it gratifies.' Besides, he enjoyed the thrill of conflagration and went at it vigorously. 'I have had a great burning of papers in your room', he wrote to Wills on another occasion; 'have destroyed everything not wanted.' On one such pyre the Case Book probably met its end. But I shall go on looking.

CHAPTER TEN

Making Up the Book

'What is her history?' asked Clennam.

'Think of that, Maggy!' said Little Dorrit, taking her two large hands and clapping them together. 'A gentleman from thousands of miles away, wanting to know your history! . . . Her old grandmother was not so kind to her as she should have been; was she, Maggy?' Maggy shook her head, made a drinking vessel out of her clenched left hand, drank out of it, and said, 'Gin.' Then beat an imaginary child, and said, 'Broomhandles and pokers.'

Little Dorrit, Book I, Chapter 9

For now, I shall have to accept that the Case Book is out of the picture. It is tantalising to speculate about its contents: what Dickens was writing when he was out at Shepherd's Bush all day 'making up the book'. But if we cannot have the real thing, we do have a few alternatives, some suggestive parallels. An array of manuscript notebooks and reports survive from refuges and asylums opening in the years around the time of Urania Cottage. On their pages individual cases slide suddenly into focus.

At the end of 1848 a Spanish woman called Mariquita Tennant, the widow of an English clergyman, met a homeless tramp called Marianne George. Twenty-four-year-old Marianne, who had been badly abused by her step-father, had just had a baby. Mrs Tennant scooped Marianne up and took her into her home at Windsor: this was the beginning of the House of Mercy at Clewer, a religious community and penitentiary for fallen women. Run by the Sisters of Mercy, it was supported by Gladstone and disparaged by Dickens and Miss Coutts. While it was close to the Oxford Movement, the Bishop of Oxford had reservations. Did the Sisters carry crucifixes concealed in their clothes? That would never do.

The Clewer archive preserves a manuscript notebook entitled 'History of the Penitents'; here seven of the first inmates tell their stories in their own words. Marianne's own tale is one of temper met by violence. When she refuses to go to church, Mariquita Tennant 'shook me and put her hands to my mouth to stop me, and gave me three or four knocks and sent me upstairs.' Twenty-one year-old Harriet Street commented, 'she do knock hard!' The inmates quarrel and throw plates at each other. Mrs Tennant locks them up and 'give us every day for dinner for three days coarsest cabbage leaves; we could hardly eat them they were so tough and we had no meat with 'em nor salt.'

The account which 21-year-old Elizabeth McIntosh gave of her past life sounds classic Urania material. Elizabeth lived in Uplyme in the West Country with her grandparents. After a quarrel with her elder sister, Elizabeth got a job as a servant and was soon on the move. 'We stayed at Jersey going on for three months and then we went to the Cape of Good Hope. I was only between 13 and 14; we was 18 months going and coming back . . . They were kind good people.' But then Elizabeth's mistress was taken sick. 'She was ill 7 weeks and then she died – I was very fond of her and never leaved her till they buried her . . . My Mistress left me £20 and all my clothes. I was 17 years and 3 months old and I lived with her 3 years and 3 months.' Her next job was as kitchen-maid at an officers' mess, then marriage to a soldier who took her twenty-pound legacy and deserted her.

How inevitable Elizabeth's next steps seem. 'One morning I got up between 2 and 3 and went off to London with one of the officers.' Three months later he abandoned her, and then it was drink, prostitution and nearly the end. Elizabeth threw herself into the Thames, to be fished out and brought to trial for attempting suicide. The Magistrate sent her to the Magdalen Hospital (where Martha Goldsmith had been), but Elizabeth was too violent for them, and they expelled her after only a month. Back on the streets again, life took its toll. 'I was ill and got the Brain Fever and went into the Fever Hospital in London. I was very kindly taken care of there and the clergyman used to come to me and I never used to take no notice of him then.'

At this time Windsor was a garrison town with good pickings for prostitutes. Elizabeth went down there prospecting and was recognised by a soldier who had known her in her servant days in Jersey. Shocked to see what she plainly was, he introduced her to Charles Johnson, the curate at Clewer. Johnson 'took me by the hand and asked me a great many questions, then he took me into his schoolroom, Mrs Cox's and had prayer with me.'

The efforts Johnson made on her behalf were impressive. First he persuaded her to return to the Magdalen Hospital, but 'when I got there it wasn't taking in day'. So he found her another temporary refuge. Then back to the Magdalen, but this time Elizabeth was not strong enough: applicants had to be able to lift a substantial weight in order to pass as fit. Johnson managed to get her into Guy's Hospital and, after constantly visiting and writing letters on her behalf, he finally suggested the 'dear motherly Lady' at Clewer.

Elizabeth did not settle easily into the strict regime. She found herself at odds with the other inmates: 'I went out to look for Mary to give her a slap in the face, but she did keep out of my way till supper time.' She was also at odds with herself. 'I found my conscience so full that I catched up a knife to cut my throat and I throwed myself on the ground.' Mrs Tennant met it all with severity. She was in the business, as she said, of 'training these unhappy souls along the thorny path of a perfect repentance.' Or, as Elizabeth saw it: 'The lessons I have had to learn were terrible and hard, and I used to cry about them, but the hardest lesson of all was to give up my pride.'

Clewer kept its records and rule-books carefully, and wrote its own history. Equally assiduous historians worked at another institution starting around this time. The House of St Barnabas in Soho began as the House for Charity for Distressed Persons in London. Its first

Prospectus dates from June 1846, the very moment Dickens and Miss Coutts were hatching Urania Cottage. But the two places were quite different.

A House, never a Home, St Barnabas had its eye as much on the helpers as the helped. The impetus came from a group of friends with their own needs. Well-off and well-intentioned, they wanted to do good in a hands-on way. The plan for the House was, they explained candidly, 'To give a definite sphere of united action to persons engaged in various worldly callings, who desire to give a portion of their time, as well as of their substance, to the poor, under fixed regulations, consistent with the discipline of the Church of England.' These men – this was an all-male organisation – formed a brotherhood for 'personal service'. The Visitors' Report Books testify to their hard work and personal involvement with the inmates. Gladstone was an Associate from the beginning; there are long entries in his hand during the first two years.

Constantly in and around the place, the Associates, as they called themselves, helped the inmates find work. They brought in Bibles and prayer-books for them, and were not above listening to fireside gossip. 'I learn from Mrs Saxby', wrote the distinguished educational reformer Thomas Dyke Acland, 'that the inmates do not wash up their tea things, plates etc themselves. I would suggest attention to this point.' The House offered 'temporary relief' to the destitute of all ages, male and female, including families. Outnumbering all the others by a long way were the 'Servant Maids'. These might be girls as young as seven-year-old Jane Macaulay from Knightsbridge, whose father had walked out on the whole family. The House of St Barnabas was the first stop for Jane on coming out of hospital, as it was for many. Jane stayed three nights and then, with help from an Associate, 'got a place'.

St Barnabas was definitely short stay, especially if you were of questionable character. The casebook entry for twelve-year-old Elizabeth Emery makes that clear. Elizabeth is described as 'a nursemaid from Shrewsbury'. She was admitted at the beginning of January 1853 and left in mid-February. Here is the account of her case:

At service in Shrewsbury, then in Hammersmith. Her sister about eight months ago having paid her passage up, – herself in service. She had £9 a year – left the latter place about three months ago, to get better wages; said she had lived upon what remained of her wages, after repaying her sister for the journey and some clothes, and upon pawning her clothes. Unable to take a place at present, having an abscess in the neck. She was quite unknown to Mr Swayne [the Vicar at St Giles] until the day of her application. An orphan of both parents since infancy.

She was admitted provisionally by Mr Chapman, Acting Warden, as her case appeared an urgent one. On close questioning next day by the Warden, and subsequently by the Matron she acknowledged she had been enticed to give up her situation, and had been deliberately seduced by a gentleman about ten weeks ago, and had since been living by prostitution.

It was agreed by the Council that she should be removed as soon as possible to another Institution, and her admission was made provisional meanwhile.

Elizabeth was one of St Barnabas's failures. They would send her out on kitchen-maid jobs and she would be returned as unsuitable. Back in the St Barnabas kitchens the twelve-year-old 'did her work very well . . . though very childish'. But she could not be allowed to stay. 'The poor child was extremely attached to the House but it was evidently injuring her to let her feel herself (as she did) especially favoured.' Five weeks after she had arrived she was sent back to Mr Swayne, the vicar she had first appealed to, with five shillings from the Alms Fund to buy a lodging.

Reading these casebooks, you see the well-known philanthropic men of the day faced by a flood of desperate young women and girls. Each one would be a different emergency. Take 26-year-old Margaret Scott for instance.

A very sad case. She was only here for one night: to see if anything could be done for her. She had left her father's house at Yarmouth and become a prostitute in London. The Rev Christopher Smythe (from Great Yarmouth) immediately came up after her: and begged us to let her stay here, only for one night, that he might see what had better be done.

Not much, unfortunately. Under 'Conduct in the House' the entry for Margaret reads: 'She was quite hard. Nothing could be done for her: though we tried every means we could think of. She left the next morning.'

Well-trained in their professions as clergymen, MPs, doctors, schoolmasters and lawyers, the Associates were diligent record keepers. There are minute books, account books, casebooks, petty cash books, subscription books, visitors' report books, chaplains' report books, and the *liber vitae*: the roll of deceased benefactors commemorated on the Feast of St Barnabas. All this paraphernalia of support Urania Cottage did not have. By comparison it leaves a light footprint.

Maybe that is why it did not last long after the lifeblood of its main progenitor ceased to run through it. Once Dickens withdrew from Urania its days were numbered, whereas the House of St Barnabas is still thriving, continually evolving to meet the needs of its changing neighbourhood in the middle of Soho. Dickens himself knew St Barnabas; it is the setting for Dr Manette's 'tranquil house' in *A Tale of Two Cities*. The quiet courtyard, 'where a plane tree rustled its green leaves' is still there; the Council Room on the first floor is known as Lucie's room. St Barnabas and Urania shared the same target group but with a different philosophy. St Barnabas did a little for a lot; Urania aimed to do a lot for a few.

Or perhaps the target group was not quite the same. St Barnabas offered protection to the 'deserving' poor, and in 1852 the Associates argued over whether they should take 'penitent women'. If they did the degrading label would stick to every woman leaving their care. On the whole they preferred not to, and they were not alone. Another charity from this time, Sidney Herbert's Fund for Promoting Female Emigration, addressed itself exclusively to the 'distressed needlewomen' constituency. What this really meant was: ex-prisoners and prostitutes not welcome. Successful applications to the Fund, which started at the end of 1849, were admitted to a short-stay Home in Hatton Garden, while they waited for a ship to take them to Australia. A team of volunteer ladies interviewed the candidates and entered their details into elegant Visiting Books, designed presumably with country house weekends in mind. The top recommendation is: 'very respectable'.

Writing in round, decisive hands, the ladies look for the best in their material. 'Eliza Allen: a nice little girl of 15.' Descriptions are brief and to-the-point. 'Margaret O'Dowd RC can neither read nor write. Has no outfit. Has been in a lead factory. Hard working old woman.' With her was Emily Dench: 'has been in service, C of E, can't write. Knows housework. Lost one eye in infancy. Appears cheerful.'

Many of the women and girls they saw could neither read nor write, but the ladies were keener on confirming them than teaching them to read. And anyway, the inmates would not be staying long enough for a realistic programme of education. There is an edge of impatience to some of the entries: 'Martha Fossard, St George's in the East age 20 deaf and stupid, maid of all work. Did not behave well, left the Home without leave and dismissed.' Hannah O'Connor could be 'a little troublesome'; someone has added later 'and ill-tempered'. Jane Craig is described as 'needlewoman, steady looking and very well conducted but acknowledged later she had had a child and showed great want of proper feeling on this subject. Dismissed from the Home.'

Dickens's letters show him less judgemental, more melodramatic. 'Of the cases I saw yesterday,' he writes to William Brown in 1848,

> I would greatly desire, with Miss Coutts's sanction, to take in one – Adelaide Thomas, aged 17 – ignorant – poor in the last degree – her history most awful – and her fall, in its beginning, impossible to be attributed to herself. Mr. Chesterton, his matron and I, saw the girl's mother (her father went mad, in his grief for this child) and are acquainted with her story from her cradle. We strongly believe she may be saved without much difficulty. If we reject her, nothing on earth can stop her in her course to destruction.

While he was writing in his Case Book to the young women's dictation he was already turning their lives into fodder. 'I have', he told Miss Coutts, 'a reasonably good little anecdote in reserve, of Rachael Bradley, whom I "booked" today.'

The anecdote, like the book, is now lost. But the book did leave some trace. Dickens was clearly plundering from it while he drafted his article about Urania Cottage for *Household Words*. 'Home for Homeless Women' was given prominence on the front page of his magazine in April 1853; by then Urania was five and a half years old. It is a useful piece of evidence. However much Dickens may fantasise in his fiction, we can trust to the truth of the magazine article. This is because it had to earn the approval of Angela Burdett Coutts before it could see the light of day.

Dickens had wanted to write about Urania for some time but Miss Coutts resisted. She finally agreed only on condition that she could check the proofs and make alterations, which she did in profusion. We can be sure that she would not let any departure from the truth or flight of fancy on Dickens's part go unchallenged. 'Everything shall be stated as you wish,' he told her, 'and I will take care to relieve it of all the little points in doubt.' The piece went to and fro between them. He begrudged the many alterations she insisted on. 'They will not improve the paper by any means,' he told his assistant Wills, 'but on such a question of feeling, nothing is to be said.'

His cast-list of inmates at the Home divides impartially between the young women 'who had already lost their characters and lapsed into guilt', and those who were in danger of doing so. The odds – or rather the economics – were simply stacked against the single woman in the city, as Dickens had acknowledged from the beginning. 'It is dreadful to think', he had written to Angela Burdett Coutts in 1847, 'how some of these doomed women have no chance or choice. It is impossible to disguise from one's self the horrible truth that it would have been a social marvel and miracle if some of them had been anything else than what they are.'

By 1853 he is struck by the variety of the Home's fifty-six inmates so far. They have belonged, he says, 'to no particular class'. Deliberately mixing together the fallen and the poor, the hungry and the despairing, he cannily forestalls readers who might want to pick and choose worthy recipients of sympathy. He knows his audience well enough to start with the 'starving needlewomen of good character'; he can then move on to the less deserving 'poor needlewomen who have robbed their furnished lodgings' and even to the 'violent girls' from prison and, unambiguously, to the 'young women from the streets'. He did, though, make out that they were older than most of the inmates seem to have been: early twenties rather than mid to late teens. Perhaps he wanted to soft-pedal on the idea of child prostitution.

The article ends with 'a specimen or two of cases of success', and we can see Dickens flipping through the pages of the Case Book in search of suitable material. He finally picked eight, and assigned each one the case number she had in his book. They make fascinating reading: similar to the street women and girls Henry Mayhew questioned for his *Morning Chronicle* journalism, but with more back-story.

Number twenty-seven, the one Dickens starts with, is the girl from Drouet's infamous orphanage who did not know her own birthday. Dickens gives her brief history.

> She had been apprenticed to a small artificial flower maker with three others. They were all ill-treated, and all seemed to have run away at different times, this girl last, who absconded with an old man, a hawker, who brought 'combs and things' to the door for sale. She took what she called 'some old clothes' of her mistress with her, and was apprehended with the old man, and they were tried together. He was acquitted; she was found guilty. Her sentence was six months' imprisonment, and, on its expiration, she was received into the Home.

What intrigued Dickens was not only her past, but also her progress once at Urania. 'She was appallingly ignorant, but most anxious to learn, and contended against her blunted facilities with a consciously slow perseverance.' He observes her closely to see how she does it. 'She showed a remarkable capacity for copying writing by the eye alone, without having the least idea of its sound, or what it meant. There seemed to be some analogy between her making letters and her making artificial flowers.'

Next his attention was drawn to an earlier case, number thirteen, whose memory for detail was a boon. She had, she said, supported herself and her sick mother by doing plain needlework.

> At last her mother died in a workhouse and the needlework 'falling off bit by bit', this girl suffered, for nine months, every extremity of dire distress. Being one night without any food or shelter from the weather,

she went to the lodging of a woman who had once lived in the same house with herself and her mother, and asked to be allowed to lie down on the stairs. She was refused, and stole a shawl which she sold for a penny. A fortnight afterwards, being still in a starving and houseless state, she went back to the same woman's, and preferred the same request. Again refused she stole a bible from her, which she sold for twopence. The theft was immediately discovered, and she was taken as she lay asleep in the casual ward of a workhouse.

The account ends with three months in prison and a PS from Dickens: 'She had never been corrupted.' This was her answer to the question he always asked.

To one of the specimen cases in Dickens's article we can actually put a name. This was Campbell, the girl who had to have her head shaved. Commiserating with her as he did, Dickens gets her words verbatim into the pages of his family magazine.

Case number fifty was a very homely, clumsy, ignorant girl, supposed to be about nineteen, but who again had no knowledge of her birthday. She was taken from a Ragged School; her mother had died when she was a little girl; and her father, marrying again, had turned her out of doors, though her mother-in-law had been kind to her. She had been once in prison for breaking some windows near the Mansion House, 'having nowheres as you can think of, to go to'. She had never gone wrong otherwise, and particularly wished that 'to be wrote down'. She was in as dirty and unwholesome condition, on her admission, as she could well be, but was inconsolable at the idea of losing her hair, until the fortunate suggestion was made that it would grow more luxuriantly after shaving. She then consented, with many tears, to that (in her case) indispensable operation.

As he leafed through his case book, was Dickens on the lookout for the 'never gone wrong'? He does seem to have selected quite a few: three out of the eight. But about some of the others he is as explicit as he can be. Case number fifty-one, 'a little ragged girl of sixteen or seventeen, as she said; but of very juvenile appearance . . . answered some searching questions without the least reserve, and not at all in her own favour.'

Case number forty-one was 'a pretty girl of a quiet and good manner, aged nineteen.' After she stayed 'out beyond the prescribed hours one night when she went with some other young people to a Circus, [the dressmaker she was apprenticed to] positively refused to admit her or give her any shelter from the streets. The natural consequences of this unjustifiable behaviour followed.' Case number fourteen seems to have suffered from sexual abuse: 'an extremely pretty girl of twenty whose mother was married to a second husband – a drunken man who ill-treated his step-daughter.'

The young woman he expresses most sympathy for is case number fifty-four, 'a good-looking young woman of two-and-twenty, first seen in prison under remand on a charge of attempting to commit suicide'. Her story, which he can write here, would never get into any of his novels.

> She had been a travelling maid with an elderly lady, and, on her mistress going to Russia, had returned home to her father's. She had stayed out late one night, in company with a 'commissioner' whom she had known abroad, was afraid or ashamed to go home, and so went wrong. Falling lower, and becoming poorer, she became at last acquainted with a ticket-taker at a railway station, who tired of the acquaintance. One night when he had made an appointment (as he had often done before) and, on the plea of inability to leave his duties, had put this girl into a cab, that she might be taken safely home (she seemed to have inspired him with that much enduring regard), she pulled up the window and swallowed two shillings' worth of the essential oil of almonds which she had bought at a chemist's an hour before. The driver happened to look round when she still had the bottle to her lips, immediately made out the whole story, and had the presence of mind to drive her straight to a hospital, where she remained a month before she was cured. She was in that state of depression in the prison, that it was a matter for grave consideration whether it would be safe to take her into the Home, where, if she were bent upon committing suicide, it would be almost impossible to prevent her. After some talk with her, however, it was decided to receive her.

One of the reasons Dickens had for going into such detail in this article is that he was using it as a covert advertisement. He was scouting for more varied material to work on at Urania, and a 'little account' of it, he explained to Miss Coutts, '*might* lead to our finding strange cases, hardly to be got at otherwise'. When the article finally appeared two years after he had first suggested it to a reluctant Miss Coutts (such was Dickens's persistence), the post-bag did indeed sag obligingly, although mainly with people wanting to look round the Home or send money. Three years later Dickens came up with another wheeze: writing to the Duty Inspectors at London Police Stations, as a way of reaching 'some wretched cases at the very crisis of their fate'. Yet more experimentation.

For eleven years Dickens questioned, listened and wrote, as the young women disclosed to him the most intimate details of their lives. Was this the price they had to pay for their warm beds and the passage out to Australia? Or was there anything in it for them? A study conducted a few years ago in America would suggest that there was. A team of developmental psychologists examined the 'narratives of people who were so disturbed as teenagers that they had to be confined to the locked wards of a residential psychiatric hospital'. The psychologists were interested in the life-stories told by those who successfully bounced back from experiences which defeated others. What they found was that the act of shaping and telling your autobiography can be a force for good. 'When mistakes become stories, people can learn from them.' It is a variant on the talking cure: 'stories help us to bring order out of chaos'. In asking the Urania women to tell him their life-stories Dickens was giving them the opportunity to get another kind of handle on themselves. As for how he used their narratives, that is another story.

6 **Student teachers at Whitelands College in Chelsea taught little girls to sew samplers:** simple stitches at the top followed by more ambitious exercises. Dickens and Miss Coutts borrowed from Whitelands methods and 'books of instruction', so the Urania inmates probably produced samplers like this.

7 **Dickens sent parcels of books to Urania Cottage,** and ordered lessons and pictures set out on 'stiffened sheets' from the Society for Promoting Christian Knowledge. They used engravings by Josiah Wood Whymper: here is his kangaroo.

8 **Susan Nipper fearlessly challenges Mr Dombey for his neglect of his daughter Florence** in Chapter 44 of *Dombey and Son* (1846-48). 'The Nipper . . . was singularly brisk and bold, and all her energies appeared to be braced up for some great feat.'

9 **Arthur Clennam 'resolved to watch Little Dorrit and know more of her story'**; he follows her through the London streets on the front of a children's version from 1946. Dickens spoke to young women on the streets about Urania Cottage and emigration 'in the course of my nightly wanderings into strange places'.

10 **Charles Dickens by J E Mayall**, Daguerreotype (1855?). Dickens during the Urania Cottage years.

11 **Two angry young women** in *Little Dorrit* (1855–57). Tattycoram rages on her bed while Miss Wade watches 'as one afflicted with a diseased part might curiously watch the dissection and exposition of an analogous case'.

CHAPTER ELEVEN

Using the Plot

What would it be to see a woman going by, even though she were going secretly? They are all secret. Mr Tulkinghorn knows that, very well.
  Bleak House, Chapter 16

ALL THAT DICKENS saw and heard at Urania Cottage fed into his fiction – how could it not? His insider dealings would reward him a thousand-fold. The orphans, servants and child-carers, the seamstresses, milliners and theatre girls, the prostitutes, tramps and petty thieves, the half-starved apprentices and the attempted suicides: they all gave him their voices and stories. At the same time they insinuated themselves ever more deeply into his imagination. They swarm through the fiction of the late forties and fifties, to make *David Copperfield* the great novel of servants, *Hard Times* the great novel of education. Twice Dickens would hand over the story telling to them, as he experimented with their voices on the pages of *Bleak House* and *Little Dorrit*. Fiction would never be the same again.

The Urania trace might flicker through in just a glimpse. At the beginning of *Little Dorrit* Mrs Meagles describes going to church at the Foundling Hospital, where Dickens also worshipped. She remembers looking at 'all those children ranged tier above tier' and thinking, 'does any wretched mother ever come here, and look among those young faces, wondering which is the poor child she brought into this forlorn world.' For that one second with Mrs Meagles in church, we are 'wondering' through Urania eyes.

In the next chapter Arthur Clennam returns to his prison-like childhood home by way of 'silent warehouses and wharves, and here and there a narrow alley leading to the river, where a wretched little bill, FOUND DROWNED, was weeping on the wet wall'. *Bleak House*'s Esther Summerson sees that poster too, during the desperate search for her suicidal mother. Inspector Bucket is extra-vigilant on bridges. 'He stood up to look over the parapet; he alighted, and went back after a shadowy female figure that flitted past us; and he gazed into the profound black pit of water.' 'Shadowy females' haunt and darken the urban backdrop.

I have to admit, though, that readers have been less than complimentary about Dickens's women. Most out of fashion are sentimental death scenes, and the magic girls who walk the evil streets undefiled – Little Nell and Little Dorrit for instance. It is worth looking again to track the changes over the Urania years. *Dombey and Son*, the novel which Dickens started as his mind first engaged with the fallen women project, hits the most conventional notes. Alice Marwood, 'tall, well-formed; handsome; miserably dressed', flaunts a 'reckless and regardless beauty' in her face and 'a dauntless and depraved indifference to more than weather'. She is the melodramatic stereotype of 'ruin', the word she applies to herself. Sentenced to transportation, she has come back wild, 'a crouched tigress, with her kindling eyes'. '"I *am* angry,"' she tells Mr Dombey, '"I have been so, many years."' But she harms no one, and Dickens calms her with the conventional penitent's death, listening to the words of the Bible and forgiving her procuress mother.

Alice also briefly takes the floor to give us her version. Adopting an oddly stilted voice, she talks about herself in the third person. '"There was a child called Alice Marwood," said the daughter with a laugh, and looking down at herself in terrible derision of herself, "born, among poverty and neglect, and nursed in it. Nobody taught her, nobody stepped forward to help her, nobody cared for her."' The hours Dickens subsequently put in listening to the inmates at Urania taught him how to convey their stories more surely.

He also had the benefit of another's example. Elizabeth Gaskell's first novel, *Mary Barton*, which was published in 1848, is down-to-earth about the life of the prostitute in the modern city. Mary's aunt Esther serves a month in prison for 'disorderly vagrancy'. Recounting the details of her fall, she frankly admits the impossibility of changing direction. "'Don't speak to me of leading a better life – I must have drink. I can't pass tonight without a dram; I dare not.'" Full of admiration, Dickens knew where to look for contributions for his new magazine *Household Words*. Elizabeth Gaskell was one of the first to be invited. 'There is no living English writer whose aid I would desire to enlist, in preference to the authoress of *Mary Barton*,' he wrote to her persuasively. He even offered to visit Manchester 'for a few hours, and explain anything you might wish to know' about his new venture.

Gaskell obliged with 'Lizzie Leigh', the story of a prostitute and her child. Its subject matter and opening words – 'When Death is present in a household on a Christmas Day' – made it an unlikely proposition for Dickens's family magazine. But he rose to the challenge, giving it pride of place straight after his 'Preliminary Word'. He told her it made him cry and pressed her for more, with a lower death count if possible. 'I wish to Heaven', he complained to Wills, 'her people would keep a little firmer on their legs!' Three years later he supported her courageous attempt in *Ruth* to put a seduced woman at the heart of a Victorian novel.

David Copperfield, the first novel which Dickens planned and wrote during the Urania years, bears its mark in two massive preoccupations: prostitution and emigration. Little Em'ly is doomed from start, even in the childhood paradise on Yarmouth beach. Running fearlessly along a 'jagged timber' high over deep water, she seems to be 'springing forward to her destruction' in the eyes of the horrified young David. It is inevitable that she will be seduced by the faithless and charming Steerforth. Looking back, as he so often does, David asks himself, 'Would it have been better for little Em'ly to have had the waters close above her head that morning in my sight?' He has to confess there was a time 'when I have answered Yes, it would have been.'

David's creator disagreed. As he sat at his desk with 'the first page of Copperfield No. 10 staring at me with what I may literally call a *blank* aspect', he broke off to 'plung[e] energetically' into his Christmas letter to his old friend William de Cerjat. He had already discussed his work at Urania with de Cerjat, and together they nailed the crux of the problem. 'In all you suggest with so much feeling of their return to virtue being cruelly cut off, I concur with a sore heart', Dickens told de Cerjat. Now is the hour for practical solutions. Fiction must move on to the front foot. Copperfield No. 10, so difficult to begin, will break the news of Emily's elopement with Steerforth.'I have been turning it over in my mind for some time, and hope, in the history of Little Em'ly (who *must* fall – there is no hope for her) to put it before the thoughts of people, in a new and pathetic way, and perhaps to do some good.' Fall, yes, but not death. There is going to be a way forward. A month later, with the episode written and its proofs corrected, he writes to Forster, 'I feel a great hope that I shall be remembered by little Em'ly, a good many years to come.'

Like the girls at Urania, Emily has a 'black shadow' in her wake. Martha Endell is the one of the ghost girls Dickens imagines wandering the streets, while her sister sits saved inside. Martha is 'lightly dressed . . . bold and haggard, and flaunting, and poor'. She edges into the book, the spectre of Emily's future, a voice under the window whispering "'I was once like you!"' Gradually she emerges from the shadows. An illustration shows her hiding behind the door listening to Mr Peggotty as he tells David about Emily.

Eventually the prostitute takes centre stage. Dickens dedicates a whole chapter to her, instating her firmly in its title: 'Martha'. Hoping she may be able to help them find Emily, David and Mr Peggotty track her through London's midnight streets. The pursuit itself exhilarates David; he describes 'the strange fascination in the secrecy and mystery of so following anyone'. With the two men behind her, Martha draws past 'the melancholy waste of road near the great blank Prison' that was Millbank, and inexorably on to the river's edge. This is hell's gateway, a slimy nightmare sinking in 'ooze and slush'.

David the budding novelist observes her attentively. 'She had been ill, probably for a long time . . . her sunken eyes expressed privation and endurance.' It is, though, the 'stronger hand' of the practical Mr Peggotty which pulls her from the water. His trust will redeem her, as he enlists her in the quest for Emily. The despised 'image of humiliation' now has an 'object' and ultimately salvation. Rescuing Emily from what sounds like a brothel, Martha Endell will end well, flying the flag for other Marthas back at Shepherd's Bush.

In handing their histories to Dickens for him to plunder, the Urania women ultimately did far more. They bestowed upon him the gift of confession. He had been a street child himself, and he blessed the young David Copperfield with his own habit of creating 'stories for myself, out of the streets, and out of men and women'. Now he would bring the story out of himself. As he sat in Shepherd's Bush 'making up the Case Book' out of the mouths of the girls he had rescued, Dickens chose this moment to go confessional. Listening to them prompted him: here was dividend he did not anticipate.

It was the end of January 1849 when John Forster, Dickens's friend and biographer in waiting, recorded in his diary first seeing the famous autobiographical fragment. In its pages – lost long ago alas – Dickens recounted his father's imprisonment for debt and his own trauma in the blacking warehouse. All of this he had kept perfectly secret, 'from that hour until this at which I write'. 'That hour' being the point at which his mother interceded for his return to the warehouse after a family quarrel. 'I never shall forget, I never can forget, that my mother was warm for my being sent back.' Since then 'no word of that part of my childhood which I have now gladly brought to a close, has passed my lips to any human being.' Even at the end of his life his children did not know the details. Something happened in the late 1840s to make Dickens start drawing together bits and pieces of autobiography – at the beginning of the Urania years.

The impetus seems to have come from 'the accident of a question' which Forster put to him. In March or April 1847 he asked Dickens whether as a boy he had seen Mr Dilke, a friend of Dickens's father. Dickens said yes, he had seen him once at his uncle's house. 'Never at any time.' It must have been someone else then, said Forster, because Dilke had mentioned the boy as 'having had some juvenile employment in a warehouse near the Strand'. Dickens was 'silent for several minutes'. Some weeks later he told Forster that he had 'struck unconsciously upon a time of which he never could lose the remembrance while he remembered anything.' 'Very shortly after this' Forster 'learnt in all their detail the incidents that had been so painful to him.'

When was that: 1847, or some time later? According to Dickens himself, 'just before Copperfield I began to write my life'. That is what he told Mrs Winter (his first love Maria Beadnell); it points to late 1848 or early 1849. Forster's evidence is fuzzy. The conversation may have been in 1847, but what he saw written down as a connected composition – 'No blotting, as when writing fiction; but straight on, as when writing an ordinary letter' – he dates to the beginning of 1849. It would soon find its way into the childhood of David Copperfield, as the novelist adopted the 'I' of the first person narrator for the first time.

Whenever it was in the late forties that Dickens began to produce his own traumatic past, one thing is clear. From the summer of 1847 onwards he was interviewing young prostitutes, thieves and attempted suicides to find candidates for Urania Cottage. From the autumn of that year he was asking them to divulge their pasts for him to write into his Case Book. He found it a powerful experience, 'interesting and touching in the extreme'. On his walk back home, sometimes through rain or snow – 'I returned from Shepherd's Bush, like Lot's Wife after she became the pillar of Salt' – he would carry the young women's histories with him. And now he could revisit his own past and articulate it for the first time. His confessions are spurred by theirs. *David Copperfield* is the novel of Dickens's own childhood. It is the novel in which memory is required and finally allowed to complete its arduous work. No surprise that this is the novel Freud gave his fiancée.

The next step would be more experiments in story telling. The narrative strategy of *Bleak House* is high risk. After two opening chapters rolling with wonderfully extravagant rhetoric there is an unexpected lurch. 'I have a great difficulty in beginning to write my portion of these pages, for I know I am not clever', begins Esther Summerson. Her self-deprecating 'little woman' goody-goodiness has infuriated many readers. So why did Dickens want to use her voice to tell half the story? It is the voice of the neglected and needy child who has 'brought no joy, at any time, to anybody's heart'. The words 'far better that you had never been born' ring in her ears. She has no one to confide in but her doll; she is desperate 'to win some love to myself if I could'. It is Dickens ventriloquising Urania.

In fact, Esther's opinions can be blistering. She unerringly gets the measure of the sponging Skimpole, of Mrs Jellyby with 'her hair looking like the mane of a dustman's horse', of Mrs Pardiggle 'applying benevolence . . . like a strait-waistcoat', and of the 'something of the Vampire' in Vholes. She gets 'angry' with Mrs Jellyby for neglecting her daughter, and 'irate' with Mr Turveydrop and his 'very disagreeable gallantry'. Her one-liners – '"Indeed?" said I' – can be devastating. This is a girl with an acid tongue in her head. When Miss Flite suggests that her 'brave physician' Allan Woodcourt should have a title awarded to him, 'I said it was not the custom in England to confer titles on men distinguished by peaceful service, however good and great; unless occasionally, when they consisted of the accumulation of some very large amount of money.'

But when it comes to talking about herself, Dickens puts Esther on the back foot. Her diffidence, so irritating to some, reminds us that she feels she is someone without the right to speak. Hers is the voice of the illegitimate, the cast out, which Dickens drags from the margins. In the plot too, he has pushed the unloved girl to the centre. Esther herself – her identity and her existence – is the secret at the core of the novel. The woman as the secret, the woman with the secret: their backstories of forbidden experience would power Dickens's fiction throughout the 1850s and herald the dawn of a new genre, sensation fiction.

Dickens was always fascinated by the secrets which the young women at Urania had to tell him. If he thought there was a gem to be unearthed he was prepared to drop everything. 'My dear Miss Coutts', he wrote at the beginning of 1848, 'My anxiety to know that secret reason of Sarah's, is so intense that I will call on Monday between one and two, on the chance of finding you at home, and becoming a party to her mystery.' This was one of his busiest times, but then which were not? In the month of Sarah and her secret he has the current instalment of *Dombey and Son* on his hands, he is organising the amateur theatricals he adored so much – producer, stage-manager and leading actor, he threw himself into them all – he is lobbying for the General Theatrical Fund, and he has the staff and inmates at Urania to interview and manage. Yet Sarah gets a whole letter to herself.

Who was she, what was the 'mystery' that Dickens so longed to discover? The only Sarah we know at Urania during this period is Sarah Wood: Dickens had just entered the 'sequel' to her history in his Case Book. Now more was emerging and he had reason to be interested. Sarah had already caused him considerable trouble as 'disappointment Number One', which he had been 'summoned out, as I was going to bed last night, to see to, and have been busy with all night and ever since.' She had probably been caught stealing some of matron's things. That is how he remembered her two years later when another girl did a bunk with Mrs Morson's bonnet and shawl. It did not happen often. 'Leave nothing open, or about' was Dickens's often-repeated practical advice to the staff.

Eighteen-year-old Sarah had come from Chesterton's prison. Her choice of scam involved calling at upmarket shops, fashionably dressed. Here she browsed the stock, picking out mourning clothes, muslin dresses and gloves for herelf and her three sisters, the court heard in due course, and 'a silk mantle for her mamma, Mrs Warner, the wife of Captain Warner'. The goods should be delivered to the family home in Finsbury Square; meanwhile she would take some flannel and a mantle or two with her on account. Smooth-talking Sarah managed to deceive at least three shopkeepers with her fictional family and address before she was caught and sent down for four months. By January 1848 she had left Urania Cottage, and because her name is a common one she is impossible to trace for certain.

By 1855, when he started planning *Little Dorrit*, Dickens had been watching and listening to the Urania women for eight years. This book is the full harvest. Its streets teem with damaged women, such as the child-like Maggy with her 'large bones, large features, large feet and hands, large eyes, and no hair . . . Her face was not exceedingly ugly, though it was only redeemed from being so by a smile; a good-humoured smile, and pleasant in itself, but rendered pitiable by being constantly there.' Or there is the young woman whom she and Little Dorrit meet while they are wandering homeless on the terrifying night streets, 'far too young to be there, Heaven knows! – and neither ugly nor wicked looking'. When Maggy asks her what she is doing she answers '"Killing myself"'.

The book heaves with angry servants, child carers, theatre girls, foundlings, abused children, distressed needlewomen, sexual adventurers and deviants. If they sound like victims, think of Fanny Dorrit the lively young dancer, so bustling, prickly and forthright in comparison with her sister Amy. Immoral in her pursuit of that dolt Edmund Sparkler she may be, but there is logic in her game of getting even. As for Little Dorrit herself: look at her in another light and she is someone who knows prison from the inside, like the Urania girls. In common with many of them, she earns her living as a needlewoman and supports other family members. With a practical sense of using what is to hand she scouts new bankrupts in the Marshalsea to organise career training for her sister from a dancing master and for herself from a milliner.

Weirdest of all is Miss Wade. We have already met her: she is the handsome and reserved young woman 'travelling quite alone' at the beginning of the novel, who is on hand to witness Tattycoram's crying jag. Tattycoram herself, ex-foundling and Urania girl, later describes Miss Wade as 'my own self grown ripe', but she is an altogether stranger proposition. In a way she is easy to grasp, the hating woman who is the polar opposite of Amy Dorrit. Like Esther Summerson, she is an illegitimate unloved child, but she is an Esther gone rancid.

She was, Dickens insisted, drawn from life. He vehemently rejected a reader's suggestion that she resembled a character in one of Amelia Opie's novels. He had observed her 'in real life', he said, and knew 'the character to be true in every respect. It quite fascinated me in its singular anatomy.' The manuscript of *Little Dorrit* bears witness to this fascination in the heavily revised introduction of Miss Wade in a 'gloomy veil' of shadow. The cuts and reworkings Dickens inflicts on her throughout the manuscript suggest that he originally had other plans for the woman he has endowed with a pun for a name. His number outlines often raise her as a possibility, to be followed by 'no' or 'not yet'.

Miss Wade is not a Urania girl: she comes from a higher social class. But their world stands behind hers. And just as they told their stories to Dickens, so Miss Wade tells hers to Arthur Clennam, in the extraordinary chapter 'The History of a Self Tormentor'. It is a tale of passion, with girl on girl bedroom scenes – 'she would cry and cry and say I was cruel, and then I would hold her in my arms till morning' – extramarital sex and black brooding. She may be a lesbian *avant la lettre*. "'I'm old enough to have heard of such,'" Mr Meagles tells her.

Dickens struggled with his experiment in story-telling, describing 'his knitted brows now turning into cordage'. In the manuscript Miss Wade speaks directly to Arthur Clennam; this is revised into a written account which we read over Arthur's shoulder. And then what? As discreet as his author, Arthur never mentions it again and nor does Dickens. It is a Urania story. You listen to it but you cannot pass it on.

Some women's buried lives never make it to the surface. We do not even hear the name of the orphaned singing girl who becomes Arthur's birth-mother. There is a box of her papers winging its way round the book, but no one reads them and the woman herself is locked up in Antwerp as a madwoman. Offshore is best for some of these appalling histories. If part of this violent undertow came via Urania, no wonder Dickens guarded his special privilege so fiercely, punctiliously observing 'the promise of confidence under which they have yielded up their secrets'.

There was to be one exception to all his rules, and this was what Dickens called the 'remarkable case' of Caroline Thompson. It started in the autumn of 1854 with a letter from Caroline's brother Frederick Maynard, a respectable young architectural draughtsman. He was appealing to Dickens for help. 'I have heard much of your goodness to unfortunate people and your writings have emboldened me to pray for your advice.' Caroline was the apparently impossible combination: an innocent whore. 'A more virtuous minded woman never lived' said her brother; yet she was earning her living, and that of her child, by prostitution. 'In the very house to which this brother goes home every night of his life', Dickens emphasised to Miss Coutts. He thought Frederick's unbounded respect for his sister was 'one of the strangest and most bewildering spectacles I ever saw within my remembrance'.

The phenomenon amazed him even more when he met Caroline in person. 'I very much wish you would see her,' he told Miss Coutts, 'and judge for yourself of its peculiarity. There is nothing about her from which you could suppose she had come to this. You might see her and her brother a thousand times – you might meet them in the street, every day in the year – and only notice them as brother and sister who were no doubt living together and taking care of one another. I cannot get the picture of her, out of my head.'

Why Dickens was breaking his customary silence to write at length to Miss Coutts was because he needed her money. There was no question of putting Caroline into Urania: 'Her manner, character, and experiences are altogether different.' And besides, there was her two-year-old daughter, to whom she was passionately devoted. The Urania solution though – emigration – is the one Dickens first suggests.

Initially Caroline was to go to South Africa with her daughter, but brother and sister did not want to be parted. So Dickens arranged for her to keep a lodging house, and when that did not work out he fixed for her to emigrate with daughter and brother to Canada. He kept in touch and went to see her before she left. So much time and effort for one case. Equally striking is Dickens's notion of Caroline, from the first mention of her, as story. 'The astonishing story' is how she first appears to him, albeit one he will never be able to use in his fiction. Caroline herself does it too, in a letter to Dickens about 'my Story' with a capital S. How tempting and forbidden it was to Dickens, this 'romance at once so astonishing and yet so intelligible as I never had the boldness to think of'.

But what he would soon be starting to think of was his next novel. *Little Dorrit* was conceived at the beginning of 1855, while Caroline Thompson was exercising him so profoundly – 'I cannot get the picture of her, out of my head'. Amy Dorrit is not the Caroline Thompson paradox of the virtuous whore, but both young women look small, meek and young for their age. Both of them educate their siblings, both are extolled by Dickens as good housekeepers, patient and gentle in the face of adversity. There is just one Caroline Thompson moment in the novel, when Little Dorrit's father basely hints to her that she might encourage the advances of simple John Chivery, the turnkey's son. She should 'lead him on', in order to make her father's life in prison more congenial. Further than that Dickens could not go.

PART FOUR

AFTERWARDS

CHAPTER TWELVE

Vicious Frances Cranstone

'She's mortal high and passionate – powerful high and passionate; and what with having notice to leave, and having others put above her, she don't take kindly to it.'

Bleak House, Chapter 18

IF IT WAS doing its job well Urania would, Dickens guessed in the flush of his first vision, hit a success rate of fifty per cent. So he was pleased with the balance sheet he could present after five years. Out of the fifty-six inmates who had been through the Home for Homeless Women, his *Household Words* article reported, thirty had emigrated and sent back good accounts of themselves. What about the others? What happened to the women who did not do so well? Were their lives better or worse for Dickens's intervention?

The Duke of Wellington had his doubts from the start. He tried to steer his friend Angela away from the whole idea. 'Irreclaimables' was his word for the women she wanted to help. 'Alas', he said, the statistics were inexorable. They demonstrated that there was 'little if any hope of saving in this World that particular Class of Unfortunates'. Angela was not deterred. She had been profoundly struck by the women and child prostitutes using the steps of her grand house in Piccadilly. As she lay in her warm bed she thought of them just outside her window. That was what she told Dickens, and he told the women they invited inside their new Home. 'There is a lady in this town', ran his Appeal which the prison governors were to read out, 'who, from the windows of her house, has seen such as you going past at night, and has felt her heart bleed at the sight. The thought of such women has troubled her in her bed.'

But Dickens knew that however much the heart bled, however carefully they screened the candidates, and however diligently he and the staff worked, there were bound to be some failures. Seven out of the first fifty-six he was reporting on in 1853 decided the place was not for them, and left of their own accord. Another seven absconded dramatically and ten were expelled. Some of the failures were spectacular. Sad of course, but great copy for the novelist.

Before the Home opened, Dickens was already projecting himself into the emotional lives of his prospective charges. 'There is no doubt', he holds forth to Miss Coutts in 1846, 'that many of them would go on well for some time, and would then be seized with a violent fit of the most extraordinary passion, apparently quite motiveless, and insist on going away. There seems to be something inherent in their course of life, which engenders and awakens a sudden restlessness and recklessness which may be long suppressed, but breaks out like madness; and which all people who have had opportunities of observation in Penitentiaries and elsewhere, must have contemplated with astonishment and pity.'

Uncontrollable emotion is exactly what intrigues Dickens and marks these women out for him. To begin with, he is all for second chances and for allowing those who depart in anger to repent in hindsight. Later he realised that this was playing with fire. Anger was the emotion most likely to disrupt his little kingdom and expose it to harm.

When it came to Frances Cranstone, Dickens had reason to regret not showing her the door soon after she arrived. She makes her first appearance during a routine committee meeting in May 1853. 'All was quiet'; Dickens paid the bills, and 'administered encouragement to the vicious Cranstone who seems to have been trying to do better'. Seventeen-year-old Frances had a temper: part and parcel of many such girls, and always a liability. Six months earlier they had had to expel an inmate known as Stallion. That may have been her nickname; at any rate she 'turned out to be [*sic*] a ferocious temper, and probably would have done some serious damage to somebody if she had remained.' It was very wet that day and Stallion had no clothes to leave in, so they gave her 'an old but decent bonnet and shawl'. Pugnacious to the end, Stallion 'immediately threw them away in the Lane'. Now Frances Cranstone seemed to be getting the better of her temper so Dickens let her stay. She managed to hang on for almost a year, and even looked like being ready to emigrate.

But when Dickens paid a Saturday afternoon call in April 1854 – this time on his own and not for a committee meeting – he was approached by Louisa Cooper and Ellen Venns on behalf of all 'the quiet ones'. Frances was, Louisa and Ellen told him, 'so constantly irritating and mischief-making' that they had all been 'made perfectly miserable (as indeed they looked).' Frances was 'making a party in the house, against all who were disposed to do well – and that whenever Mrs Marchmont's or Mrs Macartney's back was turned, there was no disguise about it.' Newcomers were especially susceptible, and 'the last but one seemed to be going in Cranstone's way as a mere matter of necessity.' It was Isabella and the gang all over again, except that Frances had none of Isabella's charm. Dickens himself immediately sensed the 'unsettled' atmosphere, he told Miss Coutts later.

The crisis compelled Louisa Cooper, who was a timid young woman, to explain it all to Dickens. Mrs Marchmont had only been at Urania a couple of months and Frances was running rings round her. Once Louisa got started she went on at some length, self-appointed defender of the faith. 'That the house was perfectly changed and made unlike anything it had ever been within her knowledge of it, and that she felt that whoever should have the misfortune to be sent out in the same ship with this girl never could hope for peace and quiet.' Dickens already recognised Louisa and Ellen as 'the two best conducted girls in the house'. Taking his cue from them he turned to the two matrons: did they agree with Louisa's version of Frances? Yes, they said, 'they had no doubt of its truth, but the girl was so extraordinarily sly in getting others into trouble and keeping herself out of it – just an inch outside – that they could never catch her.'

That was enough for Dickens. He took command and sternly ordered Frances to appear before him. Putting her on severe warning, he told her 'positively once for all, that such conduct could not be allowed'. It would be 'monstrous' for him to advise Miss Coutts to 'send out a girl so suspicious and full of mischief'. Unless she altered altogether in the next ten days 'my recommendation to the Committee would be to discharge her; which I was perfectly sure, they would do: such complaint against her, still existing.' How unfair! Frances rushed back to her claque of friends in the long room, 'protesting and lamenting'; Mrs Marchmont was there to witness it all and relay back to Dickens. What happened next redoubled Frances's crime, because 'that moment (you may see what her influence is) up gets Eliza Wilkin, that girl with the unhappy Father, and boldly says before them all "If you please Mrs Marchmont, if Frances Cranstone is to go *I* wish to go"'.

Frances was one thing, Eliza quite another. She had been a favourite since she arrived eighteen months ago. Dickens first met her when she called on him at his home accompanied by her father: they had been recommended by Dickens's magistrate friend Gilbert A' Beckett. There was something about her bruised face and her fondness for telling stories to little children which attracted his interest. He was also affected by her father, 'a very decent man indeed, and very sorrowful about her'. Eliza was a pathetic scrap: undersized, filthy and ragged. Dickens accepted her on the spot with some necessary conditions. He directed Mrs Morson to send Eliza 'under-clothing' plus 'money for her to get a warm bath – or two would be better, and instructions to her to do so, that she may be perfectly clean and wholesome'. Mindful of the rituals he had established years ago, he also asked Mrs Morson to send Eliza 'a bonnet and so forth', and to fix the appointment to collect her in a private fly.

Eliza began with a wobble. Dickens found her 'a little dubious', unnerved by two girls being expelled just as she arrived. They were the ferocious Stallion and Little Willis of 'the Key and Bible business'. Dickens took time to speak to Eliza 'very seriously, telling her that if she once got outside the gate we knew, better than she might think for now, what she would give, if she could, to come back'. This was in November 1852. The last sentence of his letter, which dealt at length with Eliza, Little Willis, and Stallion's tantrums, reminds us with a jolt what else he had on his plate. 'I have been so busy, leading up to the great turning idea of the Bleak House story, that I have lived this last week or ten days in a perpetual scald and boil.' He is referring, the editors of his *Letters* note, 'to the revelation to Esther that Lady Dedlock is her mother'; *Bleak House* is midway through its course.

Now, a year and half later here was Eliza, cleaned up, firmly on her feet, about to emigrate and on the verge of ruining everything. The 'wretched creature' maintained that 'she and Cranstone have "always kep" together, and that they mean to go together, and that she has been tired of the place this long time."' This was the downside of the buddy scheme Dickens was so enamoured of. Eliza and Frances were best friends; losing Frances meant losing Eliza. But threats like this always galvanised him. He 'immediately had Eliza in, and said "You want to go?" – "Yes Sir." – "Then Mrs Marchmont please to write to her father and tell him she is to be discharged on Monday."' Eliza's fall from grace could not have been swifter.

This was Urania the drama, as it had been for Rhena Pollard five months before. Rhena herself was still hanging on by the skin of her teeth. She was the sort of 'troublesome' which Mrs Marchmont wanted to recommend for mercy. Eliza was not, so Dickens put her in the limelight. 'I went into the long room and said before the others "If that unhappy father of yours does not come here by Monday afternoon, you will be discharged alone."' Having created the stir he wanted ('Wilkin's being taken at her word, evidently struck the rest with amazement and consternation'), Dickens left them to it. He was furious that Eliza had eliminated herself: 'better to lose a wilderness of Cranstones'.

He spent that Saturday evening at home. As always he had a pile of letters to answer. Three of tonight's batch begged his interest for a variety of charitable causes. Despondent though he was after his visit to Shepherd's Bush, he nevertheless rallied one of his correspondents towards the Urania way of doing things. We should do what we can 'as quiet individuals', he said, rather than 'forming a whole army of societies'. He ended his letter with a short homily all the more moving for coming after the disappointments of the afternoon. 'Sow the seed. It will come up in the spot where it is sown – it will be carried on wings we know nothing of, into chance places – not a grain of it will ever die out.'

Back at Shepherd's Bush the fur was flying. Frances was incandescent with rage against Louisa for snitching on her. After the door closed on Dickens she lashed out at Louisa, and attacked her with such 'violence' that Louisa '(half frightened to death) intreated to be locked up for safety'. A good idea: it seemed the only way to protect her from physical harm. Frances was completely out of control. She stormed round the house, loudly demanding to leave straightaway. Mrs Marchmont remembered Dickens's policy of trying to calm girls down for a cooling off period in case they might reconsider. But she got nowhere with Frances, who was proclaiming to the whole establishment that she intended 'to be a Devil'. The only thing to do with her was to lock her up too.

The house simmered with resentment. Sporadic warfare erupted in spats between the 'quiet ones' and the rowdy friends of Frances. In post barely two months, Mrs Marchmont had a revolution on her hands. Her years of experience as a prison matron warned her to bang down all the hatches; on the other hand her recent induction into the Urania philosophy preached kindness and tolerance. But could kindness keep this crew in order? Early next morning she crossed town to ask Dickens for advice. He told her to expel Frances now; Eliza could wait till Monday. To Miss Coutts he could not resist a little dig about the need for firmness. If only they had expelled Frances 'on that old occasion' they might have been able to save Eliza now. He made one last bid to keep her, with a special trip out to Urania, and a final interview with her father, to whom he advanced three pounds from the Burdett Coutts kitty. To no avail and Dickens's great regret. 'I think nothing that has ever occurred at Shepherd's Bush has disappointed me so much as Wilkin's defection at last.'

Failure was of course always on the cards. Two of the first, most minutely vetted inmates let them down badly. Frances Bewley, listed in Miss Coutts's note of the first girls into the Home, is never heard of again. She vanishes completely; perhaps she could not settle. The other failure, Mary Ann Stonnell, arrived along with Rosina Gale as one of the first four. A year earlier she had been convicted for her part in a pre-dawn burglary of a watchmaker's shop in Bloomsbury, not far from Dickens's house.

Described in newspaper reports as 'a slight girl of thirteen', sixteen-year-old Mary Ann was the smallest member of her gang of teenage delinquents, and the obvious choice for posting through the fanlight over the front door, much as Oliver Twist had been under Bill Sikes's brutal hand during the robbery at Chertsey. Dropping noiselessly into the blackness, Mary Ann swiftly made a clean sweep of all the watches in the shop window. Then she exited through the fanlight, which she reached by standing on a chair. The other three were waiting to haul her down into the street. Unlucky for them, an alert policeman was waiting too, and watching from a dark alley as 'all four walked away together, laughing and joking.' He told the court that he had 'sprung his rattle', whereupon they 'ran like little deers', with Mary Ann leading the chase around Bloomsbury Square. She and the other sixteen-year-old, Elizabeth Redding, were given short prison sentences; their male accomplices, youths of eighteen, were both transported for seven years.

Mary Ann was no Oliver Twist. After such excitements, Urania afforded her little except temptation. While Rosina kept her head down and applied herself to all the skills and education on offer, Mary Ann could not break her old habits. She came from Coldbath Fields prison and within a few months she was back there. Miss Coutts felt sorry for her. 'Bad Parents' she noted beside her name. She visited her in prison, something she rarely did, and wanted to give her a second chance at the Home. This was because she had been touched by the letter Mary Ann sent her from prison, as was Edward Illingworth, the chaplain from Coldbath Fields who worked at Urania.

Surviving among the Coutts papers, Mary Ann's letter is a precious remnant directly from the hand of a Urania girl, or in this case an ex-Urania girl. Illingworth was particularly impressed that she had written 'without dictation or assistance from others'. She writes neatly and so much more legibly than her benefactress; her spelling and humility are impeccable:

Madam
I take the liberty of writing a few lines to thank you for the kindness you have shown to such an unworthy creature as I have been to leave such a good home and I thank you taking the trouble you have to come and see me who am not worthy of such a kind benefactress I

hope Madam that you will forgive me for I am very sorry for what I have done.

Mary Ann Stonnell.

Dickens agreed that she was genuine but remained unmoved. 'Stonnell, *in prison*, will always, I think, be tolerably good. Out of it, until – perhaps – after great suffering, I have no hope of her.' Although he refused to allow her back, she did give him an adjective. 'Stonnellian' got to be his word for incurability.

Three years later another Mary Ann was proving a bad bet. Mary Anne Church was the eighteen-year-old who had been arrested wearing the frock she stole from her mistress. She lasted a year at Urania, but Dickens always had his doubts. He recognised her as a girl who liked to steal, not one who did it out of necessity. Things would go missing and Mary Anne would be suspected. Watch out for her 'pilfering propensities', Dickens warned Mrs Morson. These light-fingered Mary Annes could lead to a rare, though never acute, parting of the ways between Miss Coutts and Dickens. He had more experience of jail-birds than she did and it made him charier of second chances. But if she wished, he would certainly put himself out for cases he had probably given up on.

Mary Anne Church could not seem able to turn herself round. She made more trouble and would have been expelled were it not for the season. It was winter, and Miss Coutts hated the idea of turfing her out 'into the bare streets'. On her behalf Dickens contacted Tracey, the governor of the prison where Mary Anne had served her sentence, to check out the respectable relatives she referred to so glibly. 'She speaks of an Aunt "in Turks' Head Court" – which I rather believe to be a non-existent place.' He thought that if she did have any relations they were all 'sick of her' by now. Nevertheless, to satisfy Miss Coutts, all efforts should be made to 'hunt out' someone willing to give the girl shelter.

Tracey duly did his stuff. Dickens was right: there was no Aunt. 'It's all moonshine'. Mary Anne was a confidence trickster with 'a great capacity for taking in the chaplains'. Her departure looked imminent but she clung on, still pulling the wool over Miss Coutts's eyes. This went on until the spring, with Mary Anne making herself a 'consistent botheration'. Even then Miss Coutts wanted her to have 'some sort of a possibility of a chance', so Dickens turned to Chesterton for a fall-back. 'Haven't I heard you mention some place where they take all sorts and conditions of impracticable girls in, if they will work?' All this for slippery no-hoper Mary Anne Church.

The next time she surfaces is in the columns of *The Times* three years later, where she is described as a 'well-known prostitute'. She and Emma Hamilton were charged with stealing a hundred and forty pounds in bank-notes from Mr Henry Gray, 'a gentleman living in South Street, Grosvenor Square'. Under examination Mr Gray, who 'made a profession of the turf', gave 'a vague and unsatisfactory account' of the night's events. He had been with the women in different pubs and 'lastly at a brothel'. He said 'he was not strictly sober, and not positively drunk, although he had been dining late with some friends before meeting the girls'. The magistrate decided that Gray's recollections were insufficiently distinct and discharged the prisoners.

A month later Mary Anne was back in court. The reporter described her as having been 'convicted of felony at least fifty times'. Her booty this time was only half a crown. To her victim the magistrate put his customary question: 'Were you sober, Sir?' When he answered 'Yes, certainly', the magistrate hazarded the guess that 'You must be a foreigner, then?' Yes, Mr Roder was from Germany. 'Ah, that accounts for it', said the magistrate. 'If you had been an Englishman you would have been drunk for a certainty.' His two preceding cases had collapsed after drunken prosecution witnesses failed to appear. Dickens subjected the magistrate's witticisms to some heavy-handed satire in the next number of *Household Words*. He cannot have been surprised by Mary Anne's role in the proceedings.

All things considered – given the huge life changes which these young women were being asked to make – it is inevitable that temptation occasionally got the upper hand. Then a pair of inmates (this was usually something they did in pairs) would abscond with some of the matron's nice things. In 1850 two seventeen-year-olds, Ann Davis and Mary

Humphreys, fled the premises with Mrs Morson's cloak and 'other articles' belonging to her worth £7.10s, which sounds like a sizeable haul. 'The disaster' Dickens called it, as he rushed over to investigate. He faffed about with cupboards, drawers and keys, and worked himself up into a 'mighty state of indignation'. Had all his precautions about keeping valuables locked up been followed? He recognised that temptation should be part of the reform process, but you had to be realistic. Mrs Macartney's purse had also disappeared. Suspecting other inmates of being involved, Dickens instigated a programme of ruthless undercover surveillance. 'I have directed all the beds to be narrowly and secretly examined this evening while the girls are in the long room – in case it should have been taken and secreted by any one but the runaways.'

Ann and Mary were not convincing villains. Within days they walked into a police station in the City to give themselves up. If they were hoping to be taken back into the fold they were wildly mistaken. All that was on Dickens's mind was how to keep the case out of the newspapers. When it came to trial, he instructed his solicitor that there should be no mention of 'my very notorious name'. 'No unnecessary sensation will be made' he assured Miss Coutts, aware of her aversion to publicity. The lawyers and the judge were all briefed to mention neither of them. Dickens could manage things discreetly when he wanted to. The girls pleaded guilty and got six months each.

How were the lives of these Mary Anns who ended up in prison or back on the streets affected by the Urania intervention? Had Dickens made life worse for these discards from his experiment? It is undeniable that some of them would have been in and out of prison anyway. After all, that is where many of them had come from. Knowing such women would be hard material to work with, Dickens preferred to take first-time offenders. That is why the application procedures entailed extensive enquiries to check out the applicant's story. Was this, as she claimed, her first time in jail, the first time she had been seduced or sacked by a cruel employer? Even so, old lags like Mary Ann Church could slip through the net.

At least the time they spent at Shepherd's Bush gave these young women some respite. If they had come straight from prison many of them – then as now – would have nowhere to go, no job or family. And if they could not take the total vision of the new life abroad, they could enjoy a break from the streets. They could also enjoy the cheerful atmosphere which distinguished Urania from other refuges. That might be vital. Some of the Urania inmates had been imprisoned for attempting to kill themselves. They may have tried to kill unwanted babies too. In 1853 Miss Coutts sent Dickens a cutting from *The Times* about Mary Anne Copson, a milliner who had jumped into the Regent's Canal with her newborn baby. The child drowned, she was saved. *The Times* reported her as 'dreadfully depressed and agitated'. Dickens agreed with Miss Coutts that it was a 'pitiable' case, saying he would see 'if we cannot get her after a short imprisonment'.

Whether they did, we do not know; we do know that four years later Miss Coutts interceded to good effect with another attempted suicide. Seventeen-year-old Lydia Stanley was taken into custody for disorderly behaviour in the street, and while at the police station she suffered a number of fits. Recovering with the help of some medical attention, she 'requested permission to walk in the yard, and while there made a determined effort to strangle herself, which she subsequently avowed her intention of repeating whenever opportunity presented itself.' The article in *The Times* recorded the fruitless 'endeavours' to find any friends or family. Lydia 'declined' to say, but did allege, 'in the most solemn manner that her father had been her seducer.' It seems to have been through the magistrate, Mr Paynter, who 'took much interest in the poor girl's case,' that Miss Coutts came to hear of Lydia and invited her to Urania. After only a few days on remand, Lydia was discharged to Miss Coutts's 'asylum', expressing 'her sincere gratitude for the kind exertions which had been made in her behalf'. *The Times* referred to it as a 'House of Detention': Urania was still playing its cards close to its chest.

In the mid-1850s Shepherd's Bush got its first local newspaper, the *West London Observer*. Its reporters cut their teeth on sensational stories of infanticides, young women on trial for murdering their babies. Three cases in the first six months of the newspaper set the pattern. Twenty-three-year-old Hannah Brumwell was homeless and starving. Her baby, who was found floating in the Serpentine, had died from 'want and misery', according to the judge. Eliza Fowler had given birth to a baby girl and concealed her in a 'bandbox', a cardboard box used for collars and hats. Mary Ann Swan was also charged with concealing the birth of a baby girl, again in a bandbox. These young women were all servants, and their cases were all dismissed.

Dickens and Miss Coutts swapped cuttings, discussed cases, did what they could. In 1855 Dickens paid a visit to the City in response to an advertisement in *The Times* asking 'WHO will RESCUE a PENITENT aged 14?' The Protection Society appealing on her behalf trusted that 'she may not have to be turned away for want of funds'. Dickens called on the secretary of the Society 'in a sort of china-closet at the back of the first floor in the Poultry' and was highly suspicious. 'They clearly want to use the case as an advertising Puff of their establishment, and don't desire to part with it – evidently looking upon the girl as so much Capital.' He told the secretary, who 'enunciated a great deal of perilous nonsense', that he would certainly consider the case on its own merits if the girl wished to apply to the Home but refused point blank to give the Society any money. 'I fear a good deal of trading Cant prevails in the concern.'

On other occasions, acting independently of Miss Coutts, Dickens would follow up what he had witnessed while gathering material for a *Household Words* article. 'I have thought a great deal about that woman,' he wrote to the MP Jacob Bell after they had visited a workhouse together: 'the Wardswoman in the Itch Ward, who was crying about the dead child. If anything useful can be done for her, I should like to do it. Will you bear this in mind, in confidence, and if you can put me in the way of helping her, do me the kindness of telling me how it can be best done?'

Dickens was adroit at keeping Urania out of the news. The only time it appeared in the *West London Observer* was after his reign, in 1860. 'Disturbing Miss Burdett Coutts's "Home"': how the headline must have annoyed her. The story was of drunken mothers and violent stepfathers. The local vicar was requisitioned to sort it all out. The mother and stepfather wanted to remove their sixteen-year-old daughter from Urania, and Mrs Marchmont said fine, she would just need to change into her old clothes. For her part, the girl burst into tears. She said she was happy where she was; the abusive stepfather was the reason she and her sister had left home in the first place. Despite all the 'kind endearments' the parents showered on her, she refused to budge. Next day the mother returned, much the worse for drink and 'using fearful language'. Summoned again, the vicar watched as she tried to barge through the parlour window. When that failed she resorted to non-stop ringing on the doorbell. She got her day in court for creating a disturbance and made the most of it, declaring 'she would go to prison, but she would have her child in spite of them'. In the end she settled for the ten shilling fine and the girl stayed where she was.

Frances Cranstone, whose wild rage impelled Mrs Marchmont to lock her up for the night, would not leave them alone. Two months after she was expelled she wrote a begging letter to Miss Coutts, who asked Dickens to follow it up. He accordingly dispatched 'a man on whom I could depend' to check out the address. It was in Whitechapel and looked quite respectable, 'being one of four or five neat little houses'. The amateur sleuth peered in at 'a man and his wife – apparently – in the parlor whom he "saw doing nothing, through the blinds"'. They had only just moved in, and no one in the area knew anything about them. Enquiries at the pub and the police station drew a blank.

What could Frances be up to? Back at the *Household Words* office, Dickens and Harry Wills mulled over the 'odd account'; they could not work out what the set-up was. Eager to gratify his curiosity, Wills volunteered to call on Frances 'in the kitchen'. Playing detective made a good break from sub-editing.

By the time he started snooping round Whitechapel, Frances had flown. Wills exerted his talent for geniality to worm his way into the confidence of the woman who was now living in the house, 'a bright clean goodlooking woman in mourning'. The man of the house was a widower; was this woman his sister or his new wife? Wills did not like to ask, but managed to establish that Frances had been living there with the widower since she left Urania. She was caring for his three children, and 'had the entire management of his little household to the paying of the weekly bills'. She was reported to be honest, and seems to have settled down rather well to the responsibilities of domestic life, though her standards of house-keeping fell way below those of Wills's bright clean informant. In her eyes Frances was 'wretchedly deficient in washing: having been idle and dirty "to an unbelievable degree"'. Wills did a quick scan of the place: 'There are other lodgers in the House, and I doubt the respectability of the parlor but cannot swear against it.'

It was not to last, Frances could not change her spots. Once again her temper got the better of her. Wills's informant had arrived to run the show, and the two women clashed violently. Frances apparently '"couldn't abear fur to have any one put over her"', which spelled the end. Three days earlier she had '"in an artful way" asked leave to go out for an hour and . . . forgotten to return'.

Dickens forwarded Wills's report on to Miss Coutts, together with his opinion that 'It seems pretty clear that it will be best not to answer her letter'. But Frances was not one to give up easily. Four months later she wrote again, this time to Dickens. He knew Miss Coutts would be interested. 'Do look at the enclosed from Cranstone. There is a remarkable kind of ability in it.' While he recognised that nothing more could be done, there is an edge of regret to his final question: 'I suppose it would be useless to write her any reply?' He could probably already foresee Frances's unstoppable downward spiral. Two years later she was lying dead of laryngitis in the workhouse at Shoreditch; she was twenty-two years old.

Two Urania letters

August 81st 1848

Madam

I take the liberty of writing a few lines to thank you for the kindness you have shown to such an unworthy creature as I have been to leave such a good home and I thank you for taking the trouble you have to come and see me who am not worthy of such a kind benefactress I hope madam that you will forgive me for I am very sorry for what I have done

Mary ann Stonnell

12 **Mary Ann Stonnell** was one of the first inmates at Urania Cottage in the autumn of 1847, and one of the first failures. By May 1848 she was back in prison again. Somewhere Mary Ann has learned to write beautifully.

13 'I often think of Urania Cottage and the many happy hours I have spent there', wrote **Louisa Cooper** to Miss Coutts on the eve of her departure to South Africa in the autumn of 1854.

Tillington
nr Petworth Oct 21

Honored Madam,

As I am about to leave England I am most anxious that one of my last acts should be to thank you my kind Benefactress for all your goodness to me I cannot find words to express my gratitude but with the help of that kind Providence who will never leave me nor forsake me if I pray to him I will by my future life try to prove it I often think of your kind and gentle words and the thoughts of them has many times been a comfort to me

14 **Emily displaces David** on the title page of his own story in early editions.

16 **Emily had a vigorous afterlife** on the stage: a playbill from 1869.

15 **Miss Jessie Winter as Little Em'ly** in *David Copperfield* at His Majesty's Theatre in January 1915.

17 **Phiz (Dickens's illustrator, Hablot K. Browne) was fond of her**: he designed this vignette of her running over the swirling waves at Yarmouth for the Library Edition of 1858.

Chapter Thirteen

Pioneers

My aunt mused a little while, and then said:
    'Mr Micawber, I wonder you have never turned your thoughts to emigration.'
    'Madam,' returned Mr Micawber, 'it was the dream of my youth, and the fallacious aspiration of my riper years.' I am thoroughly persuaded, by the by, that he had never thought of it in his life.
    David Copperfield, Chapter 52

B EFORE THE YOUNG women crossed the threshold of Urania Cottage they had to agree that emigrating was what they most wanted to do in all the world. This was asking a lot of them, since they could have little idea what it meant. They would have a year at Shepherd's Bush to find out, and to prepare themselves for playing their parts in one of England's dreams, the brave new colonies on the other side of the globe. Pioneers in more senses than one, they were at the forefront of the great emigration craze which was to grip the country in the middle years of the nineteenth century,

Where would they be going, how would they get there, and what would they do when they did get there? And who would be the first to go? The choice was for Dickens to make. Of the early intake at Shepherd's Bush, Jane Westaway impressed him as particularly steady and responsible. She headed his list at the beginning of 1849, which then determined the make-up of the first convoy. Urania policy dictated that the friendship bonds forged inside the Home would be the building blocks for the life ahead.

As the young women sat sewing in the evenings or chattering in their bedrooms at night, a popular topic of conversation was who would be going out on the next ship, and with whom. Friendships formed, broke up, re-established. Jane Westaway's best friend was Martha Goldsmith, the plain country girl from Berkshire: that ensured Martha's place on the list. Also in their group was the volatile Julia Mosley. She had settled down well but might, Dickens thought, 'become restless, if she be left behind'. So she had to be included. By now Julia, Martha and Jane had been at Urania for over a year.

Their year of intensive training had transformed them from ex-cons, street-walkers and destitutes into top-flight domestic servants. They made their own clothes, baked their own bread and grew their own produce; they could run a house. Perhaps, some observers thought, rather too much attention had been squandered on them. It was admirable that they could read and write, but were poetry and part-singing essential to the life of a servant in the outback?

As the young women prepared their emigration outfits they were encouraged to learn about where they were headed. Extra evening lessons from experts were fitted in two or three hours a week to '"finish off" those young women who are likely to go soon'. Where that would be? Australia stood out as the obvious destination; and as early as August 1848, before any Uranians had even set foot on gangplank, word of their impending arrival preceded them. The enterprise was so novel and the celebrities so newsworthy (Dickens and Angela Burdett Coutts) that the *Maitland Mercury and Hunter River General Advertiser* in New South Wales was moved to reprint a surprisingly accurate article from the London *News of the World* about the 'experiment' at Shepherd's Bush, under the heading 'Women for Australia'.

Dickens himself never went there, though he often flirted with the idea. 'Thank God there is a Van Diemen's-land', he wrote to Forster at the beginning of the 1840s in a facetious fantasy of social climbing. 'Now, I wonder if I should make a good settler! I wonder, if I went to a new colony with my head, hands, legs, and health, I should force myself to the top of the social milk-pot and live upon the cream! What do you think: Upon my word I believe I should.' Twenty years later he was tempted again. An Australian visitor to London in 1862 offered him ten thousand pounds for an eight-month reading tour. Dickens was 'dazzled by the great chances' and by the lure of 'com[ing] back rich'. Then the long absence struck him as 'a penance and a misery, and I dread the thought of it more than I can possibly express.'

But he would get there by proxy. The voyage he would never make was vouchsafed to sons and fictional characters alike. Alfred was the first son to go. At the age of twenty he was exiled to manage a sheep station in New South Wales. This was in 1865. Three years later it was Edward's turn to be consigned to the outback, after eight months' training at Cirencester Agricultural College. Edward, or Plorn as he was nicknamed, was Dickens's youngest and favourite son. He did not want to go but Dickens was implacable. He had diagnosed what he called Plorn's 'want of application and continuity of purpose'. Australia would be the solution for these lacklustre boys of his. 'Unformed', Dickens called him – Plorn was only sixteen – as he threw him in at the deep end, though with much emotion. Plorn was so embarrassed by the tears Dickens shed when bidding him goodbye at Paddington that he pretended to look the other way until his train pulled out of the station.

Plorn and Alfred had one-way tickets. Dickens would not think of them coming back, even when he knew all was not going well. Which it did not. Neither of his sons fulfilled his dreams of them 'becoming proprietors, and aspiring to the first positions in the Colony'. Plorn made a rocky start, and had to be cautioned against his 'wretched habit' of drinking nobblers (half-glasses of spirits) in the morning. For a while the brothers worked together as stock agents. When that business failed, Alfred ended up giving lectures about his father to tiny audiences in small outback towns. Plorn, known in later life as Ted, went into parliament but was not a success. He borrowed money from his family back in England and never repaid it. He was an amiable and popular chap; his sister Katey's friend Gladys Storey hinted at his love of gambling. His biographer suggests a resemblance to Mr Micawber.

For Mr Micawber himself, emigration was to be a comic triumph. At the time when the first Uranians were setting out for Australia at the beginning of 1849, Dickens was 'revolving a new work', *David Copperfield*. Its final chapters would offer emigration as a mass-solution. Repeatedly arrested until the moment of departure, Mr Micawber takes his farewell of England – with the punch he and his creator enjoyed so much – in a pub at the foot of Hungerford Stairs. This was where the twelve-year-old Charles had been so humiliated in the blacking warehouse.

The fictional emigrants all prosper. Mr Micawber takes to the work ethic as he never had before. "'I never wish to meet a better gen'lman for turning to with a will,'" says Mr Peggotty. "'I've seen that theer bald head of his a perspiring in the sun, Mas'r Davy, till I a'most thowt it would have melted away. And now he's a Magistrate.'" David himself and Tommy Traddles cut rather staid figures at the end of the book. They are well balanced by the antipodean Saturnalia ruled over by Wilkins Micawber Esquire. Everyone thrives, including the lugubrious Mrs Gummidge, who receives an offer of marriage from a ship's cook turned settler. Hearing about it sets even po-faced Agnes laughing.

Emigration also brings life after the fall for Martha and Emily. They are luckier than the Urania women in having the substantial protection of the avuncular Mr Peggotty. Once in Australia Martha soon achieves the golden future which Dickens wished for his Uranians. She is, however – in deference to squeamish readers, Miss Coutts included – morally segregated from the general population in an outback quarantine zone. Mr Peggotty tells David all about it.

'A young man, a farm-labourer, as come by us on his way to market with his mas'r's drays – a journey of over five hundred mile, theer and back – made offers fur to take her fur his wife (wives is very scarce theer), and then to set up fur their two selves in the Bush. She spoke to me fur to tell him her trew story. I did. They was married, and they live fower hundred mile away from any voices but their own and the singing birds.'

As for Emily, 'She might have married well a mort of times, "but uncle," she says to me, "that's gone for ever."' But if her sexual history casts too long a shadow for marriage, Emily does attain something approaching a maternal role. The flighty girl becomes steadfast, a tender of the sick. Her future will be exemplary and laudable: she is the one who is "'sowt out by all that has any trouble.'"

Emily, Martha, Mr Peggotty, Mrs Gummidge and the Micawbers had all joined what turned out to be a rush. By the late 1840s emigration was proving itself the nation's top cure: for problems as various as urban overcrowding, the starving poor in Ireland, surplus women in the population, and the victims of the highland clearances in Scotland. 'The Time is big with this' declared Thomas Carlyle. A 'free bridge for emigrants' could disperse the threats posed by the potentially violent and revolutionary Chartists.

In a dramatic revision of transportation, the British Government now sponsored groups of 'assisted emigrants': the healthy and fit young (with not too many children or old folk in tow) who could contribute to colonial prosperity. Propaganda spread the word about Australia as the land of fresh beginnings. Lecturers toured the land; eye-catching black-letter posters sang the praises of official schemes and wooed eligible applicants. Women's magazines carried stories of starving young women sailing from London to blossom in the outback. 'Lucy Dean; The Noble Needlewoman' inspired readers of *Eliza Cook's Journal* in 1850 with visions of the 'prolificness' awaiting them down under.

Emigration fever seized the country. A new brand of literature did brisk business. 'How to emigrate' manuals told you how, where, with whom and with what to do it. Much of the stir came via the Colonization Society founded by William Kingston in 1847. Kingston was a journalist and popular writer for boys. He had a well-attuned feeling for what prospective emigrants wanted to know. 'How To Emigrate', 'The Emigrant Voyager's Manual', 'Arrival in the Colony': his handy pamphlets brim with facts, tips and assurance. With them in your pocket you could sail away with some borrowed confidence.

Of course not everyone was welcome. Feast was followed by famine; there would be mismatches between what was wanted and what was sent. For Australia, women were often targeted to even up the balance between the sexes. But not all women. Refuge and Reformatory inmates fell into the 'not wanted' category. They would serve only to swell the ranks of the prostitutes, and according to an observer in Hobart, 'these women already exist in numbers almost beyond belief'. A doctor trying to raise funds for a refuge for unemployed servants in Adelaide in the 1840s claimed that the 'frequency of prostitution' had 'generated a mistrust with regard to all' single female emigrants. Dickens's advice to his emigrants to stay 'profoundly silent' about their past lives was well-judged. They would need to keep the distance, in every sense, between themselves and the world they had left behind.

Off to Australia then, but where in Australia should they go? Luckily Miss Coutts had many irons in the fires of philanthropy, and one of them was sponsoring new bishops in the colonies. In 1847 she dispatched the Reverend Augustus Short and his young family from a cold draughty vicarage in Northamptonshire to Adelaide in South Australia, a colony which had been established only eleven years earlier. Life there could be hard. The Shorts' ten-month-old daughter died of heat and dysentery within two months of their arrival; another child died a few years later.

Short was distrusted for being too high church. He was stubborn in matters domestic and social as well as clerical. He insisted on designing the new family home himself, which was a disaster: the rooms faced the full afternoon sun and heated up unbearably. He refused invitations to parties at the Governor's house because the Governor had married his housekeeper (he later relented, conceivably his wife's doing: social life must have been limited). He rowed with the Catholic bishop about whose cathedral should enjoy prime position in downtown Adelaide; he rowed with visiting Congregationalist ministers, and he was always rowing with his own staff. 'A more unfortunate wicked fool I never saw', he exploded in his diary after one set-to. 'Will there never be an end to quarrelling in this diocese?'

More to the bishop's liking were the six-hundred-mile rides into the bush, when he slept under canvas and conducted services in primitive woolsheds. 'You ought to have been a fag at Westminster' he told people who complained about hardship in Adelaide. As a schoolboy he had enjoyed boxing, and this came in handy when he saw a heavy-weight sheepshearer laying about him. At length, says his biographer, 'the bishop stepped into the arena, and after he had overcome the natural reluctance of the shearer to "put on the gloves" with a prelate, administered a scientific pummelling to the champion of the shed'.

Miss Coutts also sponsored Robert Gray, the first bishop of Cape Town, and some Urania Cottage women would be sent there in the

1850s, but it was to Augustus Short in Adelaide that Urania's first fleet was entrusted in 1849. He was supposed to look out for them when they arrived: find them somewhere to live and someone to work for. How would they get on?

From its birth in 1836 Adelaide was a convict-free zone and proud of it. During the 1840s it had its teething problems, and even went temporarily bankrupt. The wrong sort of emigrants would only make things worse, and to the authorities in South Australia most emigrants looked like the wrong sort. 'Many clerks and shopmen are reported to be wandering about the streets of Adelaide unable to procure employment' grumbled the governor in 1849. Female orphans from Ireland were not welcome either. Reporters on the *South Australia Register* filed colourful columns about the government depot which took in these girls on arrival. 'Government Brothel at Native Location' trumpeted the headlines. 'Disgusting scenes are nightly enacted . . . bacchanalian orgies every night . . . no wonder that our streets should be swarmed with prostitutes.' But still came the demand for respectable female servants, with the predictable lament that the only ones who were any good promptly married and pressured the market even more by demanding servants of their own.

Domestic service: just what the Uranians were training for, although sometimes Dickens was stopped in his tracks by a sense of vagueness in theirs.

> I asked Goldsborough what work she supposed she *was* to do, when she went abroad. To which majestic enquiry she replied with a very limited sense of Committee dignity, 'that she did not suppose, Mr Dickerson, as she were a goin to set with her ands erfore her'.

Or there was the St Pancras Vestry Clerk's daughter, 'better brought up than the usual run of our inmates', who worried about the hard work being too much for her and hoped 'she might get a nurse's place when she emigrated'. Dickens told her, kindly enough, that she would have to reconcile herself to housework. He and Miss Coutts never agreed about the potent incentive of marriage, and 'what the force of that suggestion secretly is' in motivating the young women. The farewells he sent via Mrs Morson as she accompanied the 'girls who go tomorrow' to

Gravesend in 1850 could not have been clearer: 'as my last message, that I hope they will do well, marry honest men and be happy'.

Whether nor not marriage was in the offing for the well-trained servant who kept her mouth shut about her past, the energetic young city of Adelaide beckoned promisingly. Its growth from nothing to urban civilisation was amazingly rapid. Back in Shepherd's Bush the girls read all about it in *Sidney's Emigrant's Journal*. Samuel Sidney contributed dozens of articles to *Household Words* on emigration, John was his 'Bushman brother'. Their *Journal* featured letters from new arrivals to Adelaide: 'Ann very often cries at meals, and says she wishes the poor souls left at home could raise the same to eat.' A tradesman in Hindley Street boasted, 'We have some splendid shops in Adelaide, and among them drapers are particularly conspicuous. We have theatres, concert rooms etc just like London.'

In fact, the shock of the old was palpable. 'Familiar-looking inns and shops', commented the *Working Man's Handbook to South Australia* in 1849, 'genuine England bar-maids or shopmen, the glass of beer drawn out of a London engine, take one quite by surprise.' By the late 1840s the city supported three daily newspapers and sported what William Deakin (whose son would become Prime Minister) called 'a kind of Yankee independence of manners'. The Ladies Column of the *Emigrant's Journal* eulogised the 'good husbands' to be had among the Colonists. 'They are all rather rough in their language to each other, but no one ever heard of a Bushman beating his wife. In the towns there is as much gaiety as in England. Rather more.'

What no one then could have foreseen was the bombshell about to hit Australia. This was the discovery of gold near Melbourne in 1851, with immediate and drastic consequences. By then the first Urania women should have been in Adelaide, and Catherine Helen Spence, one of Australia's first women novelists, has left us a good account of life there. *Clara Morison: A Tale of South Australia during the Gold Fever* is set in 1851. 'The entire male population' has decamped to the diggings in Victoria, leaving the women to run the town. 'None but women and children were to be seen, the entire vintage of that year was gathered and the wine made by them; and never was there better made.' The milkman is now the milkgirl; for women prepared to pitch in the future looks bright.

It is the survival of the adaptable. Clara Morison is a timid middle-class orphan from Edinburgh whose job horizons are limited to governessing. Here governesses are not wanted, and Clara must learn self-confidence and push. A seasoned settler advises her, 'Don't run yourself down or you'll never get anywhere.' Clara finds back-breaking work as a domestic servant – unthinkable for a heroine back in the old country – and by the end of the book she is more or less running the farm single-handed. Clara's creator, Catherine Spence, was herself the perfect model of a pioneer woman. She arrived in Adelaide from Scotland in 1839 at the age of fourteen, and went on to enjoy a distinguished political career as a writer and government adviser. She met John Stuart Mill and campaigned for women's suffrage; South Australia was the first Australian state to introduce votes for women.

Spence was not the only one. Eliza Davies was also from Scotland and emigrated to Australia in the same year as Spence. Only nineteen years old, she went on her own, and the demure title of her autobiography, *The Story of an Earnest Life*, is deceptive. Earnest she may have been but dull she was not. While working as a teacher and missionary Eliza managed to pack in gratifying doses of romance and excitement. Manoeuvred by a scheming Frenchwoman, she marries a drunk 'with the lurking demon of jealousy in his eye'. He hits her on the head with his boot, commanding her: '"Pray, for this night you must die." He left me to go for a knife. I heard him in the knife box.' Luckily he cannot find the knife he wants and Eliza escapes. She is a vigorous young woman who swims in the sea, explores the outback and has an adventure on every page: bush fires, storms, snakes, monster centipedes, and a rash of marriage proposals. Along with all the other terrors (and more knives) comes the obligatory madwoman in the bush. '"They sleep; 'tis well. Now is the time to strike home." Oh horror! Her hand was raised, and in it a knife gleamed in the lamplight.'

Meanwhile Charlotte Brontë's own friend Mary Taylor was forging her future in New Zealand. 'I have set up shop!' she proudly announced in 1850: she is credited with introducing the first sewing machine into New Zealand. The freedom from class taboos suited her. 'We have been moving, cleaning, shop-keeping until I was really tired every night – a wonder for me. It does me good, and I had much rather be tired than ennuyée.' She tried to persuade the conventional Ellen Nussey to join her. 'It is all my eye seeking society without the means to enjoy it. Why not come here then? and be happy.' Ellen quailed, Charlotte marvelled. 'Mary Taylor sits on a wooden stool without a back in a log house, without a carpet, and neither is degraded nor thinks herself degraded by such poor accommodation.'

Mary might not have a carpet but she did have capital – and brotherly assistance – with which to launch herself on her new life. Women who posted upbeat accounts like Mary's usually were bolstered by family support: Ellen Clacy, for instance, who published her eyewitness account, *A Lady's Visit to the Gold Diggings of Australia in 1852–1853*, or Louisa Meredith who called her dog after her best-loved Dickens character (Dick Swiveller) and wrote for *Household Words*. Their voices ring out confidently; and at the other end of the economic scale, actions could speak louder than words. Among the earliest female settlers were the rebellious convicts known as the Flash Mob, their finest hour the famous incident in 1833 when three hundred of them 'at Divine Service in Hobart, in the presence of the governor's wife, Lady Jane Franklin, pulled up their clothing and smacked their bare bottoms'. Miss Coutts's pampered pets would have no financial safety nets: how would they measure up to the tough life ahead? Would they fall victim to Dickens's wilful fantasy, so many Little Nells to be sacrificed to his myth of colonial bliss?

Back in London they dragged their feet. The American writer Ralph Waldo Emerson dined with Dickens in the spring of 1848 and listened as he vented his frustration. 'When it comes to embarking for Australia they prefer to go back to the London street, though in these times it would seem as if they must eat the pavement. Such is the absurd love of home of the English race, said Dickens.' Undaunted, he ploughed on, his faith in emigration unshaken. Quite the reverse. The beginning of 1850 – midway into *David Copperfield* and the eve of publication for the first number of *Household Words* – saw him reporting on detailed research for Miss Coutts on the expenses of chartering a ship. A hundred and fifty emigrants bound for Sydney would, he told her, cost £1,581 and 5 shillings.

Household Words would be loud in its support of emigration projects. The special relationship was cemented in its first number with a heroine for the cause and an article entitled 'A Bundle of Emigrants' Letters'. It began: 'A scheme has been propounded by Mrs Chisholm, a lady to whose great exertions in reference to the emigration of the poor, especially of her own sex, the public is much indebted, – for the establishment of what it is proposed to call "A Family Colonisation Loan Society."'

In 1847, while Dickens and Miss Coutts were hatching Urania Cottage, Caroline Chisholm was touring England to promote her new scheme. Families reunited: this was Mrs Chisholm's big idea. She had spent her early married life in India, where her husband was a lieutenant in the East India Company army. When he was granted sick leave the young family decided to try a spell in Australia. Here Mrs Chisholm was struck by the quandary of newly arrived single women, who had been promised jobs but were stranded on the quayside. So she opened a Home for them, with a job centre. Then she realised that the women would not leave Sydney on their own, for the farms and cattle stations waiting for them in the interior; so she organised a wagon train.

As she dropped the girls at the farms (a useful travelling companion, she was blessed with a gift for water divining), Mrs Chisholm's trips assumed a dual purpose. Men who had been transported as convicts, and who were now well settled, wanted their wives and families to join them. Families who had left behind young children or elderly grandparents in order to qualify for government assistance now wanted them to come out too. Would Mrs Chisholm pass on their messages? Nothing would please her more. In her eyes the family was the force to tame the wild colonies; wives and young children were, she said, 'God's police'.

When she arrived back in England at the end of 1846 she had a son born on the voyage tucked under one arm and a stack of seven hundred letters under the other. Like Dickens, Caroline Chisholm appreciated the power of the individual voice. She exploited the settlers' letters in propaganda for her brainchild, the Family Colonisation Loan Society.

Families would be lent money to emigrate, which they would repay when they could. Unsurprisingly, the repayments came in slowly if at all, but thousands benefited from her work.

She had a canny eye for publicity, and gave her leaflets titles like 'Comfort for the Poor! Meat Three Times a Day!!' First to join was a Chartist carpenter, whom Mrs Chisholm persuaded to give up beer and tobacco so he could put by a shilling a week. Families were invited to meetings at her house in Charlton Place, Islington, now commemorated by a blue plaque. Here they could bond with other families and form groups to safeguard single women travelling alone. A corner of the room was kitted out as an emigrant berth, and meetings opened with a short practical speech from Mrs Chisholm. 'On one occasion', her biographer recorded, 'she began her discourse straight off with: "The best shoes for wearing on board ship have moderately stout soles, and no heels."'

The Chisholm strategy worked. Her postbag averaged three hundred letters a day. They could be addressed to 'The Emigrant's Friend' and find their way to her. At one time she was as well known as Florence Nightingale, who called herself Chisholm's 'friend and pupil'. Once she had raised enough money to charter a whole ship for her emigrants, she set about redesigning it to her own specifications, which included what sound like the first couchettes in the history of travel.

The operation was all bustle, as her biographer noted. 'From morning until evening the pen hands of the Chisholms seemed never to cease moving, except when relieved in order to shake hands with their numerous unknown friends. Callers came, asked their questions, and departed; the door was always on the swing; no one was asked to give name or address.' In 1850 one of the callers was Charles Dickens. He was on the lookout for copy for his new magazine, and pounced on the emigrants' letters which he printed verbatim, 'surely very pleasant to read, and very affecting'.

During his visit they talked about Urania Cottage and she asked him about the pianos. While he was quick to applaud her work, and the ship's berth would have appealed to him, other aspects of the Islington house appalled him. There were five children, one a sickly newborn baby, and almost no domestic help. 'I dream of Mrs Chisholm, and her housekeeping,' Dickens wrote to Miss Coutts. 'The dirty faces of her children are my constant companions.' Two years later the philanthropist Mrs Jellyby amused readers of *Bleak House*, 'sitting in quite a nest of waste paper' with her eyes fixed on Africa. Esther counts four envelopes in the gravy.

Mrs Chisholm herself returned to Australia with more schemes for improving emigrant life. She spent the money that was collected as a testimonial for her on hostels for travellers, known as Chisholm's Shakedowns, and had to make ends meet by selling sweets and giving English lessons to Chinese workers. She ended her days back in England, poor and obscure.

Household Words continued to support emigration. In 1852 it challenged readers to 'prove their sincerity' by sending subscriptions to Sidney Herbert's Fund for Promoting Female Emigration. This charity ran true to Victorian form in its gathering together of the well-heeled and the well-connected. Herbert himself was the son of an earl, a Tory MP by the age of twenty-two; his biographer testified to the 'delicate aroma' of his personal charm. Stirred by Henry Mayhew's path-breaking reports in the *Morning Chronicle* on street life throughout the autumn of 1849, Herbert wrote letters to the newspapers and marshalled an impressive committee composed of Right Honourables, Most Nobles and Right Reverends. 'Let those who have much, give much,' he urged. And they did. Top of the subscription list came Queen Victoria and Prince Albert with five hundred pounds.

Herbert appreciated the sensitivities of his patrons and assured them, 'In the selection of emigrants one condition must never be lost sight of. None but women of good character must be assisted to go. There must be no taint or discredit upon them to mar their prospects when they arrive at their new home.' The money duly came in, and the women went out. Although Disraeli mocked – 'thirty-five thousand needle-women to be deported at five pounds a piece!' – in its first four years the Fund helped over a thousand women to emigrate to Australia, New Zealand and Canada.

By the time of the fervent endorsement in *Household Words* in 1852, the Fund was already facing criticism. Despite the best efforts of the ladies who interviewed the applicants, some of the young women were not at all the 'distressed needlewomen' of unblemished character the Fund was designed to help. They were in fact prostitutes who thought they would prefer working in a warmer climate.

To the Fund's embarrassment the affair reached the London stage, where it was satirised in Joseph Coyne's one-act farce *Wanted, One Thousand Spirited Young Milliners for the Gold Diggings!* A lawyer's clerk and a medical student dress up as Madame Vanderpants and her assistant Miss Smithers, and advertise an emigration scheme in order to entice girls to their rooms. 'What are the prospects for young women in our line in Australia?' enquires plucky young needlewoman Angelica. 'Why my dear', replies Tip the lawyer's clerk, 'there's in the first place a prospect of seven thousand disconsolate diggers waiting with open arms upon the beach . . . and what with drinking rum and hunting kangaroos, the men die so fast there that an active young women may calculate upon six husbands per annum at least.' 'Oh', says Angelica, 'I'm sure the place will suit us.' It is all good clean fun – 'Don't Miss Smithers swear uncommon strong?' 'Bless me, Madame Vanderpants has a chin like a nutmeg grater' – and the milliners revenge themselves by sticking their needles into the two young men.

Official enquiries dogged Sidney Herbert's Fund, and he subsequently targeted more middle-class women to assist. They would not be plain sailing either, as Maria Rye found with her Female Middle-Class Emigration Society a decade later in the 1860s. 'The country is teeming with unemployed Governesses', complained one arrival to Australia in 1865. From New Zealand a woman ended her letter to Miss Rye with a heartfelt PS: 'Oh tell the young women to work hard at home and remain there.' On the other hand, Miss Jackson reported from South Africa that 'English servants are very scarce they never stay long in a place and do as they like and give themselves great airs generally.'

Dickens and Miss Coutts wisely stuck to their domestic servants. They took in a few of Sidney Herbert's rejects, one of them 'above the general run of our girls, but she can't write'. As ever, Dickens was more interested in literacy and motivation than morality. He was swayed by 'her trembling very much while I was talking to her, and being extremely grateful when I gave her hope'. In these young women Dickens was investing hopes of his own. He dramatised the moment of their departure and gave it to David Copperfield to witness, as he makes his farewells at Gravesend:

We went over the side into our boat, and lay at a little distance to see the ship wafted on her course. It was then calm, radiant sunset. She lay between us, and the red light; and every taper line and spar was visible against the glow. A sight at once so beautiful, so mournful, and so hopeful, as the glorious ship, lying, still, on the flushed water, with all the life on board her crowded at the bulwarks, and there clustering, for a moment, bare-headed and silent, I never saw.

CHAPTER FOURTEEN

Urania Afloat

> Among the great beams, bulks, and ringbolts of the ship,
> and the emigrant-berths, and chests, and bundles, and
> barrels, and heaps of miscellaneous baggage – lighted up,
> here and there, by dangling lanterns; and elsewhere by the
> yellow daylight straying down a windsail or a hatchway
> – were crowded groups of people, making new friendships,
> taking leave of one another, talking, laughing, crying,
> eating and drinking; some, already settled down into
> the possession of their few feet of space, with their little
> households arranged, and tiny children established on
> stools, or in dwarf elbow-chairs; others, despairing of a
> resting-place, and wandering disconsolately.
>
> *David Copperfield, Chapter 57*

First into Urania, first out to Australia. When the *Calcutta* weighed anchor off Gravesend in January 1849, her decks were crammed with emigrants bidding their farewells to the last of England. Among them were Julia Mosley, Martha Goldsmith and Jane Westaway. Jane was the mainstay of the advance party, Julia had been in the first intake and Martha – well, Dickens still wasn't sure about her. What sort of voyage did they have?

Steam came late to the Australia run, and the voyage usually took between three and four months. The *Calcutta* was a three-masted sailing ship, known as a barque. A slow old ship, she had been built in 1819. This was one of her final trips and lasted five months, 'an unusually long voyage' commented the *South Australian Register*. She arrived in Port Adelaide on 21 June, one day after the *Posthumous*, which had set out nearly two months later in the middle of March.

The *Posthumous* was carrying a second Uranian flotilla. Rosina Gale, the quiet London orphan in the first intake, had made the most of her year's training. She was now an excellent needlewoman. Rubina Waller was with her, also one of those first girls. 'Father in law bad' noted Miss Coutts. Rubina had been in prison but not, as most of them were, for theft. Perhaps she was one of the many prostitutes convicted under the Vagrant Act. Her past life left its mark and she took a while to find her feet at Shepherd's Bush. Dickens monitored the progress of these girls carefully, and claimed to know them 'very well'. Rubina, he reported more than once, was laid up with the gout. Over the months her health and spirits improved. By the time she had been there a year she was throwing her weight about. It was Rubina who was 'principal belligerent' in the fight with the grim assistant matron Mrs Furze, the 'nutmeg-grater' as Dickens called her.

With Rosina and Rubina was Emma Lea, another girl from that first intake, 'of whom I am disposed to be hopeful' wrote Dickens; he thought she seemed so 'sincerely anxious' to be admitted. She did have a temper though, which landed her in trouble for calling 'another girl by opprobrious names' and being 'violent and defiant'. Under the proposed marks regime Dickens was expounding to Miss Coutts, Emma would have been punished with loss of earnings times four: it was an elaborate tariff. As it was, he had to make do with freezing her into docility by the 'severity' of his dealings with her. It seems to have worked; Emma mended her ways.

The *Calcutta* and the *Posthumous* were passenger ships, not government-sponsored ones. When Dickens and Angela Burdett Coutts first embarked on their Urania venture they did have government schemes in mind. Then Dickens instantly qualified this approach with 'a doubt of all Governments in England'. He did, however, start a correspondence with Alfred Engelbach at the Colonial Land and Emigration Commission, the body in charge of government-assisted emigration. There were two Engelbach brothers working at Coutts's Bank, one as Angela's secretary; this sounds like a third. Later the wife of one of them enjoyed calling at Urania Cottage to dispense advice and generally depress everyone there. Dickens requested Miss Coutts as tactfully as he could, 'if you would deem it right, gradually to soften down the frequency of Mrs Engelbach's visits'.

Throughout the autumn of 1848 Dickens investigated Emigration Companies and government grants. The forms he was sent went into exhaustive detail. They demanded references from the minister of the would-be migrant's parish plus two more up-standing householders, not including publicans. The more Dickens discovered the more he was dismayed. The prospect of shiploads of needy emigrants *en masse* did not match his founding vision of forward-looking pioneers in their twos and threes. Besides, he considered his well-groomed Urania graduates were a cut above the rest. He fell into hot water for bad-mouthing assisted emigrants in *Household Words* as 'the refuse of the workhouse' and had to apologise, but that did not alter his opinion.

In the end Dickens decided to go it alone, as he usually did. He chose private rather than public, which was a mistake. Government ships carrying assisted emigrants were closely regulated, with an eye to both physical health and mental well-being. Over ninety-eight per cent of the government emigrants who made the voyage to Australia in the second half of the nineteenth century arrived in good physical shape. In some cases emigrants enjoyed better diet than they had at home during the famine years. This may have been why over half of the two hundred and twenty adolescent girls on board the *Roman Emperor* bound for Australia menstruated for the first time during the voyage.

If Dickens had been a little less high-handed he could have made life easier for his young women – and for later researchers, since government ships were meticulously documented. More to the point, single women were segregated at the other end of the ship from the single men, and supervised by matrons specially appointed and paid for their work. Unless they were accompanied by a chaperone, single women on ordinary passenger ships would be unsupervised. Martha, Jane and Julia had to be trusted to look out for each other, and then left to their own resources.

It could have been Dickens's antipathy to officialdom which swayed him most. The Government Emigration Office was at Park Street in Westminster, and 'If red tape were a plant', scoffed *Household Words* on its front page at the end of February 1852, 'the Park Street office would carry off a medal at a flower show'. (The article celebrated the work of Caroline Chisholm, during the week which also saw the publication of the first number of *Bleak House*.) But it also happened that a wave of bad publicity was crashing down on government projects, with single women as prime targets. Most infamous were the fifty-six women known as 'the Belfast girls'.

Their arrival in Australia on the *Earl Grey* in 1848 triggered a chain of enquiries between London, Sydney and Dublin. Accusations flew thick and fast. According to one witness the women had been 'violent and disorderly, with habits of pilfering, grossly profane and obscene language, many of them had been common prostitutes'. Mrs Cooper, the matron in charge of them on the voyage, protested, 'I was led to believe they were nice orphan girls.' Orphan girls, snorted another witness: some of them were nearer thirty than thirteen. As the evidence stacked up, one thing was clear. The women on the *Earl Grey* had careered out of control. Witnesses testified to intimacies between the women and the ship's officers, to fights between the women and the ship's cooks, and to threats to knock Mrs Cooper's teeth down her throat. She herself was to blame, concluded the Poor Law Commissioners back in Ireland. She had not marked the women's clothes properly so they stole each other's. She had not organised anything for them to do on the voyage, in the shape of work or school. And she had 'failed to prevent constant and unrestrained intercourse on deck between the crew and the orphans'. Although the London office defended Mrs Cooper, they had to agree that better arrangements were needed in future.

Meanwhile, trouble was erupting on two more emigrant ships. So 'heinous' were the crimes on the *Sobraon*, reported the *South Australian Register* in Adelaide, that 'they led to the death of one individual, who had been seduced by one of the persons on board'. On the *Ramilies* the captain and ship's doctor both faced accusations of physical abuse. Four girls were stripped to the waist and flogged 'sailor fashion' by the captain himself. The subsequent enquiry heard how the ship's carpenter 'made cages, by the direction of the captain, so constructed that the girls could neither stand, sit upright, nor sit down, till the carpenter removed a board on his own responsibility'. To clinch his case for the prosecution, Lord Mountcashel pulled from his pocket 'the very rope which flogged, and had come back as a witness against this country'.

Stricter legislation was now inevitable. The tighter regulations, the better supervision of single women, and the Passenger Acts of the next few years put an end to most of this anarchy and abuse. Fellow passengers would continue to grumble about noisy and promiscuous female emigrants, but the crimes they cited, of 'larking with the darkies' (Lascar sailors) or serenading Chinese passengers with choruses of 'Chinky Chinky Chinaman' showed how much things had changed.

For Dickens, the picture of his young women going out with quantities of yet more young women never appealed, whether they were sailing public or private. Anti-Irish prejudice – standard issue for the time – may have played its part too. But he was ambitious for his young women. He shied away, as always, from the idea of them mixing with their peers. If possible, he would pretend they were quasi-middle class. He would provide chaperones for them if he could, and was relieved to find Miss Morris, an emigrating nursery governess, whom he engaged to accompany Rosina, Emma and Rubina.

He also wanted to protect them from travelling steerage (third class), even if it cost more. A steerage passage would be about twelve pounds, against fifteen to twenty-five for intermediate, the next class up. Above that was second, then first. Intermediate passengers travelled on the same deck as steerage passengers, and organised as they did into 'messes' of between six and ten for their meals. But they enjoyed the privacy of cabin accommodation. By comparison, steerage sleeping quarters were crowded, cramped and communal; single women slept in shared berths. Indeed, Miss Rye's middle-class emigrants sometimes protested at anything less than first class: 'Do not Miss Rye send any more ladies out Second Class I shall never forget the passage in my life.'

Which class did the Uranians travel? Dickens's preference for intermediate led to a tussle with Mr Engelbach at the government emigration office. Engelbach advised steerage, but Dickens thought he was over-influenced by his work with the government paupers. Writing to Miss Coutts on the day the *Posthumous* sailed, Dickens voiced his own distaste. 'I have no doubt myself that it [steerage] is very bad, that Miss Morris had no idea what it was, when she shipped herself with that order of passengers.' Aware of the extra expenses which intermediate passages would cost, he marshalled his brief skilfully.

I never was so much astonished in my life as when I saw the Steerage of an American Liner – *on the passage* – and I remember Mr Tracey's face assuming a most extraordinary appearance when I told him the young women were going in the Steerage of the Posthumous. I mention this, as he is a naval officer of considerable experience, and universally respected.

On the other hand, he was annoyed with the girls who had already written to Miss Coutts to complain about the conditions in steerage. 'I doubt their delicacy very much indeed, and I think they should have undergone anything short of actual offence, before they dreamed of taking such a step.' Shipboard life meant roughing it a bit, and 'That about the washing is sheer nonsense'. In the end it looks as though the *Calcutta* women wangled an upgrade, trusting Miss Coutts to pay the difference.

These were not the only bills landing on her desk. The chaperone was another expense to add on, as was the substantial kit for each emigrant. The government stipulated a 'decent wardrobe' for their passengers. For women this included two dresses, six shifts, two pairs of shoes, sheets, towels, bedding and mess utensils, as well as a good supply of soap and brown paper. The Urania women could hardly have been given less. They packed their smart new trunks full of the stout clothes they had made themselves, plus all the bits and pieces which agents in London advised for the well-equipped emigrant. In their pockets was the money they had earned from the marks scheme.

Though Martha, Jane and Julia had thought of little else for months, leaving Urania was a wrench. Mrs Holdsworth accompanied them as far as Gravesend. Nothing could have been arranged more kindly, Dickens thought. She and the girls cried heartily: there could be no turning back now. And without a chaperone, this first trio would have to fend for themselves.

After the steady Urania routine the noisy sprawling lower decks of the *Calcutta* came as a shock. Best to treat it all as an entertaining panorama, to take the line favoured by Lucy Edwards, an out-of-work servant from Holborn who had her passage paid for by Sidney Herbert's Fund. She evoked her temporary billet in a reassuring letter to her father.

> The Ship when it was rocking afforded me great pleasure for to see the things rattling about plates and dishes rattling the Children crying the girls a going into fits the Captain a giving orders the Matron ordering the girls to be quiet because of the Captain.

Born in the busy port of Plymouth, Jane Westaway might have some nautical experience, though she was a farmer's daughter. Julia and Martha were both country girls who had grown up far inland and never even seen the sea before. Once they had found their sea-legs they had to settle in for the duration. The ancient *Calcutta*, snail of sailing ships, would be their home for nearly half a year.

Long haul under sail was a unique experience, as a passenger in the 1860s remarked: 'Three months at sea welded us into a community. The passengers did not spend their time counting the days to the next port, as passengers on a steamer do. They settled down to a daily round.' Already used to communal life, the Urania girls adapted well to the 'little village' of the steerage decks, where 'in one of the corners', wrote a young emigrant called Fanny Davis in 1858, 'will be about two dozen singing, in another a lot talking scandal about everybody . . . In another place will be a lot of Scotch girls dancing with one of them imitating the bagpipes.'

The voyage was a hiatus, a moment of limbo between two lives. There might be little to do. For government ships a new organisation, the British Ladies' Female Emigrant Society, had the bright idea of providing materials, needles and cotton for making shirts. This would keep the women busy, and they could sell the shirts when they landed. The society also provided tracts, Bibles and matrons: not always for the better 'harmony and discipline of the ship', noted a report by Charles La Trobe, superintendent of Port Phillip in Victoria. The ladies' committee asked the matrons to report back to them, which he thought 'tended to produce a system of espionage'. The atmosphere was soured further by 'religious rancour'. The Protestant tracts upset the Catholic girls, the Catholic matron annoyed the Protestant ladies' committee.

Looking like the respectable servants they had reinvented themselves to be, Urania girls were well placed to exploit the short-term market. The orphan from Drouet's orphanage who had been apprenticed to an artificial flower maker earned good money by making flowers for the ladies on board, who in turn made a pet of her. Ladies also propositioned likely servants for the voyage. Plain Martha Goldsmith was snapped up to work as a nurse by a woman called Mrs Harris who was travelling first class with her husband and child. More money in Martha's pocket, which might not be a blessing. Alcohol was readily available on passenger ships like the *Calcutta*. Martha, Julia and Jane were travelling unsupervised, after a year's surveillance in Shepherd's Bush. The freedom might well go to their heads.

Midway through the voyage the responsible Jane thoughtfully took the trouble to send back a progress report, much to Dickens's relief: 'very encouraging and hopeful indeed'. That they wrote letters at all was, to him, a good sign. He was surprised when the *Posthumous* girls asked for more writing paper. Their spelling and handwriting – and this went for Jane's too – were dreadful, he thought, even after a year's lessons. Although he agreed with Miss Coutts that the young women should not get into 'the habit of asking', he liked the idea of them having more paper. He explained why:

> Some of them may have nobody to write to; but the separation even from so much Earth that they have been used to, is a tremendous one, and the feeling that they *can* connect themselves with England by a few pothooks, twenty times or thirty times, instead of six or eight, is not an unwholesome one. Indeed I am inclined to believe that it has its root in a sentiment that it is desirable, with a view to our future hopes of them, to encourage.

What a shame none of these letters survive. Indeed, so few do from women's sea voyages at this time, that the discovery of Amy Henning's 1854 *Calcutta* journal looked like a great find. But this was a different *Calcutta*, a new steamship built in 1852. Amy and her sister travelled first class, read *Mary Barton* to each other, tasted their first bananas when they went ashore at Cap Verde, and had nothing to do with the women on the lower decks. Any women employed as

servants ate with the children. The men in Amy's party had more contact. Forbidden to smoke on their own deck, they 'retire among the
second class passengers and favour them'. Although Amy and her sisters
never 'went below', other ladies might indulge in some on-board parish
visiting. Jessie Campbell and her friend Mrs Macdonald 'went down to
the steerage and women and girls berths' on the *Blenheim* in 1840 and
commented: 'Quite delighted with the cleanliness of them'.

Jane Westaway's letter reached London in mid-April. After that
there would be no more news until November. Dickens and Miss
Coutts fidgeted. He asked her for 'any intelligence of any of our emigrants'; she wrote three times to Augustus Short in Adelaide. When
Short finally did have something to report, it was not good. Aware
of his patron's anxieties, he had dispatched his brother-in-law out to
the *Calcutta* even before it docked at Port Adelaide. He was armed
with a message from the bishop: Martha, Jane and Julia should wait on
board until the bishop could see them and find them jobs. Passengers
were usually allowed fourteen 'lay' days while the ship was in port, for
finding employment and lodgings. But the trio had other ideas. By
the time Short drove out to Port Adelaide the next day, the young
women had all flown, 'leaving the worst character behind them'. Mrs
Harris had sacked Martha for 'misconduct'; all three, he was told, 'had
returned to their old courses & [were] totally unfit to be recommended as
household servants'.

'And here I may say', commented the bishop annoyingly, though he
certainly had a point, 'that among a set of young men as "intermediate
passengers" they were placed in a situation the most tempting to persons
under their circumstances.' These young men are the ne'er-do-wells,
he explained, 'who go out to mend their fortunes or characters, not having done well in England. They mess with the mates, and have much
idle time on their hands.' This was just the wrong company for 'your
charges'. They should go steerage, where single women 'are more looked
after and their conduct more jealously watched by their neighbours'.

With the deepest forebodings Short moved on to the *Posthumous*,
only to find that Emma and Rubina had also already jumped ship,
much 'against Miss Morris's advice and remonstrances'. She had not
appreciated the finer points of Miss Coutts's girls and 'gave a very indif-
ferent account of them both'. The bishop tried to be sanguine. 'Tho

wilful and I believe inclined to drink they were not so abandoned as the other three.' In his opinion, all five would join forces and 'do no credit to the "Home"'. He had heard a rumour that 'Goldsmith and Lea are said to be engaged to be married' and hoped it was true. Not as keen as Miss Coutts on this mission, but after all she was paying his salary, he added: 'in this way only, have I any hope, that *here* and *there*, one may be reclaimed.' He did not mention Rosina, although she is on the list of passengers arrived on the *Posthumous*; she may have been lying low. Short was more concerned about Miss Morris, who 'seems a very respectable person, but I pity her exceedingly at her age to struggle with the difficulties of a new Colony is a fearful experiment.'

The long months of planning, the year of training and transformation: all this for nothing. The young women had not behaved well, but the organisers were partly to blame for sanctioning the lack of supervision. Too much freedom had beckoned too soon, straight after the close watches of Shepherd's Bush. And the new personas the young women were supposed to inhabit did not quite fit yet. If they looked placid and respectable, they had not yet had the chance to play out the part in reality. Prey to anxiety about the uncertainties ahead, they were now exposed to temptations hard to shut their tiny cabin door on. How inviting and comforting a spot of drink and male company must have sounded.

Back in London Dickens read out the bishop's letter to a committee chorus of 'heavy disappointment and great vexation'. He could not resist a dig about Martha – 'I must claim, once more, to have been never a believer in Goldsmith' – nor could he pass by the opportunity to ride his hobby horse: 'I think the Bishop's emphasising marriage as their only chance of reclamation, most important. That idea I have steadily had in view, always.' But it was a blow, which Dickens parried by bouncing on to the front foot. 'God send we may do better with some of the others!' And perhaps a different destination. Miss Coutts had another bishop up her sleeve, Robert Gray in South Africa. She had nobbled him in 1847, before he sailed for Cape Town. He said he would 'do everything I can' to help the women she sent out. Later he warned her that it might be tricky to find them all jobs 'in the families of Clergymen', and that colonists suspected such emigrants of being convicts 'under feigned names'.

Robert Gray was no stranger to opposition. During his time in South Africa he stoked up intense religious controversy: the heat still rises from the pages of the episcopal biographies. Most contentious was his clash with the bishop of Natal, John Colenso, who had translated much of the Bible into Zulu. 'When questioned by Zulu converts, he admitted that much of the Old Testament was not factually true.' An ardent missionary (and apologist for polygamy), Colenso was also attracted by the new German biblical scholarship and went in for some biblical commentary on his own account. Gray accused him of heresy – but did he have the right to do so? The case ricocheted round church and civil courts; the vicarages of England talked of little else. It took years off Gray's life. But while he was back in London for the squabbling he took advantage of the Urania connection to call on Dickens and finagle tickets to his public readings.

What the first Australian crossings demonstrated so graphically was the vulnerability of the young women. Good captains were rapidly becoming as essential as good colonies. 'There *are* respectable *married* captains, and surgeons who fear God!' August Short tried to reassure Miss Coutts after the shambles of the *Calcutta*. She sent her agent William Wardley down to the docks to investigate on her behalf. In May 1850 he called on the 'well respected' Captain Lidgett, who recommended Natal as a likely destination, 'but they do not consider it advisable to send more than five of that class in one vessel'. The first captain Wardley approached could smell trouble in the passengers he was being offered, and 'positively declined' them at anything less than fifty pounds a head – an exorbitant rate.

Finally, Wardley managed to reel in Captain Brown on the *Justina*, 'the same ship that carried out your young females on a former occasion'. Taking his duties seriously, Wardley went on board to 'inspect every part of the ship, which appears to be fitted up as conveniently as possible. I saw the captain who is a very respectable person. He assures me that everything should be done to protect females – a respectable and experienced matron will go with them. There will also be on board a clergyman and a schoolmaster.' Wardley relayed the captain's advice that the emigrants should travel intermediate: 'should there be three females together, they can have a separate enclosed cabin entirely to themselves.' But Miss Coutts must have blanched at the extra expense because the receipt issued to Mr Wardley lists three steerage passages at ten pounds each.

For all the precautions and inspections, these were still private ships, and Dickens had to admit that they were 'for the most part disgracefully managed'. He confessed to Elizabeth Gaskell that 'the Voyage out, has been, and still is, our great difficulty. . . . The temptations to a renewal of the old life on board, we find a most serious and disheartening circumstance.' Stubbornly, he persisted on sticking to private rather than public. In 1851 he is still asking Harry Wills to get inside information from 'our friend the Registrar of Merchant Seamen' on 'the individual characters' of ships to Australia, trustworthy captains a top priority.

Perhaps a complete change of continent would meet their needs. When I first found Rhena Pollard in Canada, I thought she was the only Uranian to go there. However, at least two other Urania graduates seem to have preceded her, although we do not have their names. Miss Coutts's episcopal network extended to Mary Fulford, wife of the bishop of Montreal: in June 1855 she noted her 'pleasure in being able to give you a very satisfactory report on the two young women you sent here last year. They are both in respectable situations and are conducting themselves well.' But she had dire warnings to deliver. 'The great danger lies in the acquaintances they make during the voyage. Several young girls from another Institution were sent out here about a month ago – and I am sorry to say the greater part have been led astray by companions they made during the voyage, and have been conducting themselves so ill that it will considerably damage the prospects of any others who may be sent out.'

In fact the answer to many of these problems lay on Dickens's doorstep. The young women should have travelled under the umbrella of a bigger organisation: with Mrs Chisholm's families or Sidney Herbert's needlewomen, when they started to go out at the beginning of the 1850s. There is no evidence of Urania women travelling with either of these groups, at least to begin with. In November 1851 three eighteen-year-olds from Urania, Ellen Glyn, Emma Spencer and Rosina Newman, made the crossing on the *Duke of Bedford*; again a private ship but not one used by Herbert or Chisholm. Why not?

It was partly, like so much else in the nineteenth century, a religious thing. Caroline Chisholm converted to Catholicism on her marriage, and her critics liked to accuse her of plotting to 'romanize' Australia. Sidney Herbert's wife Elizabeth, who introduced Dickens to Mrs Chisholm, moved in High Church circles and took spiritual advice from Henry Manning. After Herbert's death she too converted to Catholicism, thus cutting herself off from all her family and friends. Miss Coutts on the other hand was firmly Church of England. She did support Chisholm's enterprise with some funding, but one of the few surviving letters between them suggests at best a tepid relationship.

That was not the only reason why Miss Coutts kept her distance. Neither she nor Dickens wanted to see their hand-polished gems lost among the emigrants Herbert was conveying wholesale. Augustus Short told Miss Coutts he was dreading the arrival of the Herbert women because he assumed they would all be prostitutes. On the ships out the *soi-disant* needlewomen were winning notoriety for their obstreperous ways. The report Charles La Trobe sent back to Herbert after the *Culloden* docked in 1850 made poor reading. This was a passenger ship on which the women travelled intermediate, as the Urania women sometimes did, and with practically no supervision. The single men passed wine and beer down to the women through the ventilator; some of the crew joined in the fun, and the surgeon 'had to visit the single women's berths two or three times a night to guard against any improper intrusion.'

Worse was to come. Ellen Ellis, a lace transferer from Holborn, accused the captain himself of trying to 'accomplish her ruin' after their arrival in Port Phillip. Here the Harbour Master, a man with a well-developed sense of honour, investigated Ellen's claim. He established that Captain Ferguson had inveigled Ellen to the Rainbow hotel and brutally assaulted her. Another young woman came forward with proof that she had been seduced by the ship's surgeon. The Harbour Master denounced Ferguson for his 'unmanly and infamous intentions' but reserved his 'unmeasured reprehension' for the ship's surgeon, devious Dr Thompson who seemed 'a most pleasing and kind person, and particularly plausible and insinuating in his manners'.

On other ships Herbert's women sang rude songs to interrupt the ship's prayers; they set fire to their cabin in protest at the curfew imposed by the captain, and on the *Fortitude*, bound for Melbourne in 1852, they even managed to incite the crew to mutiny. No wonder that the Immigration Agent in Victoria reported 'a general feeling against the needlewomen' – many of them of course not needlewomen at all.

The Urania team had a lucky escape with Ellen Walsh, who spent just a few days at Shepherd's Bush before breaking through the fence with Hannah Myers. She gave Dickens the impression that she had 'only come into the Home at all, with the design of urging a certain young man to take her away from it'. Good riddance, he thought, to a 'very false, worthless, vicious person'. Her next port of call was Herbert's Fund, to whom she demurely presented herself as impoverished, though proficient at needlework and plain cooking. Herbert's ladies interviewed, approved, and duly sped Ellen off to Melbourne on the *City of Manchester*. Once at sea she came out in her true colours and was found to be 'tipsy' on several occasions. She turned out to be a waitress from the George pub in the Commercial Road.

It is not clear whether Dickens finally yielded to the advice of all the Emigration agents and experts, and sent his young women steerage on the well-regulated government ships. Here they would be under the protection of the doctors employed by the government to look after them. The story of these Victorian doctors at sea is, in the judgement of their historian Robin Haines, 'a triumph by any standards'. These 'medical police' patrolled their ships with a firm hand on everything to do with diet and sanitation. They also monitored the general atmosphere, intervening with practical remedies and prescriptions. Dr Ward, surgeon on board the *Wanderer* in 1851, proposed that

> a violin with a due supply of spare strings, resin etc, and perhaps also a clarionet or fife, be sent on board each ship. The expense would be very trifling, and if there were any musical amateurs on board, the promise of giving them the instruments at the end of the voyage would be sufficient inducement to ensure their services during the voyage. Two pairs of dumb-bells would also be a desirable addition.

Halfway to Australia on the *St Vincent* in 1849, Dr Strutt paused to reflect in his journal: 'The grand reason of the good state of health is the great attention I pay to cleanliness in all parts of the ship. Then we have fiddling and dancing every evening from seven till half past eight, which is good for the spirits, and excellent exercise.'

On this route shipwrecks were rare. Epidemics were the more real menace. Whooping cough, chicken pox, measles and scarlatina could cut swathes through the children: hence the government ships' restrictions on how many children each family could take with them. Private ships jeopardised their passengers by overcrowding and poor supervision – and they needed to make money by selling alcohol which was banned on government ships. In 1850 cholera swept through the *Douglas*, dubbed the Death Ship by an indignant press. On board was Edward Evans, brother of Dickens's publisher; he died of dropsy 'super-induced by habitual intoxication during the voyage'.

The smart deal was the arrangement reached by the Clark family, sailing on the *Fatima*, also in 1850. The Clarks were well-off and had eight children. Caroline Clark's brothers included the postal reformer Rowland Hill, as well as the two prison reformers, Frederic and Matthew Davenport (Dickens knew them both). Rather than risk a private ship, the Clarks paid for a special cabin to be fitted out on the upper deck of a government ship: the equivalent of a private bed in an NHS hospital. This would not have been an option for the Urania emigrants, but by 1853 Dickens does seem to have shifted ground. His *Household Words* article about the Home describes the women sometimes travelling as nurses or servants to 'individual ladies with children', or 'under the charge of a respectable family of emigrants'. This sounds like Mrs Chisholm's scheme. On one occasion though, we know that Dickens and Miss Coutts found a family through their own contacts – with disastrous consequences.

Alice Matthews was already twenty-four when she applied to Urania in 1856. A serious young woman, she and her friends Mary French and Annie Beaver asked to be baptised at the local church, St Stephen's in Shepherd's Bush. They were probably planning to be confirmed, with baptism as a necessary preliminary. Alice stayed at Urania much longer than most, most likely because of her bad health. Dickens noticed she was 'very poorly again' in July 1857.

By the beginning of 1859 she had recovered enough to set sail on the *Minerva* for New Zealand. She and Henrietta Baker travelled second class under the charge of the Bragg family, acquaintances of Miss Coutts. Mr Bragg's sister-in-law Harriet taught at St Stephen's School in Westminster, which was one of Miss Coutts's schools, and acquitted herself creditably. In 1856 she won a Four Pound Prize (The Five Pound Prize, said Miss Coutts that year, 'I think it best not to give'). Harriet Bragg impressed Miss Coutts with her 'indefatigable zeal and energy . . . to the beneficial results of her endeavours I can testify from my own observation.' Her emigrating in-laws seemed the ideal respectable family to take care of the Urania women, and employ them as nurses for their children.

The voyage proved too much for Alice. By the time they reached the equator her health had deteriorated drastically. She started coughing up blood; in the opinion of the ship's surgeon Dr Towle her death was imminent. He and the Chief Officer Mr Fitzsimmons were so outraged by 'the most scandalous treatment of Mr and Mrs Bragg towards the two poor girls' that they intercepted a ship bound for England in order to communicate their protest to Miss Coutts. Henrietta was kept on half-rations, and 'made a perfect slave' with washing and childcare. Alice, they wrote, was 'lying there dying no one to attend her: the poor girl wished repeatedly to see the Captain but was not allowed to send for him or to have any one else in the cabin but Mrs Bragg.' Mr Bragg turned so drunk and violent that all the porter and wine had to be locked up. Eventually another passenger sneaked word to the captain and he 'had the whole history of the Braggs conduct'.

It was a difficult letter to write. Towle and Fitzsimmons felt 'rather delicate in thus addressing you' but Mr Bragg was writing to her too, and 'knowing his character' they wanted to set the record straight. They reassured Miss Coutts that Alice had now been moved to a first-class cabin fitted out specially by the Captain. Mrs Cunningham, one of the first-class passengers, was nursing her, 'acting like a mother'. Her husband sat by Alice's bedside to write down her last message for Miss Coutts. She 'whispers to me to give her love and duty to Mrs Brown and yourself.' He added a few sad remarks of his own: 'Miss M now ship's favourite but dying – can't keep anything down but Death has no terrors for her.'

Alice seems to have died soon after this. Mr Bragg showed no contrition or sorrow. He sent his version of events to his sister-in-law Harriet, confident she would relay it to Miss Coutts. According to him, Alice had injured her left side by falling out of her chair, 'an easy chair similar to Mother's which I bought at Graves End'. His wife Caroline 'was up 2 nights with her, Henrietta has behaved ill'. Fortunately another passenger came forward to look after Henrietta when they arrived in New Zealand.

Alice is the only Urania girl we know of to die *en route* for the colonies. Just how many women did emigrate from Shepherd's Bush, and how many can be traced? Dickens's mid-term report for the *Household Words* article in 1853 notched up thirty-three emigrants so far, though three of these had 'relapsed on the passage out'. But their names are hard to come by. Dickens writes more about the first two groups of three on the *Calcutta* and the *Posthumous* because he naturally felt more anxious about this crucial new stage in his experiment. Apart from this first six, there is Rhena Pollard we already know about in Canada, plus two more unnamed emigrants there; Henrietta Baker in New Zealand; and possibly about half a dozen in South Africa.

Occasionally Dickens mentions a letter from an emigrant such as Rachael Bradley, 'which I retain for the present, to note it in our book'. Or it is 'delightful to hear about Watts'. After some trouble they had just experienced with a dunder-headed clergyman trying to foist an unsuitable candidate on them, Elizabeth Watts 'tasted like a sweetmeat'. Once, the briefest of mentions: 'Beaver/Daley/Chalk/and/Jones/ may now be sent abroad'. Emma Spencer, Ellen Glyn and Rosina Newman appear on the 1851 census at Urania, and then again together as a threesome on the passenger list for the *Duke of Bedford* which docked in Melbourne in 1852. When the *Justina* arrived in Durban in November 1850 the list of passengers in the *Natal Witness* has two identifiable Urania names on it. Rachael Bradley was the girl who squabbled with Isabella Gordon; Maria Cridge was the girl Mrs Morson took to St Bartholomew's Hospital, where she stayed for three months. Between them on the list is Elizabeth Nadauld, presumably another Urania graduate since we know that Miss Coutts paid for three fares on the *Justina*. And that is about all we have to go on.

More than a century and a half later, has the trail gone too cold to follow? Can we find out what happened to Martha and Julia and Jane after they'd bolted ashore to escape from the cramped lower decks of the *Calcutta* and the bishop's lukewarm welcome? I would have to go to Australia to see.

18 **Caroline Chisholm** assisted many
to emigrate to Australia in the 1850s.
She was dauntless: the governor of New
South Wales recalled that she argued
'as though she thought her reason and
experience [was] worth as much as mine'.

19 **Etching of a barque** (1829). In the decades before
1880, 1.3 million people emigrated from the United
Kingdom to Australia on sailing ships such as this.
The journey took an average of one hundred days.

20 **The 'distressed needlewomen' dispatched to Australia** by Sidney Herbert's Fund for
Promoting Female Emigration featured in the press as 'objects of deep commiseration'.
Here Herbert and 'the noble ladies who have been working so hard on their behalf' bid
farewell to some demure looking emigrants.

21 The German painter Alexander Schramm arrived in Adelaide in the same year as the first Urania emigrants. **A scene in South Australia** includes a female servant in the domestic group meeting an Aboriginal family. Urania graduates could have found themselves in scenes like this, but there is little evidence of their lives in Australia.

22 **Rhena Cole,** *née* **Pollard,** photographed some time after her marriage to Oris in Canada in 1856. Critics have suggested that Rhena was the model for Tattycoram in *Little Dorrit*, 'a handsome girl with lustrous dark hair and eyes, and very neatly dressed'.

CHAPTER FIFTEEN

Martha, Julia, Rosina

Unexpected recognitions have taken place on Sundays
in lonely churches to which the various members of the
little congregations have repaired from great distances.
Household Words, 23 April 1853

GOOD NEWS OF the pioneers was vital. It lifted morale back at
Urania Cottage, and blazed an encouraging trail for those coming next. What a relief, then, to have better tidings three months after
Augustus Short's gloomy bulletin from Adelaide. In South Africa the
first three arrivals found the niches they were designed for: domestic
service in trustworthy families. Robert Gray's report highlighted the
respectability of it all. 'They attend Church every Sunday, and have
family prayers every Evening. . . . They all looked particularly clean –
tidy – and quiet in their manners.'

Gray had extra cause for rejoicing. Miss Coutts could not have picked
a worse time for Cape Town. The colony was up in arms, embroiled in a
crisis over exactly the sort of emigrants the Uranians might reveal
themselves to be. Declaring the Cape a place 'to which convicts may
be transported', the government in London packed off a shipload of
Irish nationalists on the *Neptune*, including John Mitchel, one of the
leaders of the Young Ireland movement. The good citizens of Cape
Town were having none of it. Vehemently opposed to the reception of
any transported convicts, they formed an Anti-Convict Association,
which forced commercial and official business to a standstill. Violent
demonstrators took to the streets. When the *Neptune* finally appeared

over the horizon, the governor of Cape Town felt compelled to order her to remain off-shore. There she stayed for the next five months, until despatches from London countermanded the original instructions and rerouted her to Tasmania.

It was into this turmoil that the first Urania emigrants for South Africa sailed in the middle of 1849. Robert Gray kept his head and disposed of them diplomatically among his contacts. He could rely on the support of the governor of Cape Town, the old campaigner Sir Harry Smith and his exotic Spanish wife Juana, who were long-standing friends of Miss Coutts. Nevertheless, Juana found the obligation rather a chore.

The only two Cape Town Uranians we know by name could certainly be numbered among the most successful of the old girls. By July 1850 Caroline Canlon was comfortably established in the Cape after only a year there. She was married, and a useful first base for new arrivals. Her husband was a kind practical man who enjoyed using his hands to build a settler's version of the good life. 'We live very happy and comfortable together' wrote Caroline from the small-holding where the couple grew all they needed. She corresponded with Miss Coutts, and when Dickens wanted to end his article on the Home for Homeless Women with a ringing endorsement, it was one of Caroline's letters which did the trick. That is why it survives. Many of the emigrants did write to the 'Honnoured Ladies' as Caroline calls them, and send presents. Miss Coutts preserved them in a special box, but it vanished long ago.

It is a perfect letter, and were it not for Miss Coutts's anxious overseeing of the article you might suspect Dickens of writing it himself. Caroline comes across as an affectionate soul, weeping 'tears of joy' when she gets a letter from Miss Coutts. She conjures up the domestic rural idyll Dickens wished for them all, with the pig 'so fat that he could not see out of his eyes he used to have to sit down to eat', and 'such a nice cat' which her husband rescued as a stray and 'now peeps over me while I am writing this . . . get down Cat do'.

The other Cape Town emigrant, Louisa Cooper, had long been a favourite. Gilbert A' Beckett put her forward after she had been discharged from the Magdalen Hospital, where they had kept her nearly two years, much longer than usual. Dickens made his customary 'close enquiries', interviewed Louisa, and was impressed. This was 'a peculiar case'. While her appearance amazed him – 'How she could be *so* neat, was a marvel to me' – her modesty affected him. 'She made little of her own case, and merely said, in reference to her being pale, that she had had "a very hard winter".' He decided that proper food would do wonders (so much for the Magdalen regime), and was so predisposed towards her that he confided to Mrs Morson in a rare burst of indiscretion. 'She was seduced, but has never done anything else wrong – has tried very hard to subsist by needle-work, and can not do it, though she is a very good worker.'

Louisa justified Dickens's faith in her. Quiet, solemn and timid, she soon became one of the reliable squad at Shepherd's Bush. Mrs Morson depended on her judgement; Mrs Marchmont was grateful for her support in the face of "some of 'em", as Louisa put it: the girls who disturbed the peace in her first days as matron. It was Louisa who took it upon herself to report the rambunctious Frances Cranstone, and Louisa who wrote the touching thank-you letter to Miss Coutts, before she left for 'the Cape', about learning to love her. 'Poor little thing' commented Dickens when he read the letter, 'I hope she will flourish out there.'

It seems that she didn't. Two years later she was back in England and calling at Shepherd's Bush. She had worked her passage back as a lady's maid but was now out of a job; could they help? Self-effacing Louisa was not pioneer material, and Dickens took pity on her. 'She seems to have had a desperately hard place, with everything to do (mantua making included) for 7 children, and to have rather overworked herself.' A servant's lot could be a complicated one. She was engaged, she told Dickens in her letter, but she and her 'young man' could not marry until he had found a gardener's place as a married man. In the meantime, she had nowhere to go.

Mrs Marchmont rallied to the rescue. She tried to find Louisa a new job, and had her back to Urania. By the time Dickens met her there three weeks later her prospects seem to have improved. He was heartened by what he saw, if not by what she gave him. 'It was very pleasant to see Louisa Cooper, nicely dressed and looking very well to do, sitting with Mrs Macartney in the Long Room. She brought me for a present, the most hideous Ostrich's Egg ever laid – wrought all over with frightful devices, the most tasteful of which represents Queen Victoria (with her crown on) standing on the top of a Church, receiving professions of affection from a British Seaman.'

Caroline Canlon's marriage was one of the seven which Dickens celebrated in his 1853 article on Urania Cottage. According to his tally at this point, thirty of the fifty-six young women who had been through Urania could be clocked up as the successes he wanted. They had emigrated, 'entered into good service, acquired a good character, and have done so well ever since as to establish a strong prepossession in favour of others sent out from the same quarter.' But it had to be small-scale and undercover.

And what about Martha and Julia and co, the vanguard six who started their new lives by going AWOL in Adelaide? By abandoning their ships so hastily they evaded Augustus Short's half-hearted reception. Not that the bishop minded too much. He more or less preached Miss Coutts a sermon on the text of all he could not do for 'these poor creatures whom you have sent out'. He could not find them jobs, or anywhere to stay, and he could not put them up himself, 'my cottage is quite filled by my own family'. Miss Coutts was relying on his ladies' committee, but they had wearied of 'Emigrant Females utterly unwilling to bear any control or take advice, and so dissolved themselves'. He now mustered his wife plus attendant clerical spouses to trace the girls, and administered Miss Coutts as much hope as he could. 'I would say, do not despair of good, tho none can, *as yet*, be reported.'

Mellicent Short was a better bet than her husband. She already had working for her a girl she had chosen from St Barnabas, the House of Charity in Soho, who sailed with them to Adelaide in 1847. This girl was, said Short's biographer, 'a great success in every way, and on leaving the Bishop's service married very well'. Mellicent was also employing another English girl as governess for her three daughters. Seventeen-year-old Frances Provis, a teacher's daughter from Wiltshire, would lend her surname to Dickens's returned convict Magwitch in *Great Expectations*: it is the alias he uses. The real Provis prospered. She married the first Postmaster in Port Lincoln and had fifteen children in seventeen years.

Despite the demand for domestic servants ('*steady* women much prized' intoned the bishop), timing was bad for the first six. Moored alongside the *Calcutta* and the *Posthumous* lay two more recent arrivals. The *Florentia* and the *Sir Edward Parry* were both loaded to the gunnels with hopeful government emigrants, many of them women. They would all be looking for work. By the mid-1850s South Australia was – a rarity in early colonial history – awash with surplus single women. The government offered three hundred of them to Tasmania, but were declined. (If they're not good enough for you they're not good enough for us, said the Tasmanians.) Still, at least Adelaide provided exactly what independent women seeking work needed: a Labour Office and a depot where they could stay. So perhaps Martha and her pals could manage without the bishop and his ladies. Urania had taught them how to reinvent themselves, now they would do it again.

But even when they had found their jobs, their problems might not be over. It is clear from his *Household Words* article that Dickens had heard from young women working up-country in remote rural areas. The journey to them might be rough. A couple of ship's surgeons, who had befriended the girls in their care during the voyage to Australia, were stung to action by the harrowing conditions. George Dodd watched his shipload of emigrants being landed at Perth in 1854, and protested directly to the Home Secretary Sir George Grey:

> The young women, many of them respectable girls, were treated most shamefully, sent off, some one hundred, others near two hundred miles into the various districts to look for work; their luggage going in a wagon, themselves having to walk that distance, over dreary wastes of sand and rock, under the guidance of a drunken convict; who on being asked where he was going to take them told them, to h-ll; this occurred outside the female depot, at 6.00 in the evening of a very wet day; no convicts could be treated worse, and they told me and the captain, had they been aware how matters were in the colony, before leaving their home, they would have committed felony, preferring to be sent out as convicts rather than emigrants.

Edward Strutt, the doctor who had arranged the healthful dancing on board the *St Vincent* in 1849, decided he would have to take matters into his own hands. He accompanied his band of adolescent Irish girls, a hundred and eight of them, on their journey from Sydney to Yass (near present-day Canberra) and still further into the bush. He organised a caravan of fourteen wagons, and all the food, drink and overnight stops for the two-hundred mile journey. It was, he wrote in his journal, 'a grand thing to keep them well fed'; these girls bore the marks of the Irish famine on their bodies. At Yass and other small centres he vetted the jobs they were offered, turning down 'improper persons' and men trying to pick out wives. Before he made the return trip to Sydney he checked up on as many as he could to make sure the youngsters were well settled. The authorities in Yass formally thanked him with 'an address expressing the general satisfaction my girls have given in Yass and the neighbourhood'.

From the letters coming back to Miss Coutts and Dickens, we can assume that Urania graduates also gave 'general satisfaction' in similarly remote up-country areas. But oh how sparse is the evidence they have left behind. The women heeded Dickens's advice, kept mum about their pasts, and slipped into obscurity. You can, though, catch glimpses of what might have been their servant lives in early paintings and writings.

Louisa Meredith, whose husband was a police magistrate in Tasmania, chose nannies for her young children from the 'Factory', the female house of correction in Hobart, and found that 'with few exceptions they behave well and industriously'. They settled more easily in the 'solitude of the bush', she thought. One girl she had for eighteen 'irreproachable' months, 'until a visit to town, and the greater opportunities for showing her pretty face, caused neglect of her duty, and an alarming exhibition of pink silk stockings, thin muslin dresses, and other town vanities.' The Merediths enjoyed a relaxed open-air life, and their nannies joined in happily: rock-pooling, playing beach games and adopting novelty pets such as bandicoots and opossums. They did, though, refuse to eat kangaroo. It was as if she had offered them 'a haunch of tiger or a wolf-chop', said Louisa Meredith. When her servants left it was usually to marry. They would settle nearby to raise their families on 'little plots of land they cultivated for themselves'.

This pastoral happy ever after appealed strongly to Dickens. His article painted a rosy picture of affectionate Urania reunions in the 'distant solitudes'. He dwelt on the 'touching circumstances' of chance meetings in tiny country churches. 'Some of the girls now married have chosen old companions thus encountered for their bridesmaids, and in their letters have described their delight very pathetically.' Can any of this be traced? Might I be able to find living descendants of any of these women? And what about the Adelaide six?

Or should it be seven? 'Shipping Intelligence' columns in Australian newspapers listed all disembarking passengers and emigrants by name. If you were waiting for a friend or relative to join you, this is how you might hear that they had now arrived. The reporter taking down the names of the Urania women on the *Posthumous* for *The South Australian Register* lists a fourth among them. 'Mary ann G. Hoye' appears in his column between Emma Sea and Rowina Gale. She does not feature among the first intakes at Shepherd's Bush, nor in the index to Dickens's *Letters*. She could have been a non-Uranian who had chummed up with Emma and Rosina during the voyage. But her name sounded familiar, and eventually I found it in a letter to Miss Coutts from Dickens at the end of 1848. Something on her part has exasperated him. 'When I think of the moral indignation of Mary Anne Hoy! (of all others!) I want somebody to attack; I become so desperately vicious.' By this time the *Posthumous* was at sea. Perhaps Mary Anne had written to complain about conditions on board. She sounds like a woman who was not afraid to assert herself: she has made sure the reporter in Adelaide includes that middle G.

But that is the last we hear of her. After that she disappears completely; so does Rubina Waller, despite her unusual name. Neither of them has left a shred of evidence behind her. In September 1850, inundated by workhouse orphans, Irish famine victims and Sidney Herbert needlewomen, government officials in Adelaide ordered a major enquiry into the fate of recent female immigrants. The enquirers counted ninety-six prostitutes on the streets, and listed two as coming over on the *Posthumous* the year before. Perhaps they were Mary Anne and Rubina. Every now and then the bishop murmured about trying to trace the Urania women, 'but events, letters, business, press so quickly press on one another that many benevolent projects slip through'. He had to eat his words about Martha Goldsmith though. A year after she arrived in Adelaide he could pass on the cheering news that she 'may be said to be recovered from perdition as well as infamy'. She was not yet married – the rumoured shipboard engagement led to nothing – and was still unsettled enough to ask Miss Coutts for 'a gift of money'. But she seems to have found herself a decent job.

As for Miss Morris, the not-so-young woman who had chaperoned Rubina, Rosina and Emma on the *Posthumous,* the bishop scotched her plans to find governess work. No one could afford her, he said. 'She must be more of an upper maid than a Teacher.' An advertisement which appeared in the *Adelaide Times* around the time of her arrival might have been her attempt to prepare the ground. 'Dry Nurse' was the heading for a modest notice at the bottom of the page. 'A person in the vicinity of Adelaide who has had considerable experience in the management of children, wishes to take a child or two to nurse. Address to M.M. at the office of this paper.'

What Miss Morris had yet to learn was that she was asking for the jewel in the crown. Jobs like this were much sought after. Gertrude Gonthier, the eponymous heroine of Caroline Atkinson's 1857 novel, *Gertrude the Emigrant: A Tale of Colonial Life*, wastes no time in pursuing the nursery governess post she hears about on the servant grapevine. She calls at the 'large and elegant residence', and admires 'the stands of beautiful flowers, the books glittering with azure, crimson and gold, the choice engravings and the open piano, which told of mental culture and refinement'. But the job in this Elysium has already been snapped up, so Gertrude must adapt to dress-making and shopwork.

Miss Morris's first year was not easy. 'Poor Miss Morris', reported Augustus Short in June 1850; 'she has been on the verge of Ruin and Insolvence, more than once.' She survived on hand-outs from him and other clergymen. There was no doubting her reliability; she took her Urania responsibilities seriously and corresponded with Miss Coutts. But was she tough enough?

If so, South Australia could offer plenty of dashing role models. The young artist Edward Snell, who also arrived in the colony in 1849, was bowled over by Miss Rogers, who

> favoured us with a call in the afternoon and staid to tea, not a bad looking lady by any means but rather an extraordinary character has been in the Colony eleven years and looks after a farm herself and talks of riding a wild horse up and down the hills here as if such a thing was nothing at all. She seemed full of pluck and good spirits, admired the colony beyond everything, and appeared to entertain a thorough contempt for every thing English.

Or there was the lady magistrate interviewed by the *South Australian Register*, who 'transacts the business, hears cases, decides, makes out judgement etc, and then hands the documents to her husband to sign.'

Without capital to fortify her, where could Miss Morris find a foothold? Probably not in Adelaide itself. The only advertisement for a governess wanted around the time of her arrival was from 'a quiet domestic family, a few miles from town'. This sounds like a euphemism for the remote outback, where women like Louisa Geohagan found work in the 1860s. She loathed it at first but soon reconciled herself to the 'strange mixture of roughing and refinement'. In her view it was 'a mistake unless very strongminded to come out here without having some relatives in the Colony'. The middle-class women Maria Rye dispatched grumbled interminably: 'I never thought I should live to be in the unhappy position that I am in now.' These women were ahead of their time: governesses would come to be appreciated in Australia, as indeed they still are. 'Govies are a unique part of rural Australia', living on remote cattle stations and providing support for distance learning, claims the 'GovernessAustralia' website, which also warns: 'Conditions can be dusty'.

For now, the bishop thought that Miss Morris would do better to try running a boarding house. Miss Coutts sent her a welcome present of ten pounds to start her off. And if the establishment where Catherine Spence's Clara Morison stays on first arriving in Adelaide is anything to go by, Miss Morris could have enjoyed a pleasant livelihood. Clara's landlady hosts a sociable tea-table for her respectable gentlemen lodgers.

Cards and singing are on offer but no dancing, because Clara and her friend object to the only music available: one of the lodgers' melodious whistling. What Clara enjoys most is the 'refreshing' book talk, preferably about Dickens. Miss Morris might have enjoyed that too.

Although Augustus Short was not much use to the Urania women, he did prove himself a friend to the needy in later years. In 1856 he opened a Female Refuge of his own, run along traditional lines (prayers and laundry); it was still in business in the 1940s. None of the handful of Urania names we have appears in their records, or in those of the Adelaide Destitute Asylum. That is encouraging. Most of the women in the Asylum's lying-in ward were domestic servants, and infant mortality rates there topped eighty per cent.

Apart, possibly, from the disappeared Rubina and Mary Anne G, the first-fleeter to stay longest in Adelaide was Julia Mosley, the tailor's daughter from Stroud who cried when she saw her bed at Urania Cottage. In November 1853 she got married in Holy Trinity Church, North Terrace; the church is still there. Her husband, Henry Cranston, was a bullock driver. Their happiness would be short-lived; tender-hearted weepy Julia was not robust enough for this demanding new world. To thrive you needed the 'happy buoyancy of mind' prescribed by the Melbourne *Argus* for all immigrants. You also needed the physical stamina of the 'strong hardworking healthy girl' called Jones, whom Dickens off-loaded to the outback after only nine months at Urania. He described her as 'a little rough and not very bright intellectually – whom it seems a sort of waste to keep here'. Julia was the opposite: a highly strung, nervy and tense woman. Only three years after her wedding she died of 'inflamation of the uterus', maybe a legacy of the sexually transmitted disease about which she had hinted to Dickens. She was twenty-eight years old.

Well, at least she married. As did all the other Urania women I have managed to trace. If they had stayed in England they might very well not have done so. Marriage rates there were lower: the 1861 census revealed nearly three million single women in the population, a figure which would increase over the next decade. By comparison, 97 per cent of women in Australia in 1861 had been married by the age of fifty.

But in Adelaide the trail went dead. The Uranians had moved on. At the time of her death Julia was living in Sandhurst, soon to be renamed Bendigo, the first and fastest growing of the gold rush cities. The remaining four of the first group all decamped to Melbourne, most likely by sea. The overland route was an arduous trek of six hundred miles, taking five weeks or more. The log book which Charles Rule kept of his journey by horse and dray in 1852 describes covering swampy marsh and desert 'of as rough a nature it is possible to conceive of'. But the magnet of the goldfields to the north of Melbourne proved irresistible, and Dickens's young women were carried along with the rush.

This episode in their odyssey we can catch briefly through the eyes of Emily Skinner, a 22-year-old contemporary of the Urania women, who emigrated to Melbourne in 1854. From there she jolted out to the diggings at Beechworth where her husband was trying his luck. With her in the wagon were 'two stout young women' who told Emily 'they had many offers of a place, as it was hard to get servants. The girls had determined to go to the diggings where high wages and easy times awaited them.'

Emily Skinner's memoir captures the moment: 'I saw a new rush in all its glory – such a rowdy place it was. Extravagance was the order of the day. It was no uncommon thing for one or two of the richest bosses to give a champagne shout; that is, to stop in the middle of the day and treat all their men with champagne, then one pound per bottle.' Business boomed in the packed hotels and restaurants; at most of them 'five or six or even more girls were kept who did the work in the day and in the evening were expected to join in the dance.' And more besides, presumably. Urania graduates? Emily gave them happy landings. 'Many of these girls made very good marriages, and in a few years were the leading members of society in the town.'

Female company could be scarce on the goldfields. Emily describes going 'a whole month without seeing a woman of any description pass by'. No doctors either, so 'people trusted in Providence and Holloway's pills'. Emily lost three young children, and valued her women friends so highly that she moved house to be closer to one of them. 'How one longed for mothers and sisters at such times, and envied the poorest women at home who in sickness generally have some relative near.'

Champagne shouts seem to have been intermittent. When George Dunderdale visited the goldfields in search of adventure in 1853 he met a digger who told him: 'There's twenty thousand men on Bendigo, and I don't believe nineteen thousand of 'em are earning their grub.' Dunderdale commented: 'It was impossible to feel jolly.'

Let us hope that some of the Uranians struck lucky. By 1855 the steady Jane Westaway was working in the mining town of Ballarat. Here she met and married Thomas Stanfield, an American miner from Illinois. Their subsequent lives cannot be traced. Thomas's father was an attorney; perhaps the couple returned to his family in America, their bags stuffed with gold. Sometimes the letters the Uranian colonists sent back were incomprehensible to Dickens. How Rachael Bradley 'got the "ladies old clothes" is inscrutable to us', he told Miss Coutts as he noted Rachael's letter from Natal in his Case Book, 'but the state of society is strange and unsettled where she is, and there may be ways and means of proceeding there, that look unlikely to old-world eyes.'

Emma Lea, the girl who had once been violent and defiant, took advantage of the reporter from *The South Australian Register* misreading her name to slip into a new identity as Emma Sea. In 1853 she married William Morgan and settled in the gold-mining town of Inglewood. She did better than Julia Mosley: after ten years of marriage she managed to have one child, a son they called Henry Richard. But he died aged eight months. Trying to care for an ailing baby without the support of mothers or grandmothers cannot have been easy. Dehydration in the scorching heat was the commonest cause of infant death. Emma had no more children, but stayed on in the state of Victoria until her death at the ripe old age of seventy-five.

Among these Urania women in Australia, one common factor was emerging. Most had few or no children; others had children who died young. Were these women unusually unlucky as mothers? One way to judge this is to compare them with other emigrants at that time. Judy Georgiou, a local historian from Gumeracha in South Australia, has been researching her great-great-grandmother, Elizabeth Bennett, who arrived in Adelaide in 1849. Elizabeth was one of eighteen teenage girls from Marylebone Workhouse in London. Many of them went on to have sizeable families. Elizabeth herself had ten children; three of them died in infancy but the other seven lived to decent ages. The workhouse girls may have fared better because they were younger when they emigrated (many of them in their early teens), and less likely to have had their fertility compromised by prostitution.

There is one shining exception. Elizabeth Watts is listed at Urania Cottage in the 1851 census; she had been at Tothill Fields prison. In 1854 she sent the letter which 'tasted like a sweetmeat' to Dickens, it was the news of her marriage that year. She and William Howard settled in a remote rural part of South Australia, and went on to have thirteen children. Sadly most of them died young, but three sons, Caleb, Gilbert and Jesse, survived to have families of their own.

The other Urania graduates moved to Melbourne or went straight there. Ellen Glyn and Emma Spencer, who had grown up together in the Clerkenwell Workhouse and been friends ever since, arrived there in 1852. With them was Rosina Newman. Within a year she was married, before the end of another year she had died at the age of nineteen. Ellen married George Poppleton in 1859: that is the only record we have of her. Emma waited longer and did not marry until 1863, eleven years after her arrival in the colony. Emma and Thomas Woolgrove had three children, two of whom died in infancy. Emma survived her husband and ran a boarding house in the pleasant suburb of Carlton, now popular for its wide shady streets, Victorian terraces and Italian cafés. When she died at the age of fifty-seven she was a widow of some substance. Her daughter Alice inherited it all, including the proceeds of a life insurance policy, ten worthless mining shares, and rent owing from two lodgers, supposed by the executors 'to be uncollectable'. Alice was made of sterner stuff and managed to retrieve the thirty-two pounds owing from Mr Nightingale. By the time the will was proved she had also got her hands on the piano, valued at forty-five pounds and Emma's prize possession: it reminded her of evenings in Shepherd's Bush. Alice's daughter Lynda died unmarried at the age of ninety-four.

And what about Martha Goldsmith, the ex-prostitute from the Magdalen Hospital whose tears had persuaded Dickens to take her in? Although she found work in Adelaide she did not stay long. On Christmas Eve 1851 she married George Hamilton in the Scots Presbyterian Church in Melbourne. The church on Collins Street had already expanded once from the original building it shared with the school. It had to be rebuilt again in the 1870s as Melbourne grew and burst at the seams. David Mitchell was the builder that time; he was the father of Nellie Melba, who started her singing career in the choir there. If Martha and George were church-goers they would have heard her sing.

The Hamiltons were in Melbourne for the beginnings of the gold rush. Back in Shepherd's Bush the young women waiting to set sail read in their *Illustrated London News* of huge consignments of gold and the lawless world of the diggings. The *Posthumous*, the ship which had brought over Rosina, Rubina and Emma, returned to England laden with nuggets of pure gold said to weigh twenty-eight pounds or more. The *Posthumous* was lucky to get away. Many sailors jumped ship to try their fortunes at the diggings as soon as they berthed in Port Phillip (the port for Melbourne), and ships would lie helplessly in harbour deserted by their crews. The population of the state of Victoria leapt from eighty thousand to half a million in just one decade.

The Hamiltons settled down to married life. George was a carpenter, and times were good. He may well have been one of the carpenters and smiths of Melbourne described in the *Illustrated London News* who 'will not let their wives be seen in a gown of less cost than ten pounds, with a shawl and bonnet to match'. The city was shooting up fast. George and Martha were among the energetic practical workers building the 'Metropolis of the Southern Hemisphere' as it was dubbed, 'Marvellous Melbourne'. When they wed, George marked the certificate with a cross while Martha signed in a clear flowing hand. By the time they both died thirty years later George could write. His script looks like a smaller version of Martha's; perhaps she taught him.

When Martha died in 1884 the couple were living in Windsor, a new inner city suburb well served by a train link to the centre. Peel Street is still an attractive place to live, quiet and shady but just off the bustle of Chapel Street with its bars and cafés. Number 56, where Martha and George lodged, has been demolished but we can see what it was like from surviving houses, pretty one-storey weatherboard buildings with wrought iron lacework detailing. In the 1860s the area was developing so fast the streets did not have names and had to make do with 'Off Stokes Street' and 'Off Nott Street'. The rate books for the last years of Martha's life show houses packed with trades and professions:

stonemasons, law clerks, butchers, teachers, stationers, dressmakers. Number 56 had four rooms, each with a different tenant. The boom times of the 1850s had long gone.

Martha was fifty-eight when she died of asthma and heart disease. She and George did not have any children; she died at home without a doctor to attend her. George knew that she had originally come from Berkshire but he could not tell the registrar anything about her parents. He himself died in hospital a few months later.

So far in Australia, no living descendants. I was delighted to have found Rhena Pollard's great-granddaughter in Canada. It was Australia, though, which was the focus of Dickens's bright vision. Was nothing left there to show for it? My appeals to *The Dickensian* (the journal published by the Dickens Fellowship) and an assortment of journals and newspapers in Australia all drew blanks. I decided it was worth a trip to investigate further. But not until my last afternoon in Melbourne did I unearth the name of a possible candidate. I admit I was making things difficult, since women are always harder to track than men. But as Virginia Woolf says, 'We think back through our mothers if we are women.' I wanted to trace the Urania women down through their daughters and granddaughters. The female line.

Rosina Gale was the quiet London needlewoman who kept a low profile during her year at Urania, and slipped unobtrusively ashore at Adelaide unnoticed by the bishop. Like Martha Goldsmith she was in Melbourne by 1851, where her first son George was born. She had married George Greville, a countryman from Kent. He was, like Martha's husband, a carpenter. The Grevilles took lodgings in the town centre, on Little Bourke Street, and here Rosina gave birth to eight more children. Charles – named for Dickens? – was born soon after George but did not survive. Five of Rosina's nine children died in infancy. After a year's illness Rosina herself died relatively young at the age of forty-three, from 'corroding ulcer of uterus and vagina'. Her death certificate gives her occupation as 'tailoress': this suggests to me a woman who took pride in her profession.

Rosina's daughter Sarah was eight when her mother died. Later she followed in her footsteps and became a dressmaker. It was the details of her children which landed on my desk in the Victorian Archives Centre on my last afternoon in Melbourne, to give me a glimmer of hope. When Sarah's son Hugh died in 1973 his will left his estate to his two children Gwenyth and Colin, and named his son-in-law Jack Cadwallader as his executor. I liked the sound of Jack; Mrs Cadwallader is one of my favourite characters in *Middlemarch*. And at last I had the name of a female descendant who might be alive: Gwenyth Cadwallader.

The Melbourne phone book listed ten Cadwalladers. I copied the addresses, planning to write to them once I was back in England in a couple of days' time. But: to come all this way and not go the final few inches? I picked a G. Cadwallader and dialled. 'I'm looking for the family of Gwenyth Cadwallader,' I blurted out, expecting to have the phone banged down on me. Instead a friendly male voice answered, 'That'd be Aunt Gwen.' He did not have his aunt's number (few nephews do), but put me on to his mother, Gwen's sister-in-law. And so eventually I found Gwen, now living in a retirement village in a Melbourne suburb. She was kindness itself to the stranger coming out of the blue to question her relentlessly about long-dead relations.

Gwen did not know about the Dickens connection. His young women had covered their tracks just as he instructed. But she could remember her grandmother very well. This was Rosina's daughter Sarah. She and her husband David, a bricklayer from Sheffield, lived in Richmond, at that time a poor industrial suburb of Melbourne. Sarah's dress-making business expanded into a tidy empire. Next to her house was a workroom which Sarah would open up at weekends, in order to let her little granddaughter Gwen peep in at the rows of sewing machines. David and Sarah both lived to good ages. Their son Hugh inherited his mother's nimble fingers and stayed in the trade to become an upholsterer. The chair he made for his daughter's twenty-first birthday still sits in her bedroom sixty years later.

Rosina's descendants are doing well. The female line along which I was hunting is assured through Gwen's daughter and granddaughters. Although Gwen herself has lived in Melbourne all her life, her family spreads widely across Australia.

How many more Rosinas were there? On the Urania atlas you can colour in South Africa, Canada and New Zealand as well as Australia, and who knows where else? The numbers were of course tiny. But perhaps that does not matter: Dickens designed his ark to be compact. In 1856 Angela Burdett Coutts forwarded a letter from one of the emigrants; who it was we do not know. Dickens read it 'with great emotion' and wrote back to her the same day. For him, one was enough.

If you had done nothing else in maintaining the Home – instead of having done so much that we know of, to which is to be added all the chance and bye-way Good that has sprung out of it in the lives of these women: which I believe to be enormous – what a great reward this case alone would be!

Epilogue

Legacies

URANIA COTTAGE ENTHRALLED Dickens for over a decade. The first years were the most intense and exciting: it is like that with any project. But he never departed far from his own prescription of total immersion, 'as if there were nothing else to be done in the world'. Eleven years of hiring and firing staff, doing the accounts and organising the repairs, interviewing potential inmates, writing and updating the Case Book. Some of the business he handed over to Wills in 1856, but he continued to visit regularly and to chair committee meetings.

In 1857 he bristled with plans for more alterations. That July he was calling in builders' estimates for enlarging the house yet again. He reassured Miss Coutts. 'I know my plan is a good one, – because it is mine!' He met Mr Bird the builder on site and forwarded the estimate to Miss Coutts: 'What do you say to it?' He agitated when he did not hear from her by return. 'Hereupon I become inconsolable.' But he had more letters to write that day, including an invitation to an actress to appear in the new play he and Collins had written, *The Frozen Deep*. One of the parts would be taken by Nelly Ternan. And thus began the next chapter of Dickens's life.

He sustained his interest in Urania well into 1858. That April he chaired the committee which investigated the 'disagreeable circumstance' of Sarah Hyam's shenanigans with a policeman. Sarah's roommate Mary had found her at four o'clock in the morning downstairs in the parlour, carrying on with the Police Constable '*employed to watch the place*'. Galled by the offence of the gamekeeper turned poacher, Dickens summoned the full panoply of West London law and order: the Acting Inspector of the District, another officer, and the accused

Constable. 'I examined into the case with great minuteness and care', he assured Miss Coutts. Convinced of the constable's guilt, he issued a barrage of orders. He 'formally required the Inspector, in writing,' to report the matter to the Chief Metropolitan Police Commissioner, he discharged Sarah Hyam, and he saddled the matrons with yet more 'household precautions'. It should have been a glory moment for him, but his report lacks his usual zest.

A fortnight later he agreed to write an entry about Urania for a *Hand-Book of Penitentiaries and Homes for Females*. No copies survive so we do not know if he did. After that the Home and its inmates drop out of his world as if they had never been in it. The liaison with Nelly Ternan could have been a factor. Befriender of the fallen, knight of the new beginning abroad: was this a suitable mission for a 45-year-old man conducting an affair with a young actress the age of his second daughter?

It wasn't just Nelly. During the Urania years Dickens was increasingly leading a double life. At home he was feeling the strain. Too many children, and as for his parents and brothers, he said they were 'millstones round my neck'. In the 1840s trips abroad had been a whole-family event; in the 1850s Dickens preferred to slope off for a Paris weekend with a male friend or two. Perhaps it would be the bohemian Maclise or *Punch* cartoonist John Leech; or the aristocratic Spencer Lyttleton. The 'scapegrace' of his family and continually in debt, Lyttleton was the sort of buccaneer youngster Dickens enjoyed relaxing with. 'We have got on famously, and been very facetious.'

For a more extended European tour Dickens chose raffish fellow novelist Wilkie Collins and the painter Augustus Egg. The 'Triumvirate' went in for moustache-growing competitions (Dickens won of course), indiscreet parlour games, and exchanges of confidence. Dickens told his sister-in-law Georgina:

Collins gave us, by the bye, in a Carriage one day, a full account of his first love adventure. It was at Rome it seemed, and proceeded, if I may be allowed the expression, to the utmost extremities – he came out quite a pagan Jupiter in the business. Egg and I made a calculation afterwards, and found that at this precocious passage in his history, he was twelve years and some odd months old.

A new arena for Dickens was opening up with the public readings which were to dominate the last decade of his life. Perhaps he did not need Urania so much. Its cause cannot have been helped by Miss Coutts taking Catherine's side after the break-up of the Dickens marriage. In the spring of 1858 and again in 1860, she tried to mediate between them. This failed, and the friendship between her and Dickens understandably cooled. They kept up a diminished correspondence, in which Dickens expressed his feelings more openly than he had before: 'I think you know how I love you'. In none of his subsequent letters to her, or in his many letters to Wills, is there any trace of Urania. But then, Dickens was a dropper. As with Urania, so with his wife. Seven years after the acrimonious split he dismissed his marriage chillingly. 'A page in my life which once had writing on it, has become absolutely blank.' Urania Cottage was still going strong for the census in 1861, when ten inmates were listed. It seems to have come to an end in the following year; the last entry in the Rate Book is dated February 1862.

When Dickens did turn his back on Urania Cottage, it was not because he was disillusioned or judged it a failure. Far from it. Over the years he would buoy Miss Coutts up with enthusiastic endorsements and progress reports. In 1850 he commented on a 'delightful' note from one of the emigrants. 'Looking back on the history of your noble effort – especially with this added light – I sincerely think it has prospered as well as our most hopeful anticipations could have reasonably encouraged us to believe. – Don't you?' His agreement in April 1858 to write the entry on Urania Cottage for the penitentiaries *Hand-Book* (the last time he ever mentioned Urania) would have led to its first appearance in public under its own name. Other lists and handbooks had left it out, although it had surfaced briefly in America, where it was honoured as 'the only institution of this nature in England at present', in an appeal on behalf of a Home for Discharged Female Convicts in New York. Now Dickens agreed with Miss Coutts that an account of Urania was 'worth doing'. They were both happy, it seems, with their decade-long experiment, even though that same day Dickens was losing his temper with the excesses of the charitable community. He was being besieged by philanthropic 'bullies' in his own house, he raged with comic irritation to his young friend Edmund Yates. 'Benevolent men get behind the piers of the gates, lying in wait for my going out.' Dickens retaliated by making them 'stay so long at the door, that their horses deposit beehives of excellent manure all over the front court.'

And although Dickens did finally abandon Urania, he always kept faith by his fictionally fallen women. As early as 1855, when he was testing the water with his public readings, he was 'poring over *Copperfield* (which is my favourite), with the idea of getting a reading out of it, to be called by some such name as "Young Housekeeping, and Little Emily"'. But the story was too 'woven' and 'blended' for him to disentangle a cut-down script. After many attempts he produced a two-hour version, streamlined to an hour and a half for his American tour in 1867. It was the reading he loved best, and one of his most exhausting; he said he was 'half dead the day after'.

In his imagination, emigrant girls persisted in linking themselves to his childhood self. A story from the 1860s has the garrulous landlady Mrs Lirriper reminiscing about Willing Sophy, the hard-working servant with the dirty face.

> And I says to Sophy, 'Now Sophy my good girl have a regular day for your stoves and keep the width of the Airy between yourself and the blacking and do not brush your hair with the bottoms of the sauce-pans and do not meddle with the snuffs of the candles and it stands to reason that it can no longer be' yet there it was and always on her nose, which turning up and being broad at the end seemed to boast of it and caused warning from a steady gentleman and excellent lodger with breakfast by the week but a little irritable . . . I put it to her 'O Sophy Sophy for goodness' goodness' sake where does it come from?' To which that poor unlucky willing mortal bursting out crying to see me so vexed replied 'I took a deal of black into me ma'am when I was a small child being much neglected and I think it must be, that it works out.'

Mrs Lirriper is inspired to 'help' Sophy away to New South Wales. 'Nor did I ever repent the money which was well spent, for she married the ship's cook on the voyage (himself a Mulotter) and did well and lived happy, and so far as ever I heard it was *not* noticed in a new state of society to her dying day.'

There is no closing audit of the success rates at Urania Cottage. From the figures Dickens gives in his *Household Words* article we can make some informed guesses. Thirty flourishing emigrants in the first five years would add up to about a hundred over the fifteen years of the Home's life. A drop in the ocean of course, but worthwhile nevertheless.

Part of the Urania dividend would be indirect, through the example it offered. Domestic community on a small scale, a family for those who had none: this was its attraction. Experts were charmed by what they saw. In 1857 Mr Cork from the Education Department Council office in Downing Street called at Shepherd's Bush and was 'exceedingly struck by the gentle and modest manners of the young inmates. It is impossible to doubt the beneficial effects of such training.' Altogether, he concluded, Urania Cottage confirmed his opinion that 'a private home, resembling a family as much as possible, is preferable to a penitentiary'.

The family model slowly gained ground over the next decades. Large reformatories and prison-like institutions just did not work for girls and young women. When Thomas Barnardo opened his home for sixty destitute girls in 1873, it was a catastrophe. So many girls together were wild and unbiddable. His next idea he said, came to him in a dream. This was for cottage homes, where twenty girls would be 'mothered' by a suitably Christian housewife and taught to be servants. Barnardo was a genius at fundraising, and the first fourteen cottages of the Girls' Village Home opened at Ilford in 1876, amid a fanfare of evangelical celebrities, marquees and hymn-singing. While Barnardo might have dreamt the concept, he could also have read about it, as small family-sized homes looked like the way forward in the 1870s.

Did these developments owe anything to Urania? At the least we could see it as a forerunner, with its philosophy and practice clearly outlined in the *Household Words* article. In 1861, as Urania was coming to an end, Miss Coutts's funds supported a new short-stay home for ex-workhouse girls who were between jobs as servants and had nowhere else to go. This was the brainchild of Louisa Twining, one of the next generation of social workers. She would have read Dickens's article, as would Joshua Jebb before he opened the Fulham Refuge in 1855 for women coming from Millbank and Brixton jails.

Sir Joshua's grand title was 'surveyor-general of prisons'. The separate system at the brand-new Pentonville prison in 1842 was his handiwork – boisterously satirised at the end of *David Copperfield* with the incarceration of the arch-hypocrite Uriah Heep. Jebb and his wife grew fond of the Fulham Refuge women, who came to be known as Jebb's Pets. Lady Jebb read to them and wrote reports on the most interesting cases, in a style inclining towards the melodramatic: 'She burst into tears and spoke with unfeigned horror of her past life and a strong desire to do better.'

The Fulham regime emphasised rehabilitation, but Jebb's optimism about the young women being able to get domestic work when they left was ill-founded. In the first ten years of the Refuge only twenty-nine of the 1,047 women who were discharged were sent directly into service. A later training scheme taught the women to make mosaic blocks for pavement out of refuse marble set in cement. The floor beneath your feet in the Sheepshanks Gallery at the Victoria and Albert Museum is their work.

Angela Burdett Coutts's generosity never faltered, with emigrants always near the top of her list. She supported starving weavers from Spitalfields and fishermen from Cork in their efforts to prosper overseas. A letter addressed to 'The Queen of Costers, England' found its way to her at Stratton Street, Piccadilly; it was from a costermonger she had helped emigrate to Canada.

As for the house itself, its afterlife would have amused Dickens. In 1912 the Gaumont Film Company bought the land next to Urania Cottage, in order to build the first custom-designed film studios in Britain. The 'famous glass studio', as publicity had it, did not last long, the vagaries of the English climate saw to that. The glass walls were soon blacked out and artificial light installed.

Urania Cottage lived on in Lime Grove beside the huge studio as the Manager's House, with offices, dressing rooms and a dining room for the stars. A photograph from 1915 shows the moustachioed film-maker George Pearson at his desk in an office with a Victorian fireplace and mantelpiece, which could well have been one of the girls' bedrooms. In the 1920s Gaumont-British joined forces with Gainsborough Pictures, employing Michael Balcon as head of production. He had the foresight to sign up Alfred Hitchcock, the Dickens of his generation. Out of this corner of Shepherd's Bush came a string of 1930s classics: *The Man Who Knew Too Much* with Peter Lorre and Nova Pilbeam, *The Thirty-Nine Steps* with Robert Donat and Madeleine Carroll, *Sabotage* with Oscar Homolka, *The Secret Agent* with John Gielgud. Michael Powell worked here, so did the young David Lean. He would go on to direct two of the greatest Dickens adaptations, *Great Expectations* and *Oliver Twist*.

In 1934 Christopher Isherwood was there to polish up the script of Berthold Viertel's *Little Friend*. The experience is recreated in his 1946 novel, *Prater Violet*. Isherwood enjoyed exploring his temporary habitat, with its history dating 'back to early silent days, when directors yelled through megaphones to make themselves heard above the carpenters' hammering; and great flocks of dazed, deafened, limping hungry extras were driven hither and thither by aggressive young assistant directors, who barked at them like sheep-dogs.' With the arrival of sound the original studios were torn down in a 'rather hysterical reconstruction programme. . . . No one knew what was coming next: Taste, perhaps or Smell, or Stereoscopy, or some device that climbed down out of the screen and ran around in the audience.' The ensuing building was a cheap, ramshackle maze: 'Everything was provisional, and liable to electrocute you, fall on your head, or come apart in your hand.'

By the end of the 1930s the hazardous jumble had been replaced by a sleek white luxury block. During the Second World War Gainsborough decamped here from its Islington studio, which was thought to be at risk of German bombing because of its proximity to King's Cross and St Pancras. Shepherd's Bush entertained the nation at war with comedy from Arthur Askey (*I Thank You*, *Band Wagon*, *The Ghost Train*), Tommy Handley (*It's That Man Again*) and the Crazy Gang, and with Gainsborough's famous costume melodramas, as James Mason smouldered through *Fanny by Gaslight*, *The Seventh Veil* and *The Wicked Lady*. The Ministry of Information gave its support to Launder and Gilliat's documentary drama *Millions Like Us*, the story of British women's contribution to the war effort.

Meanwhile the studio was home to a new set of female inmates, the Gainsborough girls. Patricia Roc, Phyllis Calvert and Jean Kent were the young actresses of the time; they turned their dressing rooms into bedrooms and sheltered there during the Blitz. It was 'a sort of hotel', Phyllis Calvert recalled. 'I don't remember any sort of discord at all. The make-up room was an absolute hive of fun and gaiety and laughter. It was like a little club.' 'There was never any vanity or rivalry,' agreed Patricia Roc. The studio survived despite a direct hit. It had a water tank for staging sea battles, and long after it had been dismantled the actress Irene Handl claimed that on quiet evenings she could hear the water dripping from it.

Next on the site was the BBC: Lime Grove housed their first TV studios. Here they made path-breaking programmes such as *Tonight*, a topical magazine show buzzing with the energy of new young London – *Household Words* brought right up to date. *That Was The Week That Was*, *The Eurovision Song Contest* and *Doctor Who* all came out of Lime Grove to change the face of British culture. In the panelled hospitality rooms of the former film studios, the great, the good and the not so good were all well entertained. But old stories persisted. According to local historian Jocelyn Lukins, 'the *Blue Peter* office was in one of the adjoining houses which reputedly had been the house of a local prostitute'; this sounds like a garbled Urania trace to me.

The house itself has finally gone. But the site has come full circle, and returned to its earlier vocation as a hostel for the homeless. St Christopher's Fellowship began life as Homes for Working Boys in 1870, the year of Dickens's death. It is a charity which supports around two thousand children, young people and adults each year. In 1999 it opened its purpose built Limegrove hostel for about forty medium-stay inmates. Here they get shelter, training and support. The young people I met there praised the place, and liked the idea of their Dickensian heritage. Limegrove is the perfect endpoint for the Urania story. 'St Christopher's made me believe in myself and I feel hopeful about the future,' one youngster says on their website. The spirit of Urania lives on.

Names of Known Inmates at
Urania Cottage: 1847–1862

Eliza Akhurst**
Fanny Baker**
Frances Barclay
Lucy Barnes*
Anne Beaver
Frances Bewley
Rachael Bradley
Mary Anne Browne
— Campbell
Caroline Canlon
Ann Cattle
— Chalk
Mary Anne Church
Eliza Clayton
Sarah Cook
Louisa Cooper
Frances Cranstone
Maria Cridge
— Cummins
— Daley
Anne Davies

— Donovan
Julia Dye*
Elizabeth Ebbet**
Mary Essam
— Fisher
Mary French
Rosina Gale
Charlotte Glyn*
Ellen Glyn*
— Godfrey
— Goldsborough
Martha Goldsmith
Isabella Gordon
— Hearn
Jemima Hiscock
Elizabeth Hogg
Mary Anne G Hoye
Mary Humphries
Sarah Hyam
Heph Jenkins**
— Jessup

Anne Johnson
— Jones
Mary Joynes
Emma Lea
Elizabeth Mackin
— Mason
Susan Matcham
Alice Matthews
Susan Mayne
Ann Morris**
Julia Mosley
Hannah Myers
Elizabeth Nadauld
Rosina Newman
Rhena Pollard
Eleanor Queen**
Annie Rowe**
Elizabeth Rupkin*
Kate Russell**
Mary Ann Shadwell
Anna Maria Sisini
Emma Spencer*
— Stallion

Ellen Stanley
Lydia Stanley
Mary Anne Stonnell
Harriet Tanner
— Templin
Adelaide Thomas
Matilda Thompson*
— Trim
Ellen Venns
— Wallace
Rubina Waller
Ann Wallis
Ellen Walsh
Elizabeth Watts*
Jane Westaway
Eliza Wilkins
Anne Willdeck
Martha Williamson
— Willis
Mary Anne Wilson*
Sarah Wood
Sarah Youngman

* Listed at Urania Cottage in the 1851 census
** Listed at Urania Cottage in the 1861 census

All the other names appear in the index to this book and/or the indexes
to the Pilgrim Edition of Dickens's *Letters*

Dickens's Appeal to Fallen Women

Reprinted from The Letters of Charles Dickens, *Vol 5 pp.698–99*

YOU WILL SEE, on beginning to read this letter, that it is not addressed to you by name. But I address it to a woman – a very young woman still – who was born to be happy, and has lived miserably; who has no prospect before her but sorrow, or behind her but a wasted youth; who, if she has ever been a mother, has felt shame, instead of pride, in her own unhappy child.

You are such a person, or this letter would not be put into your hands. If you have ever wished (I know you must have done so, some-times) for a chance of rising out of your sad life, and having friends, a quiet home, means of being useful to yourself and others, peace of mind, self-respect, everything you have lost, pray read it attentively, and reflect upon it afterwards. I am going to offer you, not the chance but the certainty of all these blessings, if you will exert yourself to deserve them. And do not think that I write to you as if I felt myself very much above you, or wished to hurt your feelings by reminding you of the situation in which you are placed. GOD forbid! I mean nothing but kindness to you, and I write as if you were my sister.

Think, for a moment, what your present situation is. Think how impossible it is that it ever can be better if you continue to live as you have lived, and how certain it is that it must be worse. You know what the streets are; you know how cruel the companions that you find there, are; you know the vices practised there, and to what wretched consequences they bring you, even while you are young. Shunned by decent people, marked out from all other kinds of women as you walk along, avoided by the very children, hunted by the police, imprisoned, and only set free to be imprisoned over and over again – reading this very letter in a common jail – you have, already, dismal experience of the truth. But, to grow old in such a way of life, and among such company – to escape an early death from terrible disease, or your own maddened hand, and arrive at old age in such a course – will be an aggravation of every misery that you know now, which words cannot describe. Imagine for yourself the bed on which you, then an object terrible to look at, will lie down to die. Imagine all the long, long years of shame, want, crime, and ruin, that will rise before you. And by that dreadful day, and by the Judgment that will follow it, and by the recollection you are certain to have then, when it is too late, of the offer that is made to you now, when it is NOT too late, I implore you to think of it, and weigh it well!

There is a lady in this town, who, from the windows of her house, has seen such as you going past at night, and has felt her heart bleed at the sight. She is what is called a great lady; but she has looked after you with compassion, as being of her own sex and nature; and the thought of such fallen women has troubled her in her bed. She has resolved to open, at her own expense, a place of refuge very near London, for a small number of females, who, without such help, are lost for ever: and to make it A HOME for them. In this Home they will be taught all household work that would be useful to them in a home of their own, and enable them to make it comfortable and happy. In this Home, which stands in a pleasant country lane, and where each may have her little flower-garden, if she pleases, they will be treated with the greatest kindness; will lead an active, cheerful, healthy life; will learn many things it is profitable and good to know; and, being entirely removed from all who have any knowledge of their past career, will begin life afresh, and be able to win a good name and character. And because it is not the lady's wish that these young women should be shut out from the world, after they have repented and have learned how to do their duty there, and because it *is* her wish and object that they may be restored to society – a comfort to themselves and it – they will be supplied with every means, when some time shall have elapsed, and their conduct shall have fully proved their earnestness and reformation, to go abroad, where, in a distant country, they may become the faithful wives of honest men, and live and die in peace.

I have been told that those who see you daily in this place, believe that there are virtuous inclinations lingering within you, and that you may be reclaimed. I offer the Home I have described in these few words, to you.

But, consider well before you accept it. As you are to pass from the gate of this Prison to a perfectly new life, where all the means of happiness from which you are now shut out, are opened brightly to you, so remember, on the other hand, that you must have the strength to leave behind you, all old habits. You must resolve to set a watch upon yourself, and to be firm in your control over yourself, and to restrain yourself; to be patient, gentle, persevering, and good-tempered. Above all things, to be truthful in every word you speak. Do this, and all the rest is easy. But you must solemnly remember that if you enter this Home without such constant resolutions, you will occupy, unworthily and uselessly, the place of some other unhappy girl, now wandering and lost; and that her ruin, no less than your own, will be upon your head, before Almighty God, who knows the secrets of our breasts, and Christ, who died upon the Cross, to save us.

In case there should be anything you wish to know, or any question you would like to ask, about this Home, you have only to say so, and every information shall be given to you. Whether you accept it or reject it, think of it. If you awake in the silence and solitude of night, think of it then. If any remembrance ever comes into your mind of any time when you were innocent and very different, think of it then. If you should be softened by a moment's recollection of any tenderness or affection you have ever felt, or that has ever been shown to you, or of any kind word that has ever been spoken to you, think of it then. If ever your poor heart is moved to feel, truly, what you might have been, and what you are, oh think of it then, and consider what you may be yet!

Believe me that I am, indeed,
YOUR FRIEND.

NOTES

Most of what we know about Urania Cottage comes from Dickens's letters. The reader can trace references to the Home and its inmates in the twelve volume Pilgrim Edition of *The Letters of Charles Dickens*, published by Oxford University Press between 1965 and 2002, which has full indexes. Most of the Urania correspondence falls in Volumes Five to Eight. This edition is also available electronically, in the InteLex Past Masters, English Letters Collection, www.nlx.com.

The place of publication is London unless indicated otherwise.

Prologue

p.1 This account is partly based on Henry Morley's article, 'A Rainy Day on *The Euphrates*', *Household Words*, 24 January 1852. He was reporting on a group of Sidney Herbert's distressed needlewomen.

p.3 Dickens's article, 'Home for Homeless Women', appeared in *Household Words*, 23 April 1853, rpt *Dickens' Journalism*, Vol 3, 1851–59, ed. Michael Slater, J.M.Dent, 1998, pp. 127–141.

p.3 Urania Cottage, the biographers, critics and historians: John Forster mentions the Home 'which largely and regularly occupied his time for several years' once in his biography, *The Life of Charles Dickens*,1872–74, rpt Dent Everyman, 1927, Vol 2 p. 92. Edgar Johnson gives it a couple of pages in *Charles Dickens, His Tragedy and Triumph*, Victor Gollancz 1953, pp. 593–5, 621, 675. It has much more space in Peter Ackroyd's *Dickens*, Sinclair-Stevenson, 1990; see index for references. Angela Burdett Coutts's two biographers offer good appraisals: see Edna Healey, *Lady Unknown: The Life of Angela Burdett-Coutts*, Sidgwick and Jackson, 1978, and Diana Orton, *Made of Gold: A Biography of Angela Burdett Coutts*, Hamish Hamilton, 1980. Among critics and historians, Edward Payne and Henry Harper describe Urania Cottage as a scheme which 'ultimately failed' in *The Charity of Dickens*, The Bibliophile Society, Boston, US, 1929. Philip Collins has an excellent chapter on Urania Cottage in *Dickens and Crime*, Macmillan 1965. Michael Slater writes about it in *Dickens and Women*, J. M. Dent and Sons, 1983, pp. 341–45. Significantly, he identifies 1846–56 for Dickens as the 'period during which his novelist's imagination was most deeply engaged with women for their own sakes, rather than as "relative creatures"' (p. xii). Pamela Janes gives a helpful account in *Shepherd's Bush . . . The Dickens Connection*, published by the Shepherd's Bush Local History Society, 1992, and Selma Barbara Kanner's unpublished PhD thesis, 'Victorian Institutional Patronage: Angela Burdett-Coutts, Charles Dickens and Urania Cottage Reformatory for Women', UCLA 1972, situates it 'as exemplifying Victorian philanthropy'. Rosemarie Bodenheimer discusses Urania Cottage imaginatively, in the context of house-keeping in Dickens's life, letters and fiction in *Knowing Dickens*, Cornell University Press, 2007, Chapter 5, 'Manager of the House'.

Chapter One: Where To Go?

p.7 Julia Mosley: see 'Calendar of the Prisoners in the House of Correction at Westminster, for the Sessions at Clerkenwell, Middlesex', April 1847, London Metropolitan Archives WJ/CP/A 1–64. Other evidence from 1841 census and Certificate of Death.

p.8 Rosina Gale: evidence from Certificate of Death and Dickens's *Letters*.

p.8 Martha Goldsmith: evidence from Dickens's *Letters*. On the Magdalen, see Stanley Nash, 'Prostitution and Charity: The Magdalen Hospital, A Case Study', *Journal of Social History*, 1984, Vol 14, no 4.

p.9 Henry Mayhew's figures for servants: see *London Labour and the London Poor*, Vol 4, 1861, rpt Dover Publications 1968, p. xxvi.

p.9 Mary Anne Church: evidence from *Sessions Papers, Central Criminal Court*, September 1850, London Metropolitan Archives.

p.10 The workhouse: see Sidney and Beatrice Webb, *English Poor Law Policy*, Frank Cass, 1963, pp. 73–82; M. A. Crowther, *The Workhouse System 1834–1929, The History of a Social Institution*, Methuen, 1981; Frank Crompton, *Workhouse Children*, Sutton Publishing, Stroud, 1997; Simon Fowler, *Workhouse: The People, the Places, the Life Behind Doors*, National Archives, Kew, 2007.

p.10 The workhouse girls: see *The Times*, 12 January 1848 and 26 January 1848.

p.11 Mary Anne Smith, *The Times*, 28 January 1847.

p.11 Felicia Skene, (Francis Scougal), *Scenes from a Silent World, or Prisons and Their Inmates*, Wm Blackwood, 1889, p. 37.

p.12 Christina Rossetti, *Letters*, ed. Anthony Harrison, University Press of Virginia, Charlottesville, 1997, Vol I, 1843–1873, p. 100.

p.12 Sophia Jex-Blake: Margaret Todd, *The Life of Sophia Jex-Blake*, Macmillan, 1918, p. 73.

p.12 Dickens's untitled 'Appeal to Fallen Women' is reprinted here as Appendix II.

p.14 George Laval Chesterton, *Revelations of Prison Life*, Hurst and Blackett, 1857, pp. 25, 28, 79, 292.

p.15 George Laval Chesterton, *Peace, War, and Adventure: An Autobiographical Memoir*, Longman, Brown, Green and Longmans, 1853, pp. 23–24.

p.15 Augustus Tracey: biographical note in Dickens's *Letters*, Vol 2, p. 270.

p.15 'Objections would be raised': Chesterton, *Revelations*, pp. 309–310.

p.16 Dickens's eve-of-opening letter about 'your "Home": 28 October 1847, *Letters*, Vol 5 pp.177–79.

p.16 Penitentiaries and Refuges: see Tuckniss's Preface to *London Labour and the London Poor*, Vol 4; *The Reformation and Refuge Journal* 1861–63; Susan Mumm, *Stolen Daughters, Virgin Mothers, Anglican Sisterhoods in Victorian Britain*, Leicester University Press, 1999; 'St Mary Magdalene, Park House, Highgate', St Michael's Parish Magazine, January 1864, Archives of Highgate Literary and Scientific Institution; F. K. Prochaska, *Women and Philanthropy in Nineteenth Century England*, Clarendon Press, Oxford, 1980.

p.16 Dickens on the House of Mercy: *Letters*, 17 May 1849, Vol 5, p. 54.

p.16 Christina Rossetti at Highgate: Diane D'Amico, '"Equal Before God": Christina Rossetti and the Fallen women of Highgate Penitentiary', in *Gender and Discourse in Victorian Literature and Art*, eds Anthony Harrison and Beverly Taylor, Northern Illinois University Press, Illinois, 1992, pp. 66–83. See also Joan Schwitzer, ed. *People and Places, Lost Estates of Highgate, Hornsey and Wood Green*, Hornsey Historical Society, 1996.

p.17 Chesterton's young furies: *Revelations of Prison Life*, p. 106.

p.17 Emigration: Eric Richards, *Britannia's Children: Emigration from England, Scotland, Wales and Ireland since 1600*, Hambledon, 2004, pp. 127–43.

p.18 Anne Simons: *The Times*, 12 November 1847.

Chapter Two: Leap Of Faith

p.22 Dickens and the Model: *Letters*, 3 November 1847, Vol 5 p. 184.

p.23 Ragged schools: Claire Seymour, *Ragged Schools, Ragged Children*, Ragged School Museum Trust, 1995. Thomas Barnardo's Copperfield Ragged School in London is now the Ragged School Museum. See also John Hollingshead, *Ragged London in 1861*, Dent Everyman, 1986, p. 24; Dickens, *Letters*, 5 May 1846, Vol 4 p. 545, and p. 552n.

p.24 Dickens's first letter about a home for fallen women: *Letters,* 26 May 1846, Vol 4 pp. 552–56.

p.24 See *The Times* for 26 May 1846 and 9 May 1846.

p.26 Angela Burdett Coutts: Edna Healey, *Lady Unknown: the Life of Angela Burdett-Coutts*, Sidgwick and Jackson, 1978, p. 90 on the Duke of Wellington; Diana Orton, *Made of Gold: A Biography of Angela Burdett Coutts*, Hamish Hamilton, 1980, pp. 69–75 on Richard Dunn. Details of the pictures at Stratton Street in the archives of the Pilgrim *Letters*, courtesy of Margaret Brown. For marriage rumours see *Morning Chronicle*, 30 September 1847; *Manchester Times and Gazette* 5 October 1847; correspondent for the *Augsberg Gazette* in Berlin, quoted in *Exeter Flying Post*, 21 October 1847.

p.28 Florence on the streets: *Dombey and Son*, 1846–1848, chapter 6.

p.30 Urania Cottage Insurance documents: Records of Sun Fire Office, MS 11936/493,/995477, 9 September 1822; MS 11936/527/1103993, 3 March 1830; MS 11936/544/1178581, 2 July 1834; MS 11936/545/1199712, 1 July 1835, Guildhall Library.

p.30 Mamie Dickens, *My Father As I Recall Him*, Roxburghe Press, 1897, p. 12.

p.30 Katey Dickens, quoted in Gladys Storey, *Dickens and Daughter*, Frederick Muller Ltd, 1939, p. 94.

p.31 Ralph Wardlaw: *Lectures on Female Prostitution: Its Nature, Extent, Guilt, Causes, and Remedy*, 1842, pp. 52–53, quoted in Amanda Anderson, *Tainted Souls and Painted Faces: The Rhetoric of Fallenness in Victorian Culture*, Cornell University Press, Ithaca, 1993, p. 52.

p.32 Susan Mumm, *Stolen Daughters*, p. 105.

p.32 Marianne George at Clewer: Valerie Bonham, *A Place in Life: The Clewer House of Mercy, 1849–83*, Community of St John the Baptist, Berks, 1992, p.29.

p.32 Felicia Skene, *Hidden Depths*, Edmonston and Douglas, Edinburgh, 1866, pp. 134, 212. See also Henry Gladwyn Jebb, *Out of the Depths, The Story of a Woman's Life*, Macmillan, 1859.

p.33 The 'heap of misery': 'A Nightly Scene in London', *Household Words*, 26 January 1856, rpt Slater ed. *Dickens' Journalism* Vol 3, pp. 347–351.

p. 35 Eighty-seven Urania names: See Appendix I for the full list.

Chapter Three: Guinea Pigs

p.37 Dr Barnardo's photographs: Norman Wymer, *Father of Nobody's Children, A Portrait of Dr Barnado*, Hutchinson 1954, p. 133.

p.37 Dickens on reading 'The Chimes', *Letters,* 2 December 1844, Vol 4 p. 235.

p.40 Estimates of the number of prostitutes in London: Mayhew, *London Labour and the London Poor*, Vol 4, pp. 210–13.

p.40 The 'multitudinous Amazonian army': J.A. Miller, *Prostitution Considered in Relation to its Causes and Cure*, Sutherland & Knox, Edinburgh, 1859, quoted in Linda Mahood, *The Magdalenes: Prostitution in the Nineteenth Century*, Routledge,1990, p.121. On Victorian prostitution in the period after Urania, see Judith Walkowitz, *Prostitution and Victorian Society, Women, Class and the State*, Cambridge University Press, Cambridge, 1980. Amanda Anderson describes Alexandre Parent-Duchâtelet's 1836 study, *De La Prostitution dans la Ville de Paris*, and contemporary Victorian debates in *Tainted Souls and Painted Faces: The Rhetoric of Fallenness in Victorian Culture*, pp.1–65.

p.41 Mayhew's interviews are printed in *The Unknown Mayhew*, eds E.P.Thompson and Eileen Yeo, The Merlin Press, 1971.

p.42 F. K. Prochaska, *Women and Philanthropy in Nineteenth Century England*, Clarendon Press, Oxford, 1980, p. 188. See also Seth Koven, *Slumming, Sexual and Social Politics in Victorian London*, Princeton University Press, Princeton, 2004.

p.43 The auctioneer: Simon de Bruxelles, 'Fallen Women were all right in Dickens' book', *The Times*, 8 June 2001.

p.43 Maclise and the prostitutes of Margate: Peter Ackroyd, *Dickens*, Sinclair-Stevenson Ltd, 1990, p. 332.

p.43 Dickens prefers girls: letter to Clarkson Stanfield, *Letters*, 28 October 1845, Vol 4 p. 419.

p.43 'a Daughter after all!': *Dombey and Son*, chapter 16.

p.44 *Paradise Lost,* Book VII lines 30–31.

p.45 'A Walk in a Workhouse', *Household Words*, 25 May 1850, rpt *Dickens' Journalism*, ed. Slater, Vol 2, pp. 234–241.

p.45 Drouet: Dickens 'The Paradise at Tooting' *The Examiner*, 20 January 1849, rpt *Dickens' Journalism* Vol 2, pp. 147–155. See p. 155 for editor's account of Dickens's further articles, and Drouet's trial.

p.46 Dickens on the Drouet girl at Urania: 'Home for Homeless Women', *Household Words*, 23 April 1853.

p.47 Dickens's letters to Gilbert A'Beckett and William Broderip, 26 July 1850, *Letters*, Vol 6, pp. 135–6.

p.48 'Love must be the ruling sentiment': Mary Carpenter, *Reformatory Schools for the Children of the Perishing and Dangerous Classes and for Juvenile Offenders*, C. Gilpin, 1851, p.74. See also Jo Manton, *Mary Carpenter and the Children of the Streets*, Heinemann, 1976.

p.49 Elizabeth Gaskell, *The Letters of Elizabeth Gaskell*, eds J.A.V.Chapple and Arthur Pollard, Manchester University Press, Manchester, 1966, 8 January 1850, pp. 98–9. On the reception of *Ruth*: Jenny Uglow, *Elizabeth Gaskell, A Habit of Stories*, Faber, 1993, pp. 338–42.

p.50 Rosemarie Bodenheimer, *Knowing Dickens*, p. 148.

Chapter Four: Charles In Charge

p.55 Six o'clock rise: 'Home for Homeless Women', *Household Words*; ten o'clock bedtime, *Letters*, 3 November 1847, Vol 5 p.187.

p.56 Dickens, Lemon and Cornelius Hearne: *The Times,* 21 March 1849.

p.56 'Active management', *Letters*, 19 April 1853, Vol 7 p. 68; 'showman's pride', *Letters*, 7 March 1848, Vol 5 p. 261.

p.57 Mamie Dickens, *My Father As I Recall Him*, p. 16.

p.57 The waterfall shower bath was at Bonchurch on the Isle of Wight in 1849, *Letters* Vol 5 pp.574, 583.

p.58 Inmates at Clewer: Bonham, p. 52.

p.58 Costs: For the cheques Dickens wrote to the Urania matrons and Miss Coutts's payments to him, see Dickens's account-book at Messrs Coutts & Co. The matron's salary could not have been less than the £50, which Kathryn Hughes gives as the average for a residential governess at the beginning of the 1860s, in *The Victorian Governess*, Hambledon Press, 1993,

p. 158. There was also an under-matron. For emigration costs, see Robin Haines, 'Indigent Misfits or Shrewd Operators? Government Assisted Emigrants from the United Kingdom to Australia 1831–1860', *Population Studies*, 48, 1994, pp. 223–247. Mary MacKinnon estimates workhouse costs in 'English Poor Law Policy and the Crusade against Outrelief', *The Journal of Economic History*, XLVII (3), 1987, pp. 603–25. For Angela Burdett Coutts's annual income, see Diana Orton p. 47. The multiplier of one hundred for a comparison with today's figures is taken from the 'Composite Price Index 1750–2003' compiled by the Office of National Statistics. Foyer costs are listed by Homeless Link at www.homeless.org.uk; the Jobseeker's allowance is currently approximately £47 a week. Robert Patten analyses Dickens's finances in *Charles Dickens and his Publishers*, OUP, Oxford, 1978, see pp. 198, 228.

p.60 Miss Coutts on Dickens as 'rather overpoweringly energetic': entry on Angela Burdett Coutts in Paul Schlicke, ed. *Oxford Reader's Companion to Dickens*, OUP, Oxford, 1999.

p.60 Miss Coutts's outfit for the royal ball: Orton, p.83.

p.61 Dickens's outburst on Derry: *Letters,* 15 November 1856, Vol 8 p. 223; Johnson's comment: *Letters from Charles Dickens to Angela Burdett-Coutts 1841–1865*, ed. Edgar Johnson, Jonathan Cape, 1953, p. 328n.

p.63 'Each inmate has a separate bed': *Household Words* article.

p.63 Alexander Maconochie: John Clay, *Maconochie's Experiment*, John Murray, 2001, pp. 73–147.

p.64 Dickens's lengthy 'Explanation of the Mark Table' is reprinted as Appendix F of *Letters*, Vol 5 pp. 703–5.

p.65 Dickens to Daniel Maclise: *Letters*, 1 April 1850, Vol 6 p. 76.

p.65 Police reports, *The Times*, 5 January 1855, 16 January 1855, 7 February 1855.

p.66 *The Gladstone Diaries*, eds M. R. D. Foot and H. C. G. Matthew, Clarendon Press, Oxford, 1974, Vol 4 p. 207.

p.66 Jane Bywater: *The Gladstone Diaries* Vol 3 1840–47, p. xlv.

p.67 Susan Norton: Philip Collins ed. *Dickens: Interviews and Recollections*, Houndmills, 1981, Vol 2 p. 286.

p.67 Peter Ackroyd, *Dickens*, pp. 587, 537.

p.67 Nancy's last night: Oliver Twist, 1837–9, chapter 46; on the 'Oliver murder', see Charles Dickens, *Sikes and Nancy and other Public Readings*, ed. Philip Collins, OUP, Oxford, 1975, p. 231.

p.68 Bet's end: *Oliver Twist*, chapter 50; Nancy talks of emigration in chapter 47.

Chapter Five: Isabella's Gang

p.71 'No one should Ever be sent abroad alone': *Letters*, 3 November 1847, Vol 5 p. 186. 'I... told them to be friends': *Letters*, 1 November 1852, Vol 6 p. 792.

p.72 Dickens's praise for Mrs Morson: *Letters*, 16 May 1849, Vol 12 pp. 616–17. 'Grim and gloomy': *Letters* 15 November 1848, Vol 5 p. 440. 'They perhaps quarrel less': 'Home for Homeless Women'.

p.73 Little Willis: *Letters*, 19 November 1852, Vol 6 p. 804.

p.75 Long letter about Isabella and co: *Letters* 6 November 1849, Vol 5 pp. 637–639.

p.76 Anna Maria Sisini: 'Calendar of the Prisoners in the House of Correction at Westminster for the Sessions at Clerkenwell, Middlesex', Quarter Session April 1849, London Metropolitan Archive, WJ/CP/A 1–64.

p.77 Hannah Myers at the Middlesex Sessions: *Letters*, 12 April 1850, Vol 6 p. 83; four years later, *Letters,* 18 January 1854, Vol 7 p. 253.

p.78 Sesina: *Letters,* 7 November 1849, Vol 5 p. 641.

p.80 Martha: *David Copperfield*, chapter 22.

Chapter Six: School For Servants

p.83 Dickens and Queen Victoria: George Dolby, *Charles Dickens as I Knew Him*, T. Fisher Unwin, 1885, p. 457.

p.83 *The Posthumous Papers of the Pickwick Club*, 1836–37, chapters 22 and 57.

p.84 The Marchioness: *The Old Curiosity Shop*, chapter 34.

p.84 Susan Nipper: *Dombey and Son*, chapters 3, 56, 28. 'I rely very much on Susan Nipper': John Forster, *The Life of Charles Dickens*, 1872–74, rpt Dent Everyman, 1927, Vol 2 p. 21.

p.85 'Miss Nipper threw away the scabbard': *Dombey*, chapter 12.

p.85 Anne Brown and Macready's daughter: *Letters*, Vol 6 p. 46n. Anne as 'our friend': *Letters*, 3 April 1857, Vol 8 p. 307. Dickens's letter of congratulation: *Letters,* 23 August 1855, Vol 7 p. 693.

p.86 Instructions about the bedroom: *Letters,* 11 October 1857, Vol 8 p. 465.

The 'violated' letter: see Ackroyd pp. 814–5. The letter is printed as Appendix F (3), *Letters*, Vol 8 pp. 740–1. Anne as Catherine's 'only hope': *Letters*, 9 May 1858, Vol 8 p. 560.

p.87 The Demon at Gad's Hill: *Letters*, 20 July 1862, Vol 10 p.110. Advice on helping Anne: *Letters*, 23 January 1868, Vol 12 p. 22. Dickens's Will is printed as Appendix K, *Letters* Vol 12 pp. 730–33.

p.88 John Thompson waiting for the post: *Letters*, 21 August 1850, Vol 6, p. 153; his Irish impersonations: *Letters*, 23 August 1858, Vol 8 p. 635; his lack of prejudice: *Letters*, 21 January 1863, Vol 10 pp. 200–01.

p.88 Instructions for Nelly's baskets: *Letters*, 25 June 1865, Vol 11 p. 65.

p.89 'I have been so fortunate in servants': *Letters*, 12 June 1862, Vol 10 p. 92. The 'horrible business': *Letters*, 3 November 1866, Vol 11 p. 262.

p.89 John and the Reform Club: *Letters*, 6 November 1866, Vol 11 p. 265.

p.90 Rules for washing and dressing: *Letters*, 3 November 1847, Vol 5 p. 186.

p.90 'In every room': 'Home for Homeless Women'.

p.91 Information on Whitelands College: Whitelands College Archive, Roehampton University. See also Malcolm Cole, *Whitelands College: The History*, pub. Whitelands College, 1982.

p.91 Staymaking: letter from J. T.Atwood to Miss Coutts, 28 December 1848, in the 'Correspondence of Charles Dickens with Baroness Burdett-Coutts', MA. 1352.627, Pierpont Morgan Library, New York.

p.92 'Only *fourteen* can read': 'Ignorance and Crime', *The Examiner*, 22 April 1848, rpt *Dickens' Journalism* ed. Slater, Vol 2, pp. 92–95.

p.92 Teaching aids: *Letters*, 19 November 1847, Vol 7 p. 882. See Josiah Wood Whymper, *Zoological Sketches*, SPCK, 1844.

p.92 Eliza Clayton: *Letters*, 22 December 1851, Vol 6 p. 558.

p.93 Lesson books and schemes: *Letters*, 20 November 1847, Vol 5 p. 199; poetry: *Letters*, 15 November 1848, Vol 5 p. 440.

p.93 *Hard Times*, 1854, Book the First, chapters 7 and 15.

p.94 Children's books: *Letters*, 6 September 1850, Vol 6 pp. 164–5.

p.94 Maconochie on music: Clay, *Maconochie's Experiment*, p. 182.

p.94 John Hullah: see entry in *Oxford Dictionary of National Biography*.

p.95 Caroline Chisholm and the pianos: *Letters*, 4 March 1850, Vol 6 p. 53.

p.96 The unrecognisability of the girls after a year: 'Home for Homeless Women'

p.96 Monica Dickens, *One Pair of Hands*, Michael Joseph, 1939, chapter 8.

Chapter Seven: Toiling Dowagers

p.99 Mrs Fisher: *Letters*, 29 December 1847, Vol 5 p. 214.

p.100 The job spec: *Letters*, 28 October 1847, Vol 5 pp.178–79.

p.100 'A stern functionary': Chesterton, *Revelations*, Vol 2 p. 280.

p.100 Frederick Robinson, *Female Life in Prison by a Prison Matron*, Hurst & Blackett, 1862, Vol 1, pp. 1, 59. The book went into four editions over the next twenty years.

p.100 'The extraordinary monotony': *Letters*, 3 November 1847, Vol 5 p. 182.

p.101 'Mincing nonsense': *Letters* 13 August 1848, Vol 5 p. 392. See also pp. 223, 269, 430.

p.101 Mrs Sparsit: *Hard Times*, Book the Second, chapter 1.

p.101 Chesterton on Mrs Furze, *Letters*, Vol 5 p. 430n.

p.102 Miss Cunliffe: *Letters*, Vol V pp. 316, 480, 490, 493, 504.

p.103 The Collins and the Morsons: information kindly supplied by Sheila Fenner of Tavistock.

p.103 Josiah Conder, *The Modern Traveller*, James Duncan, 1830, Vol 30, p. 116; Richard Burton, *Explorations of the Highlands of Brazil*, Tinsley Brothers, 1869, Vol 1, pp. 435–442.

p.104 Mrs Morson and Eliza Clayton: *Letters*, 22 December 1851, Vol 6 p. 558.

p.105 Jemima Hiscock and Mary Joynes: *Letters,* 17 April 1850, Vol 6 pp. 84–5, also Vol 5 p. 504.

p.106 Mary Ann Shadwell: *Lloyd's Weekly Newspaper*, 21 August 1853; *Daily News*, 21 September 1853.

p.107 William Loaden on Mrs Morson: *Letters from Charles Dickens to Angela Burdett-Coutts 1841–1865*, ed. Edgar Johnson, p. 179n.

p.107 Mrs Morson and the Turnham Green girl: Letter from Dickens to Mrs Morson, 8 November 1852, 'The Letters of Charles Dickens: Supplement 8', *The Dickensian*, Winter 2007.

p.107 Maria Cridge: Letter from Dickens to Mrs Morson, 27 December 1849, 'The Letters of Charles Dickens: Supplement 8', *The Dickensian*, Winter 2007.

p.107 Mrs Morson on nursing Hannah Brown: letter dated 9 September 1852, in the Burdett-Coutts collection, City of Westminster Archives Centre. Mrs Morson on Anne Johnson: letter dated 12 May 1853, in the 'Correspondence of Charles Dickens with Baroness Burdett-Coutts',

MA. 1352.662, Pierpont Morgan Library, New York.

p.108 *Our Mutual Friend*, Book the Second, chapter Five.

p.109 Ellen Stanley: *Letters*, 23 May 1854, Vol 7 p. 336.

p.110 Mrs Harries at Whitelands: Malcom Cole: *Whitelands College: The History*, p. 8.

p.110 'They really seem so sorry': *Letters*, 30 October 1856, Vol 8 p. 216. 'Useful' Mrs Macartney: *Letters*, 1 January 1851, Vol 6 p. 253.

p.111 Mr Chadband: *Bleak House* 1852–53, chapter 19. Guster pats Jo in chapter 25.

p.112 Notices 'admonishing them': *Letters*, 3 November 1847, Vol 5 p. 186.

p.112 William Tennant: *Letters*, Vol 5 p. 231n.

p.112 Martha Williamson: *Letters*, 4 and 17 November 1851, Vol 6 pp. 534 and 540–42. See also *The Times*, 6 November 1851.

Chapter Eight: Audacious Rhena Pollard

p.115 Rhena's mother, Mary Pollard: see Quarter Sessions Records for April 1845, West Sussex Records Office.

p.115 *Nottinghamshire Guardian*: quoted *Letters*, Vol 6 p. 745n.

p.116 'He was reading your character': the anecdote from Dickens's American friend James Field is quoted in Ackroyd, p. 929.

p.117 The two long letters about Rhena: to Angela Burdett Coutts, *Letters*, 4 January 1854, Vol 7 pp. 237–238; to Mrs Morson, *Letters*, 4 January 1854, Vol 12 pp. 654–655.

p.117 Norstead and Judith Hughes: information kindly given by the late Robin Fenner.

p.118 Arthur Helps: 'In Memoriam', *Macmillan's Magazine* July 1870, quoted in Malcolm Andrews, *Charles Dickens and His Performing Selves: Dickens and the Public Readings*, OUP, Oxford, 2006, p. 260.

p.120 Instructions for the rough dress: *Letters*, 19 November 1852, Vol 6 p. 804.

p.123 *Bleak House*, chapter 15.

p.124 Geraldine Jewsbury, 'Canker in the Bud', *All the Year Round*, 14 November 1868.

p.122 'Motes of new books': *Letters*, 3 February 1855, Vol 7 p. 523. Susan Shatto makes the connection between Tattycoram and Rhena in 'Tough Love at Urania Cottage', *Times Literary Supplement*, 5 October 2001.

p.125 'Now, Harriet we changed': *Little Dorrit*, 1855–57, Book the First, chapter 2. 'A sullen, passionate girl!': *Little Dorrit*, Book the First, chapter 2. 'Five-and-twenty hundred': *Little Dorrit*, Book the Second, chapter 33.

p.126 Rhena in Canada: I am indebted to Rhena's great-granddaughter June Gillies; also to Kat Rytych, Dave Lee and Jim Larsen, all members of the Cole family.

p.126 'The literary and the social': Laman Blanchard, 'Charles Dickens', *Ainsworth's Magazine* January 1844, quoted in Malcolm Andrews, p. 15.

Chapter Nine: Case Book

p.132 The fence: *Letters*, 20 June 1848, Vol 5 p. 344.

p.132 'That their past lives should never be referred to': *Letters*, 3 November 1847, Vol 5 p. 182.

p.132 Description of the Case Book: *Letters*, 3 November 1847, Vol 5 p. 186.

p.133 'Making up the book': see e.g. *Letters*, Vol 5 pp. 628, 679; Vol 7 pp. 357.

p.133 Emma Lea: *Letters*, 10 December 1847, Vol 5 p. 205.

p.133 Louisa Cooper's letter: *Letters from Charles Dickens to Angela Burdett-Coutts*, ed. Edgar Johnson, 20 October 1854, p. 272.

p.134 Wilkie Collins: William M Clarke, *The Secret Life of Wilkie Collins*, Ivan R Dee, Chicago, 1988, p. 100.

p.135 Dickens describes his interviewing technique in the *Household Words* article.

p.136 Charlotte Glyn: *Letters*, 31 August 1850, Vol 6, p. 160.

p.136 Mary Boyle: *Mary Boyle: Her Book*, John Murray, 1902, p. 235.

p.136 Georgina Hogarth: *Letters*, 20 July 1853, Vol 7 p. 116n.

p.137 Georgina's later life: Arthur Adrian, *Georgina Hogarth and the Dickens Circle*, OUP, Oxford, 1957, pp. 262–3.

p.137 Francis Burdett and Lady Oxford: Orton, chapter 6.

p.138 The lost Case Book: *Letters*, Vol V pp. 186n, 205n.

p.138 Dickens on Wills: *Letters*, 22 June 1854, Vol 7 p. 359; 16 November 1855, Vol 7 p. 746.

p.138 Wills: *Letters*, Vol 1 p. 264n; Preface to *Charles Dickens as Editor*, ed. R.C. Lehmann, Smith and Elder, 1912; entry in Anne Lohrli, *Household Words, Table of Contents*, University of Toronto Press, Toronto, 1973; R.C. Lehmann, *Memories of Half a Century*, Smith and Elder, 1908; Eliza

Priestley, *The Story of a Lifetime*, Kegan Paul, 1908.

p.138 The 'evolutionary epic': James A Secord, *Victorian Sensation: The Extraordinary Publication, Reception, and Secret Authorship of Vestiges of the Natural History of Creation*, University of Chicago Press, 2000, pp. 1, 20, 21, 169.

p.138 'If there were only another Wills': Eliza Priestley, *The Story of a Lifetime*, p. 143. R.C.Lehmann described Wills as Dickens's alter ego in his Preface to *Charles Dickens as Editor*. Extracts from Wills's 1855 untitled manuscript novel were printed in Bernard Quaritch's 1996 'Catalogue of English Literature in Manuscript'. John Forster on Wills: *The Life of Charles Dickens*, Vol 2 p. 65. Wills in Hertfordshire: Wills file, Hertford County Archive. 'I won't believe it': tribute by John Edwin Cussans, Hertford County Archive.

p.140 'If she says No': *Letters*, 6 April 1856, Vol 8 .p 82.

p.140 Janet Wills: see Eliza Priestley, *The Story of a Lifetime.* The old MSS and the tin box: Eliza Priestley, pp. 115, 226.

p.141 'Yesterday I burnt': *Letters*, 4 September 1860, Vol 9 p. 304.

p.141 'Probably the most valuable bonfire': Paul Lewis, 'Burning the Evidence', *The Dickensian*, Winter 2004, pp. 197–208.

p.141 'I have no sympathy': *Letters*, 5 May 1855, Vol 7 p. 610.

p.141 'I have had a great burning': *Letters*, 30 March 1869, Vol 12 p. 321.

Chapter Ten: Making Up The Book

p.144 The Clewer archive: Valerie Bonham, *A Place in Life: The Clewer House of Mercy 1849–83,* published by Valerie Bonham and the CSJB, Windsor, 1992, pp. 28, 30, 40, 103–4. Elizabeth McIntosh: Bonham, pp. 42–44.

p.145 'Training these unhappy souls': Bonham, p. 57.

p.145 The House of St Barnabas: John Cornforth, 'The House of St Barnabas in Soho', *Country Life* 8 July 1961. The records for St Barnabas in Soho, City of Westminster Archives Centre, quoted by kind permission of Director of the House of St Barnabas, Fay Buglass.

p.148 Professions of the St Barnabas Associates: see list of the First Members of Council.

p.148 Dr Manette's house: *A Tale of Two Cities*, 1859, chapter 6.

p.148 The Visiting Books: Sidney Herbert and the Fund for Female Emigration, Wiltshire and Swindon Record Office, Trowbridge, 2057/F8/IX/1, 2.

p.154 'A little account': *Letters*, 28 January 1851, Vol 6 p. 269.

p.154 The developmental psychologists: Stuart T. Hauser, Joseph P. Allen, Eve Golden: *Out of the Woods, Tales of Resilient Teens*, Harvard University Press, Cambridge Mass, 2006, pp. 13, 297.

Chapter Eleven: Using The Plot

p.157 Mrs Meagles at church: *Little Dorrit*, Book the First, Chapter Two. Critics who have read Dickens's fiction through the lens of Urania Cottage include Amanda Anderson, *Tainted Souls and Painted Faces*, pp. 66–107; Joss Lutz Marsh, 'Good Mrs Brown's Connections: Sexuality and Story-Telling in *Dealings with The Firm of Dombey and Son*', *ELH* 58.2, 1991, pp. 405–26; Margaret Flanders Darby, 'Dickens and Women's Stories', *Dickens Quarterly* 17.2, 2000, pp. 67–76, and 17.3, 2000, pp. 127–38; and Rosemarie Bodenheimer, *Knowing Dickens*, pp. 135–142.

p.158 Inspector Bucket on bridges: *Bleak House*, chapter 57.

p.158 Alice Marwood: *Dombey and Son*, chapter 33, chapter 52, chapter 34.

p.158 Esther: Elizabeth Gaskell, *Mary Barton, a Tale of Manchester Life*, 1848, chapter 14.

p.159 'Lizzie Leigh': *Household Words*, 30 March 1850.

p.159 Dickens on Gaskell: *Letters* 27 February 1850, Vol 7 p. 900; 12 December 1850, Vol 6. p. 231.

p.159 Em'ly: *David Copperfield*, chapter 3; 'Copperfield No.10': *Letters*, 29 December 1849, Vol 5 p. 682; 'I feel a great hope': *Letters*, 23 January 1850, Vol 6 p. 14.

p.160 The 'black shadow': *David Copperfield*, chapter 22. 'Martha' is chapter 47; Martha rescues Emily in chapter 51.

p.161 'Stories for myself': *David Copperfield*, chapter 11.

p.161 'I never shall forget': John Forster, *The Life of Charles Dickens*, Vol 1 p. 32. Mr Dilke: Forster, Vol 1 p. 19.

p.162 'Just before Copperfield': *Letters*, 22 February 1855, Vol 7 p. 543. 'No blotting': see footnote in the first edition of Forster's *Life of Charles Dickens*, Bradbury and Evans, 1872–74, Vol 1 p. 20n. Nina Burgis assesses Forster's evidence in her Introduction to *David Copperfield*, Clarendon Press, Oxford, 1981.

p.162 'I returned from Shepherd's Bush': *Letters*, 9 February 1855, Vol 7 p. 528.

p.162 Freud: Ernest Jones, *The Life and Work of Sigmund Freud*, eds

Lionel Trilling and Steven Marcus, Hogarth Press, 1961, p. 116.

p.162 Esther: *Bleak House*, chapter 3, chapter 35. She comments on Mrs Jellyby and Mrs Pardiggle in chapter 30, and Vholes in chapter 60.

p.163 'I said it was not the custom': chapter 35.

p.163 'My anxiety to know': *Letters*, 20 January 1848, Vol 5 p. 236.

p.164 'Disappointment Number One': *Letters*, 27 November 1847, Vol 5 p. 204.

p.164 'Leave nothing open': *Letters*, 7 September 1849, Vol 5 p. 607.

p.164 Sarah's scam: see *The Times* 26 June 1847; the Proceedings of the Old Bailey, Reference Number t18470705-1621.

p.164 Maggy: *Little Dorrit*, Book the First, chapter 9.'Killing myself': *Little Dorrit*, Book the First, Chapter 14.

p.165 The manuscript of *Little Dorrit* is in the Forster Collection in the National Art Library at the Victoria and Albert Museum.

p.165 Miss Wade's name: if you can persuade someone, presumably you can also missuade them, which is what Miss Wade does with Tattycoram. Amy Dorrit's name also suggests a pun: A Me could be a version of the prison-child Charles. Dickens's puns on his characters' names go as far back as Master Bates in *Oliver Twist*.

p.165 The number plans are reproduced in the Penguin Classics edition, eds Stephen Wall and Helen Small, Harmondsworth, 1998.

p.166 'The History of a Self Tormentor': Book the Second, chapter 21.

p.166 'His knitted brows': *Letters,* 28 January 1857, Vol 8 p. 270.

p.166 'The promise of confidence': *Letters,* 28 March 1849, Vol 5 p. 516.

p.166 Frederick Maynard: 'Letters Concerning Mrs Caroline Thompson', Appendix D, *Letters*, Vol 7 pp. 915–19. Claire Tomalin gives a full account of the episode in *The Invisible Woman: The Story of Nelly Ternan and Charles Dickens*, Viking, 1990, pp. 87–91.

p.166 'One of the strangest': *Letters*, 17 November 1854, Vol 7 p. 467.

p.167 Mr Dorrit and John Chivery: *Little Dorrit,* Book the First, chapter 19.

Chapter Twelve: Vicious Frances Cranstone

p.171 The Duke of Wellington: Edna Healey, *Lady Unknown: The Life of Angela Burdett-Coutts*, Sidgwick and Jackson, 1978, p. 89.

p.172 Stallion: *Letters*, 19 November 1852, Vol 6 p. 804.

p.173 Frances Cranstone: *Letters*, 16 April 1854, Vol 7 pp. 315–6.

p.174 Eliza Wilkin: *Letters*, 30 October 1852, Vol 6 p. 789; 31 October,

1852, Vol 12 p. 644; 19 November 1852, Vol 6 p. 805n; 16 April 1854, Vol 7 p. 315.

p.175 'Sow the seed': *Letters*, 15 April 1854, Vol 7 p. 312.

p.176 Mary Ann Stonnell and the burglary: *Daily News*, 24 July 1846; the Proceedings of the Old Bailey, Reference Number t18460817-1573. Mary Ann Stonnell's letter: *Letters*, Vol 5 p. 403n. This letter and Edward Illingworth's are in the 'Correspondence of Charles Dickens and Angela Burdett Coutts', MA/ 1352. 647 and MA/1352.673, Pierpont Morgan Library, New York.

p.178 Mary Anne Church: *Letters*, Vol 6 pp. 559–640; *The Times*, 3 July 1855; 10 August 1855; *Household Words*, 25 August 1855.

p.180 'The disaster': *Letters*, 8 November 1850, Vol 6 p. 207.

p.181 Lydia Stanley: *The Times*, 14 October 1857.

p.181 *The West London Observer*: Hammersmith and Fulham Archives and Local History Centre, Hammersmith.

p.182 The Protection Institution: *Letters*, 8 March 1855, Vol 7 p. 558.

p.182 The Wardswoman: *Letters*, 12 May 1850, Vol 6 p. 99.

p.182 'Disturbing Miss Burdett Coutts's "Home"': *The West London Observer*, 17 November 1860.

p.183 Frances Cranstone: *Letters*, 18 June 1854, Vol 7 pp. 357–8; 22 June 1854, p. 359.

p.184 Details of Frances Cranstone's death from her Certificate of Death.

Chapter Thirteen: Pioneers

p.188 Extra evening lessons: *Letters*, 15 November 1848, Vol 5 p. 40.

p.188 Dickens as a settler: *Letters*, mid-August 1841, Vol 2 p. 358. On Dickens and Australia: Coral Lansbury, 'Terra Australis Dickensia', *Modern Language Studies*, Vol 1 no 2, Summer 1971, pp. 12–21. The invitation to Australia: Edgar Johnson, *Charles Dickens, His Tragedy and Triumph*, Victor Gollancz, 1953, p. 1001.

p.189 Plorn: Ackroyd, p. 1032; *Letters* 20 May 1870, Vol 12 p. 529; Mary Lazarus, *A Tale of Two Brothers: Charles Dickens's Sons in Australia*, Angus & Robertson, Sydney, 1973.

p.190 The fictional emigrants: *David Copperfield*, chapter 63.

p.191 Carlyle: Eric Richards, *Britannia's Children: Emigration from England, Scotland, Wales and Ireland since 1600*, Hambledon, 2004, p.136.

p.191 William Henry Giles Kingston: see entry in *Oxford Dictionary of National Biography*.

p.191 Refuge and Reformatory women: Jan Gothard, *Blue China: Single Female Migration to Colonial Australia*, Melbourne University Press, Victoria, 2001, p. 27. 'The frequency of prostitution': Kay Daniels and Mary Murnane, *Uphill All The Way: A Documentary History of Women in Australia*, University of Queensland Press, Queensland 1980, p. 95.

p.192 Dickens's advice: *Letters*, 5 February 1850, Vol 6 p. 29.

p.192 Augustus Short: Brian Dickey, *Holy Trinity Adelaide 1836–1988*, Trinity Church Trust Inc, Adelaide 1988, p. 55; Judith Brown, *Augustus Short D.D., Bishop of Adelaide*, Hodge Publishing House, Adelaide, 1973, pp. 115, 128; Margaret Dunn, *The Captain, the Colonel and the Bishop*, Crawford House Publishing, Adelaide, 2004; Fred. T. Whitington, *Augustus Short, First Bishop of Adelaide*, Wells, Gardner, Darton & co, 1888, p.140; Short Family Papers State Library of South Australia, PRG 160\1-20. Information also kindly supplied by members of the History Seminar at Flinders University Adelaide, March 2005.

p.193 'Many clerks and shopmen': Report from the Governor of South Australia, 9 July 1849, rpt *British Parliamentary Papers, Correspondence and Papers Relating to Emigration and Other Affairs in Australia 1849–50*, Vol 11, Irish University Press, Shannon, Ireland, 1969, p. 609.

p.193 'Disgusting scenes': *South Australian Register*, 21 January 1850, rpt *British Parliamentary Papers*, Vol 13 p. 253.

p.193 Goldsborough: *Letters*, 23 May 1854, Vol 7 p. 335.

p.193 The incentive of marriage: *Letters*, 11 January 11 January 1849, Vol 5 p. 472. 'My last message': *Letters* 14 July 1850, Vol 12 p. 625.

p.194 *Sidney's Emigrant's Journal*, Conducted by Samuel and John Sidney, 2 November 1848; 22 March 1849.

p.194 *Working Man's Handbook to South Australia*, 1849, quoted in John Hill Burton, *The Emigrant's Manual*, William and Robert Chambers, Edinburgh, 1851, p. 152. William Deakin: Don Charlwood, *The Long Farewell*, Penguin, Middlesex 1981, p. 248. The Ladies Column: *Sidney's Emigrant's Journal*, 5 October 1848.

p.194 Catherine Helen Spence, *Clara Morison, A Tale of South Australia during the Gold Fever*, 1851, rpt University of Queensland Press, 1987, Preface, p.238. See also Spence, *Tender and True*, Smith and Elder, 1856. For Spence's biography, see Introduction to *Clara Morison*.

p.195 Eliza Davies, *The Story of an Earnest Life: A Woman's Adventures in Australia*, Cincinatti, Central Book Concern, 1981, pp. 175, 179, 528.

p.195 'I have set up shop!' Mary Taylor to Charlotte Brontë, April 1850, rpt Joan Stevens ed. *Mary Taylor, Friend of Charlotte Brontë, Letters from New Zealand and Elsewhere*, Auckland University Press, Dunedin, 1972, p. 92. The sewing machine: Joan Bellamy, *More Precious than Rubies: Mary Taylor: Friend of Charlotte Brontë, Strong-minded Woman*, Highgate Publications, Beverley, 2002, p. 56.

p.196 'We have been moving': Mary Taylor to Charlotte Brontë, April 1850, Stevens p. 94. 'It is all my eye': Mary Taylor to Ellen Nussey, 9 February 1849, Stevens p. 81. Charlotte Brontë on Mary Taylor, 29 September 1847: *The Letters of Charlotte* Brontë, ed Margaret Smith, Oxford University Press, Oxford, 1995, Vol 1, p 500.

p.196 Louisa Meredith, *My Home in Tasmania, During a Residence of Nine Years*, John Murray, 1852.

p.196 The Flash Mob: Kay Daniels, 'The Flash Mob: Rebellion, Rough Culture and Sexuality in the Female Factories of Van Diemen's Land', *Australian Feminist Studies* 18/2, 1993, pp. 133–50.

p.196 Little Nell: the critic John Ruskin claimed she was 'simply killed for the market as a butcher kills a lamb', 'Fiction Fair and Foul', 1881, in *The Works of John Ruskin*, Library Edition eds E.T. Cook and Alexander Wedderburn, 1903–12, Vol 34 p. 275n.

p.196 Ralph Waldo Emerson, Journal for April 1848, *Journals*, Constable, 1913, Vol 8 pp. 434–5.

p.197 Dickens's research on chartering a ship is reprinted as Appendix E, 'Emigration', *Letters*, Vol 6 pp. 858–60.

p.197 Caroline Chisholm: Eneas Mackenzie: *What Has Mrs Caroline Chisholm Done for the Colony of New South Wales?* James Cole, Sydney, 1862; Margaret Kiddle: *Caroline Chisholm*, Melbourne University Press, Melbourne 1950; Anne Summers, *Damned Whores and God's Police, Women's Lives in Australia*, 1975, rpt Penguin, Victoria, 2002; Joanna Bogle, *Caroline Chisholm: The Emigrant's Friend*, Gracewing, Leominster, 1993.

p.198 'The best shoes', quoted Mackenzie, p. 7. 'From morning till evening': Mackenzie, p. 5.

p.198 'I dream of Mrs Chisholm', *Letters*, 4 March 1850, Vol 6 p. 53.

p.199 *Household Words* and emigration: see entries on John and Samuel Sidney in Anne Lohrli, *Household Words, Table of Contents*, University of

Toronto Press, Toronto, 1973.

p.199 Sidney Herbert: letter to *The Times*, 6 December 1849. See also Lord Stanmore, *Sidney Herbert, Lord Herbert of Lea, A Memoir*, John Murray, 1906, pp. 1, 110–20. Mayhew's reports in the *Morning Chronicle* were reprinted as *London Labour and the London Poor*.

p.199 Disraeli: *The Unknown Mayhew*, eds E P Thompson and Eileen Yeo, 1971, rpt Pelican Books, Harmondsworth, 1973, p. 28.

p.200 The Fund: Jo Chimes, '"Wanted: 1000 Spirited Young Milliners": The Fund for Promoting Female Emigration', in Beth Harris, ed. *Famine and Fashion: Needlewomen in the Nineteenth Century*, Ashgate, Aldershot, 2005, pp. 229–41.

p.200 Joseph Coyne, *'Wanted: 1000 Spirited Young Milliners for the Gold Diggings!', A Farce in One Act*, Thomas Hailes Lacy, 1852.

p.200 Maria Rye: Marion Diamond: *Emigration and Empire, The Life of Maria S. Rye*, Garland Publishing Inc, 1999. Extracts from The Letterbook of the Female Middle-Class Emigration Society, FL001, The Women's Library, London Metropolitan University.

p.200 'Her trembling very much': *Letters*, 20 April 1852, Vol 6 p. 648.

p.201 *David Copperfield*, chapter 57.

Chapter Fourteen: Urania Afloat

p.203 The *Calcutta* and the *Posthumous*: *Letters*, Vol 5, pp. 472n, 507n, 637n; Shipping Intelligence columns in *The South Australian Register*, information from Diane Cummings's 'Bound for South Australia website'; Advertisements in the *South Australian News*.

p.204 Rubina Waller: *Letters*, Vol 5 p. 241.

p.204 The marks scheme: Emma's bout of name-calling would earn her bad marks under four separate headings: 'temper', propriety of department', 'propriety of language', and 'improvement', *Letters*, Vol 5 p. 704.

p.204 'A doubt of all Governments': *Letters*, 26 May 1846, Vol 4 p. 553.

p.205 Mrs Engelbach's visits: *Letters*, 30 October 1856, Vol 8 p. 216.

p.205 'The refuse of the workhouse': 'Official Emigration', *Household Words*, 1 May 1852.

p.205 Emigration and the voyage to Australia: Robin Haines has produced a fascinating series of books: *Emigration and the Labouring Poor*, Macmillan, Basingstoke, 1997; *Life and Death in the Age of Sail: The Passage to Australia*,

University of South Wales Press, Sydney, 2003; *Doctors at Sea: Emigrant Voyages to Colonial Australia*, Palgrave, Basingstoke, 2005.

p.205 Adolescent girls on the *Roman Emperor*: Haines, *Emigration and the Labouring Poor,* p. 163.

p.205 'If red tape were a plant': 'Better Ties Than Red Tape Ties', *Household Words*, 28 February 1852.

p.206 The Belfast girls: *British Parliamentary Papers: Correspondence and Papers Relating to Emigration and Other Affairs in Australia, 1849–50*, Vol 11, pp. 418–420.

p.206 The *Sobraon*: *The South Australian Register,* 30 July 1850. The *Ramilies*: *British Parliamentary Papers*, Vol 11 p. 603 ; *South Australian Register*, 30 July 1850.

p.207 Complaints about fellow passengers: Gothard, *Blue China*, p. 161.

p.207 'Do not Miss Rye': The Letterbook of the Female Middle-Class Emigration Society, FL001, The Women's Library, London Metropolitan University.

p.207 Miss Morris: *Letters*, Vol 5 pp. 426n, 507.

p.208 'I never was so astonished': *Letters* 13 March 1849, Vol 5 p. 507.

p.208 'A decent wardrobe': *British Parliamentary Papers*, Vol 11 p. 130.

p.209 Lucy Edwards: quoted by Jo Chimes in *Famine and Fashion*, pp. 229–41.

p.209 A passenger in the 1860s: Helen R Woolcock, *Rights of Passage: Emigration to Australia in the Nineteenth Century*, Tavistock Publications, 1986, p. 88. Fanny Davis: Andrew Hassam, *Sailing to Australia: Shipboard Diaries by Nineteenth Century British Emigrants*, Manchester University Press, Manchester, 1994, p. 132.

p.209 Charles La Trobe: *British Parliamentary Papers Relating to Australia 1854–55*, Vol 19, p. 92.

p.210 The Drouet orphan: 'Home for Homeless Women'.

p.210 Martha Goldsmith and Mrs Harris: Letter from Augustus Short to Miss Coutts, 23 June 1849, Papers of Baroness Burdett-Coutts, Lambeth Palace Library, MS 1385.

p.210 'Some of them may have nobody': *Letters*, 13 March 1849, Vol 5 p. 508.

p.210 Amy Henning: Joan Thomas, *The Sea Journals of Annie and Amy Henning*, Halstead Press, Sydney, 1984. See also Basil Greenhill and Ann Giffard, *Women Under Sail*, David and Charles, Newton Abbot, 1970.

p.211 Jessie Campbell: Hassam, p. 124.

p.211 Augustus Short: letter to Miss Coutts, 23 June 1849, Papers of Baroness Burdett-Coutts, Lambeth Palace Library, MS 1385.

p.212 'Heavy disappointment': *Letters*, 6 November 1849, Vol 5 p. 638.

p.212 Robert Gray: Papers of Baroness Burdett-Coutts, Lambeth Palace Library, MS 1386. See also *Letters*, Vol 5 p. 591n, and entry in *ODNB*.

p.213 William Wardley, letters to Miss Coutts 27 May, 8 June and 22 June 1850, Lambeth Palace Library, MS 1386.

p.214 'The Voyage out': *Letters*, 9 January 1850, Vol 6 p. 6.

p.214 Mary Fulford: letter to Miss Coutts, 20 June 1855, Papers of Baroness Burdett-Coutts, Lambeth Palace Library, MS 1385.

p.215 See letter from Caroline Chisholm to Angela Burdett Coutts: Kiddle, Appendix F.

p.215 Charles La Trobe's report: *British Parliamentary Papers Relating to Australia 1851–52*, Vol 13 pp. 150–60; see also Jo Chimes in *Famine and Fashion*. p.208. Ellen Walsh: *Letters*, 10 March 1850, Vol 6 p. 59; Report from the Immigration Office in Melbourne, *British Parliamentary Papers Relating to Australia 1852*, Vol 14, p.58; Jo Chimes in *Famine and Fashion*, pp. 229–41.

p.216 Dr Ward: Enquiry into the *Wanderer*, June 1851, *British Parliamentary Papers Relating to Australia 1852*, Vol 14, p. 87.

p.217 Dr Strutt: Robin Haines, *Doctors at Sea*, p. 135.

p.217 The *Douglas*: Diane Cummings, 'Bound for South Australia': www.slsa.sa.gov.au.

p.217 The Clark family: Robin Haines, *Life and Death in the Age of Sail*, p. 26.

p.217 Alice Matthews: Record of Baptisms at St Stephen's Church, Hammersmith and Fulham Local Archives and Local History Centre. Alice's voyage: 'Trouble at Sea', BUR/B3, City of Westminster Archives Centre.

p.219 Rachael Bradley: *Letters*, 17 August 1851, Vol 6 p. 462; Elizabeth Watts: 22 June 1854, Vol 7 p. 359; Beaver and friends: 16 May 1856, Vol 8 p. 120.

Chapter Fifteen: Martha, Julia, Rosina

p.223 Robert Gray: *Letters*, Vol 5 p. 591n; Papers of Baroness Burdett-Coutts, Lambeth Palace Library, MS 1386.

p.223 Cape Town and the *Neptune*: see Joseph H. Lehmann, *Remember You Are an Englishman, A Biography of Sir Harry Smith 1787–1860*, Jonathan Cape, 1977, pp.309–318. I am grateful to Lady Healey for additional information.

p.224 Louisa Cooper: *Letters*, 11 April 1853, Vol 7 p. 61; 26 October 1854; Vol 7 p. 443; 5 July 1856, Vol 8 p.147; 15 November 1856, Vol 8 p. 223.

p.226 Augustus Short: letter to Miss Coutts, 23 June 1849, Papers of Baroness Burdett-Coutts, Lambeth Palace Library, MS 1385.

p.226 Mellicent Short's servant: Fred T. Whitington, *Augustus Short, First Bishop of Adelaide*, Wells, Garner, Darton & Co, 1888, p. 266. Information on Frances Provis kindly supplied by Jenny Elson, family descendant and historian.

p.227 Surplus women: see Daniels pp. 214–6.

p.227 Tasmania: see Gothard, p. 26.

p.227 George Dodd: *British Parliamentary Papers Relating to Australia, 1854–55*, Vol 19, p. 418.

p.228 Edward Strutt: see Haines, *Doctors at Sea,* chapter 9.

p.228 Louisa Meredith, *My Home in Tasmania*, p. 207.

p.229 Mary Anne Hoy: *Letters*, 9 November 1848, Vol 5 p. 437.

p.229 Enquiry into recent female immigrants: Report by Mr Moorhouse, Superintendent of the Female Immigrant Dept, 28 October 1850, *Parliamentary Papers 1851–52*, Vol 13, p. 292.

p.230 The bishop: letter to Miss Coutts, 15 June 1850, Lambeth Palace Library, MS 1385.

p.231 Edward Snell: Elizabeth Kwan, *Living in South Australia: A Social History*, South Australia Government, Netley, South Australia, 1987, Vol 1 p. 40. The lady magistrate: *South Australian Register*, 2 July 1850.

p.231 Louisa Geohagan: Lucy Frost, *No Place for a Nervous Lady, Voices from the Australian Bush*, Penguin, Harmondsworth, 1984, pp. 192–96.

p.231 'I never thought': Ellen Ollard, in Lucy Frost, p. 202.

p.231 Catherine Spence: *Clara Morison*, chapter 4, 'The Boarding House'.

p.232 The South Australia Female Refuge: information kindly supplied by Dr Brian Dickey of Flinders University, Adelaide. See also Reports of the South Australian Female Refuge 1858–1890, State Library of South Australia, and Short Family Papers, SLSA PRG 160\1-20.

p.232 Adelaide Destitute Asylum infant mortality rates: Helen Jones, *In Her Own Name: A History of Women in South Australia from 1836*, Wakefield Press, Adelaide, 1986, p. 38.

p.232 'Happy buoyancy': Melbourne *Argus*, quoted in *South Australian Register*, 3 August 1850.

p.232 Hard-working Jones: *Letters*, 16 May 1856, Vol 8 p. 120. Information on Julia Mosley, Jane Westaway, Emma Lea, Elizabeth Watts, Ellen Glyn, Emma Spencer, Martha Goldsmith, from marriage and death certificates via the South Australian Genealogy and Heraldry Society, and from wills and records in the Public Record Office Victoria, Melbourne.

p.232 Marriage rates in England: J. A. and O. Banks, *Feminism and Family Planning in Victorian England*, University of Liverpool, Liverpool, 1964, p. 27; Robert Woods, *The Demography of Victorian England and Wales*, Cambridge University Press, Cambridge, 2000, p. 89. Marriage rates in Australia: Penelope Baker, 'The Position of Women in South Australia 1836–76', unpublished thesis, University of Adelaide 1977, p. 29; Anne Summers: *Damned Whores and God's Police*, p. 352.

p.233 Charles Rule's Log Book is in the State Library of South Australia, Adelaide.

p.233 Emily Skinner: *A Woman on the Goldfields: Recollections of Emily Skinner 1854–1878*, ed. Edward Duyker, Melbourne University Press, Victoria, 1995, pp. 44, 64–5, 81.

p.233 George Dunderdale: *The Book of the Bush, Containing Many Truthful Sketches of the Early Colonial Life of Squatters, Whalers, Convicts, Diggers, and others who left their Native Land and Never Returned*, Ward Lock, 1898, pp. 81, 92.

p.234 Rachael Bradley's letter: *Letters*, 17 September 1851, Vol 6 p. 462.

p.236 *Illustrated London News*, 3 July 1852. Marvellous Melbourne and Collingwood: Graeme Davison, *The Rise and Fall of Marvellous Melbourne*, Melbourne University Press, Melbourne, 1979, p. 40.

p.236 Martha's rate book: Public Record Office Victoria, Melbourne.

p.237 Virginia Woolf, *A Room of One's Own*, The Hogarth Press, 1929, chapter 4.

p.237 Rosina Gale: papers in the Public Record Office Victoria, Melbourne. Information about her family kindly supplied by her great-granddaughter Gwenyth Cadwallader.

p.239 'If you had done nothing else': *Letters*, 13 May 1856, Vol 8 p. 118.

Epilogue

p.242 The Home for Discharged Female Convicts in New York: see Mrs C. M. Kirkland, *The Helping Hand*, Charles Scribner, New York, 1853. Mrs Kirkland's informant was a prison governor in London; the Home in New York was bigger than Urania, with a higher turnover of short-stay inmates, who were redirected into domestic or factory work.

p.244 'Mrs Lirriper's Lodgings', *All the Year Round*, 1863, rpt *Christmas Stories*, Oxford Illustrated Dickens, OUP, Oxford , 1956. p. 373.

p.245 Mr Cork: Letter to Miss Coutts, 12 October 1857, Papers of Baroness Burdett-Coutts, Lambeth Palace Library, MS 1386.

p.245 Thomas Barnardo: Gillian Wagner, *Barnado*, Weidenfeld & Nicolson, 1979, p. 79. Wagner mentions other small-scale initiatives such as Susan Meredith's Princess Mary Village Homes at Addlestone in Surrey, and William Quarrier's Homes in Scotland, p. 80.

p.245 Louisa Twining: 'The History of Workhouse Reform' in *Woman's Mission*, ed. A. Burdett-Coutts, Sampson Low, Marston & co, 1893, p. 269.

p.245 Joshua Jebb: Jebb Papers, London School of Economics.

p.246 The Fulham Refuge: Anne Wheeldon, 'Fulham Women's Prison 1856–1888, The Reformatory Vision of Joshua Jebb', MA Dissertation 1999, University of Kingston.

p.246 Angela Burdett Coutts: *Cork Examiner*, 9 February 1863; Orton p. 259.

p.246 Gaumont Film Company and Gainsborough: *Shepherd's Bush Gazette*, 7 February 1986; see also Matthew Sweet, *Shepperton Babylon: the Lost Worlds of British Cinema*, Faber, 2005; Pam Cook ed. *Gainsborough Pictures*, Cassell 1997; Michael Balcon, *Michael Balcon Presents . . . A Lifetime of Films*, Hutchinson 1969; George Pearson, *Flashback, The Autobiography of a British Film-maker*, George Allen & Unwin, 1957.

p.247 Christopher Isherwood, *Prater Violet*, Methuen, 1946, p. 67.

p.248 Phyllis Calvert: Pam Cook, p. 140; Patricia Roc: Matthew Sweet, p. 201.

p.248 The BBC at Lime Grove: Information from BBC producers of the time, and from Jocelyn Lukins, *The Fantasy Factory: Lime Grove Studios,* Venta Books London, for the Shepherd's Bush Local History Society, 1966. The *Blue Peter* office: Lukins, p. 128.

p.248 Limegrove hostel: for information on St Christopher's Fellowship, the charity which runs the hostel, see www.st.chris.org.uk.

INDEX